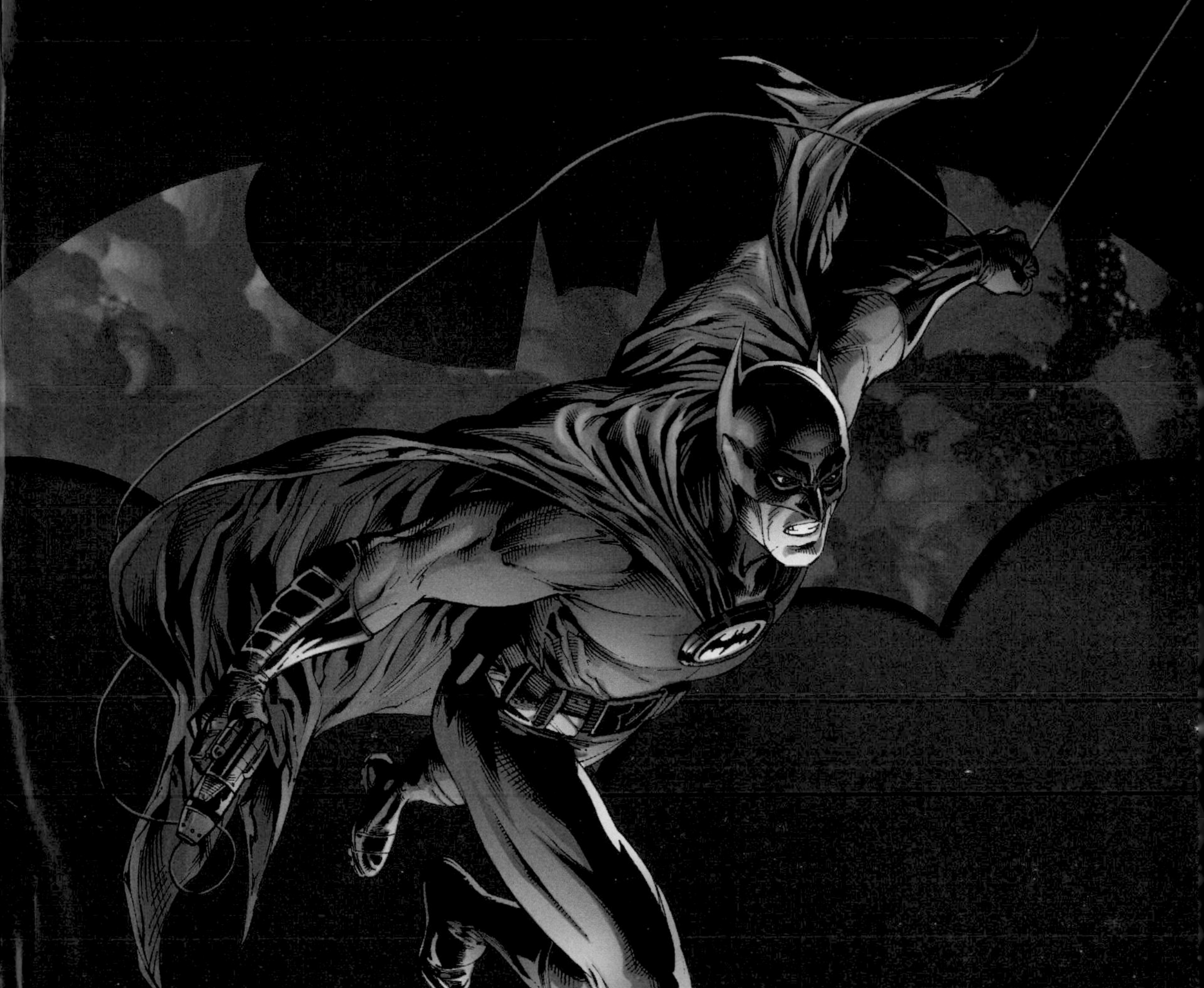

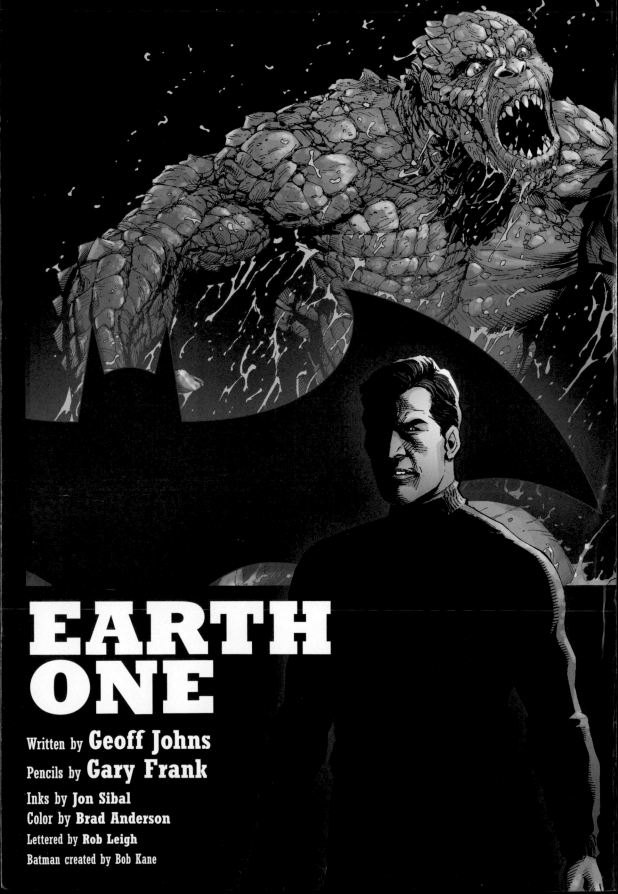

EARTH ONE

Written by **Geoff Johns**

Pencils by **Gary Frank**

Inks by **Jon Sibal**
Color by **Brad Anderson**
Lettered by **Rob Leigh**
Batman created by Bob Kane

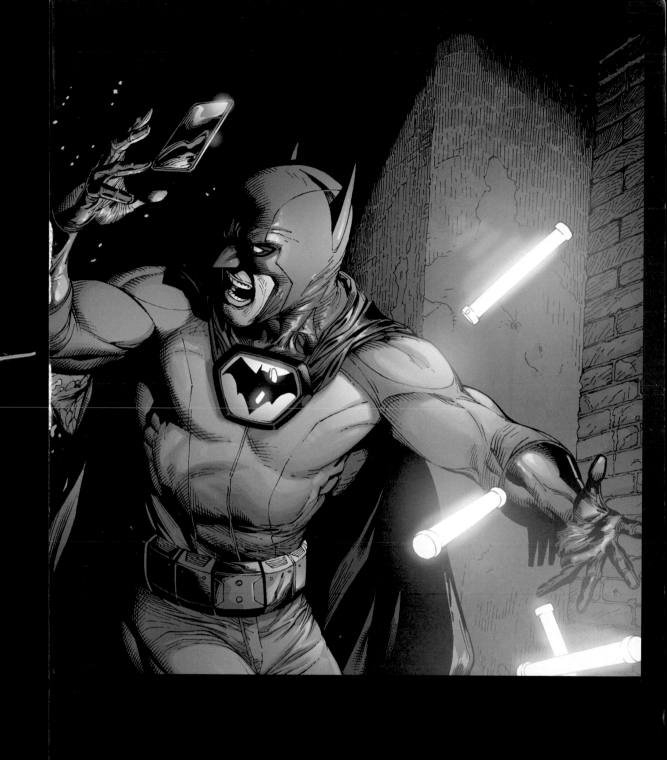

Brian Cunningham Editor – Original Series
Amedeo Turturro and **Kate Durre** Assistant Editors –
Original Series
Jeb Woodard Group Editor – Collected Editions
Steve Cook Design Director – Books
Curtis King Jr. Art Director

Bob Harras Senior VP – Editor-in-Chief, DC Comics

Diane Nelson President
Dan DiDio and **Jim Lee** Co-Publishers
Geoff Johns Chief Creative Officer
Amit Desai Senior VP – Marketing & Global Franchise Management
Nairi Gardiner Senior VP – Finance
Sam Ades VP – Digital Marketing
Bobbie Chase VP – Talent Development
Mark Chiarello Senior VP – Art, Design & Collected Editions
John Cunningham VP – Content Strategy
Anne DePies VP – Strategy Planning & Reporting
Don Falletti VP – Manufacturing Operations
Lawrence Ganem VP – Editorial Administration & Talent Relations
Alison Gill Senior VP – Manufacturing & Operations
Hank Kanalz Senior VP – Editorial Strategy & Administration
Jay Kogan VP – Business Affairs
Derek Maddalena Senior VP – Sales & Business Development
Jack Mahan VP – Business Affairs
Dan Miron VP – Sales Planning & Trade Development
Nick Napolitano VP – Manufacturing Administration
Carol Roeder VP – Marketing
Eddie Scannell VP – Mass Account & Digital Sales
Courtney Simmons Senior VP – Publicity & Communications
Jim (Ski) Sokolowski VP – Comic Book Specialty & Newsstand Sales
Sandy Yi Senior VP – Global Franchise Management

BATMAN: EARTH ONE VOLUME TWO

DC Comics, 2900 W. Alameda Avenue, Burbank, CA 91505
Printed by RR Donnelley, Owensville, MO, USA. 5/13/16.
First Printing. SC ISBN: 978-1-4012-6251-8

Library of Congress Cataloging-in-Publication Data

Johns, Geoff, 1973-
  Batman : earth one , volume 2 / Geoff Johns, Gary Frank.
  p. cm.
  ISBN 978-1-4012-4185-8 (hardback)
  1. Graphic novels. I. Frank, Gary, 1969- II. Title.
PN6728.B36J64 2012
741.5'973 — dc23
                              2012000608

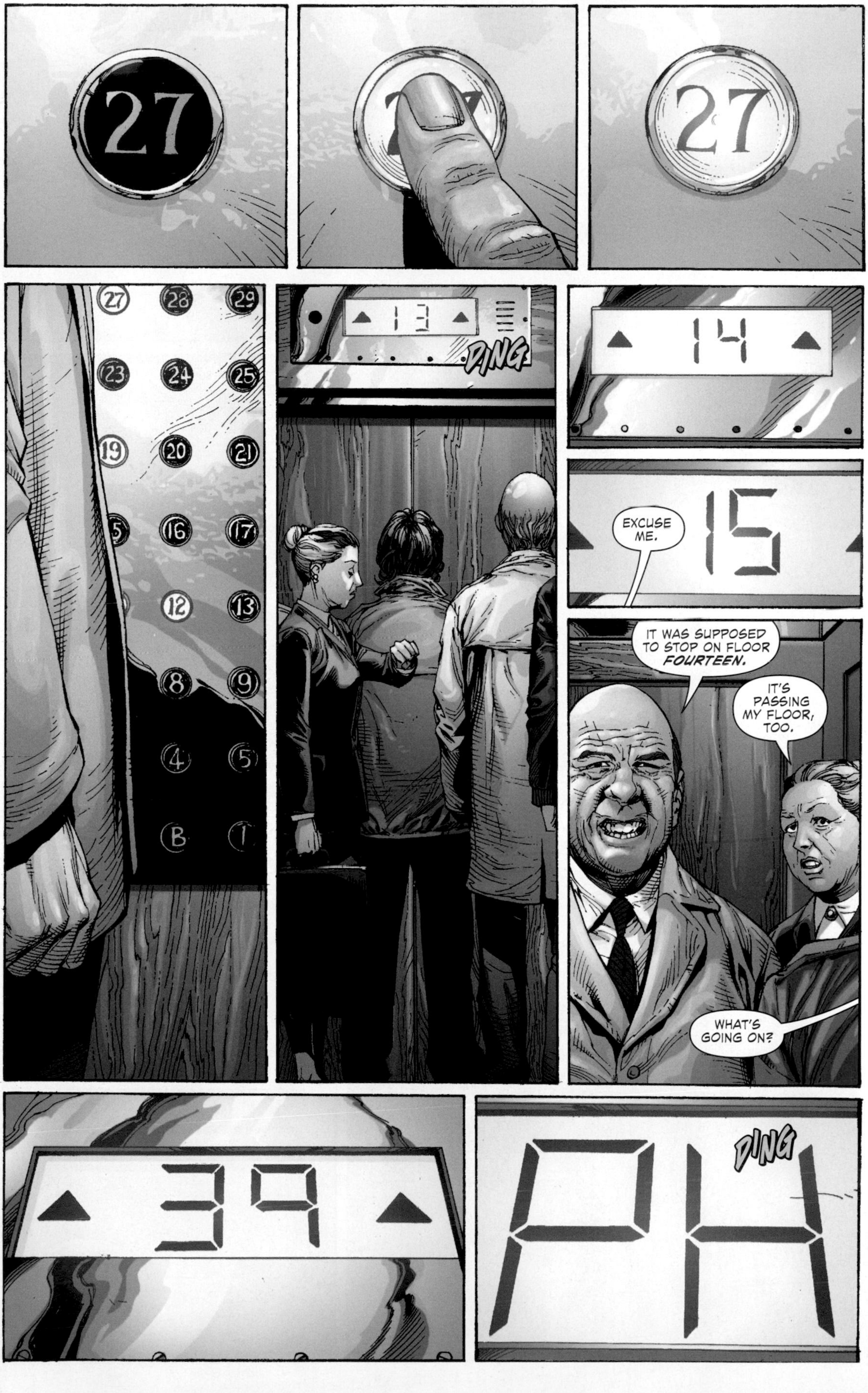
27
27
DING
EXCUSE ME.
IT WAS SUPPOSED TO STOP ON FLOOR FOURTEEN.
IT'S PASSING MY FLOOR, TOO.
WHAT'S GOING ON?
DING

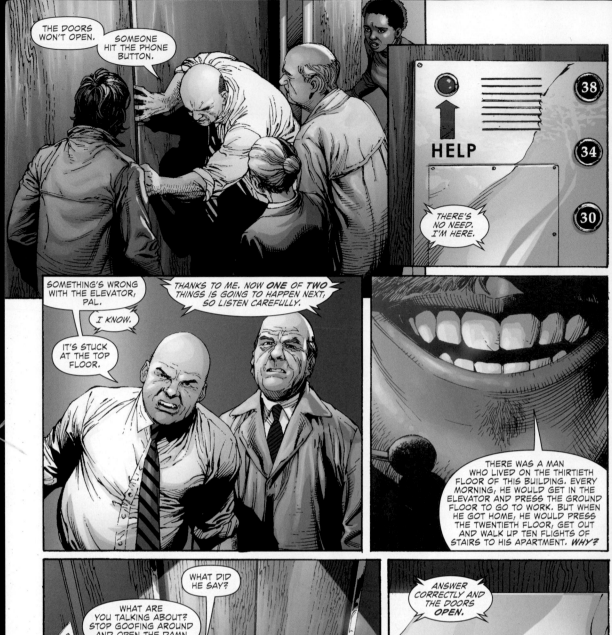

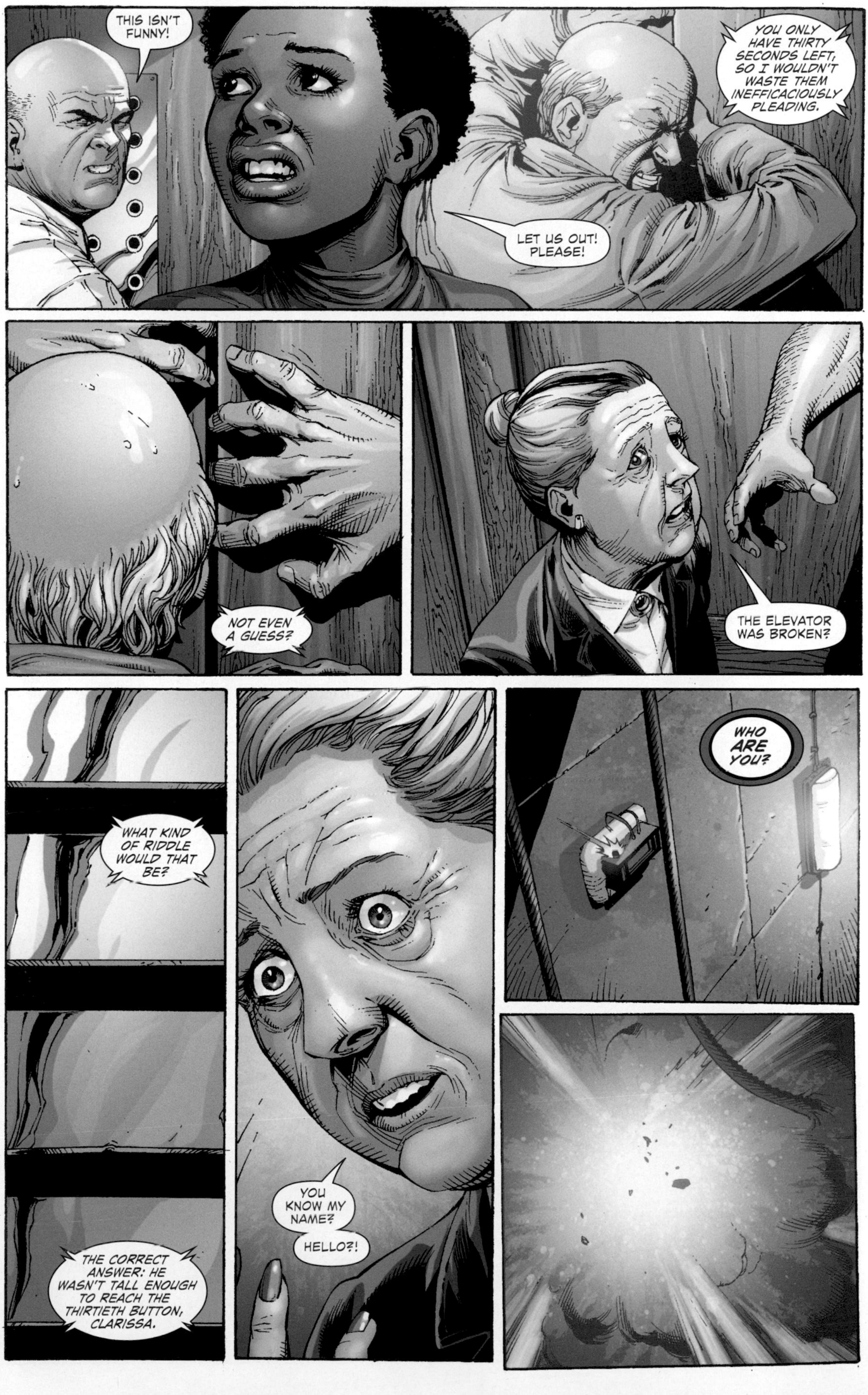
THIS ISN'T FUNNY!
YOU ONLY HAVE THIRTY SECONDS LEFT, SO I WOULDN'T WASTE THEM INEFFICACIOUSLY PLEADING.
LET US OUT! PLEASE!
NOT EVEN A GUESS?
THE ELEVATOR WAS BROKEN?
WHAT KIND OF RIDDLE WOULD THAT BE?
THE CORRECT ANSWER: HE WASN'T TALL ENOUGH TO REACH THE THIRTIETH BUTTON, CLARISSA.
YOU KNOW MY NAME?
HELLO?!
WHO ARE YOU?

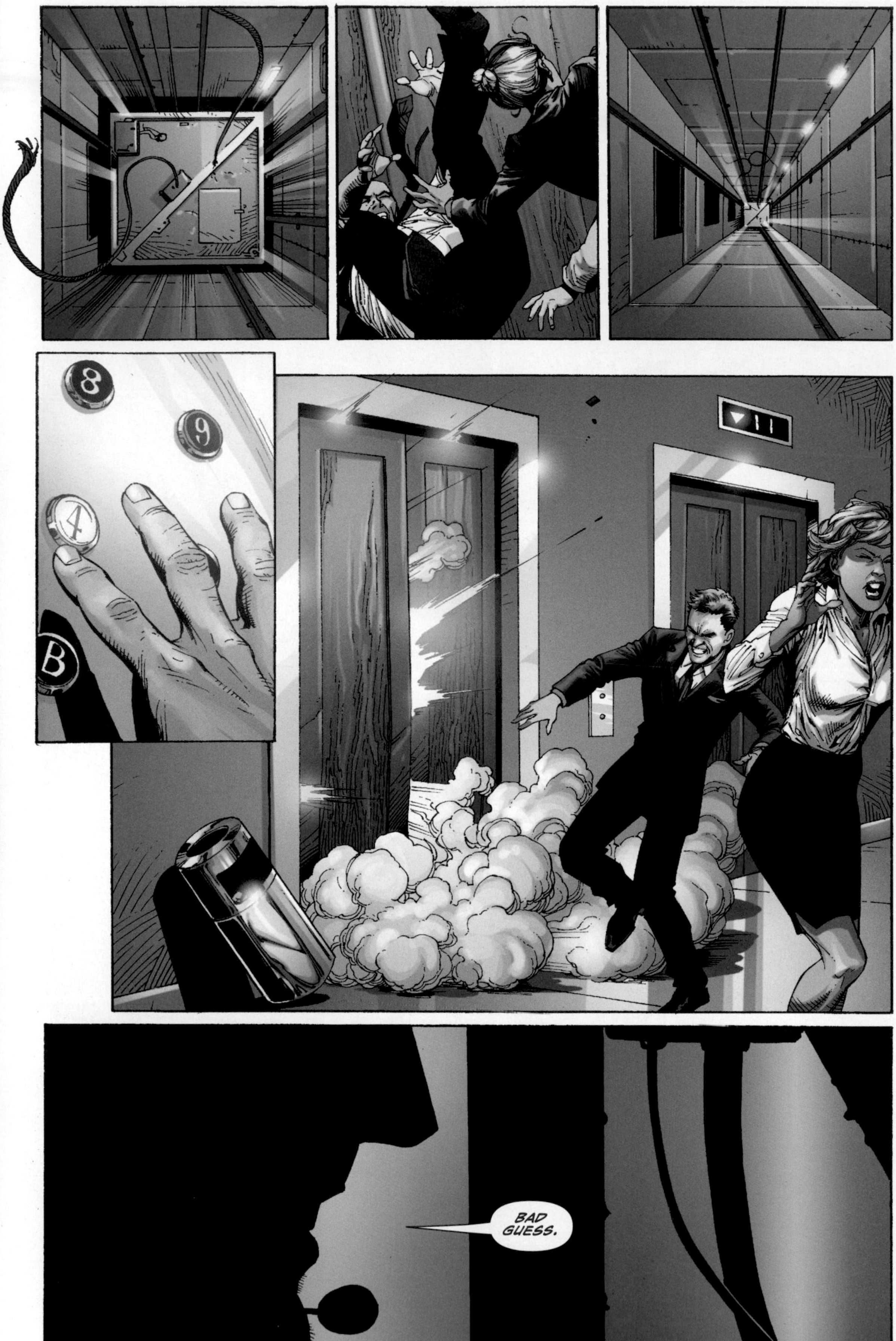
BAD GUESS.

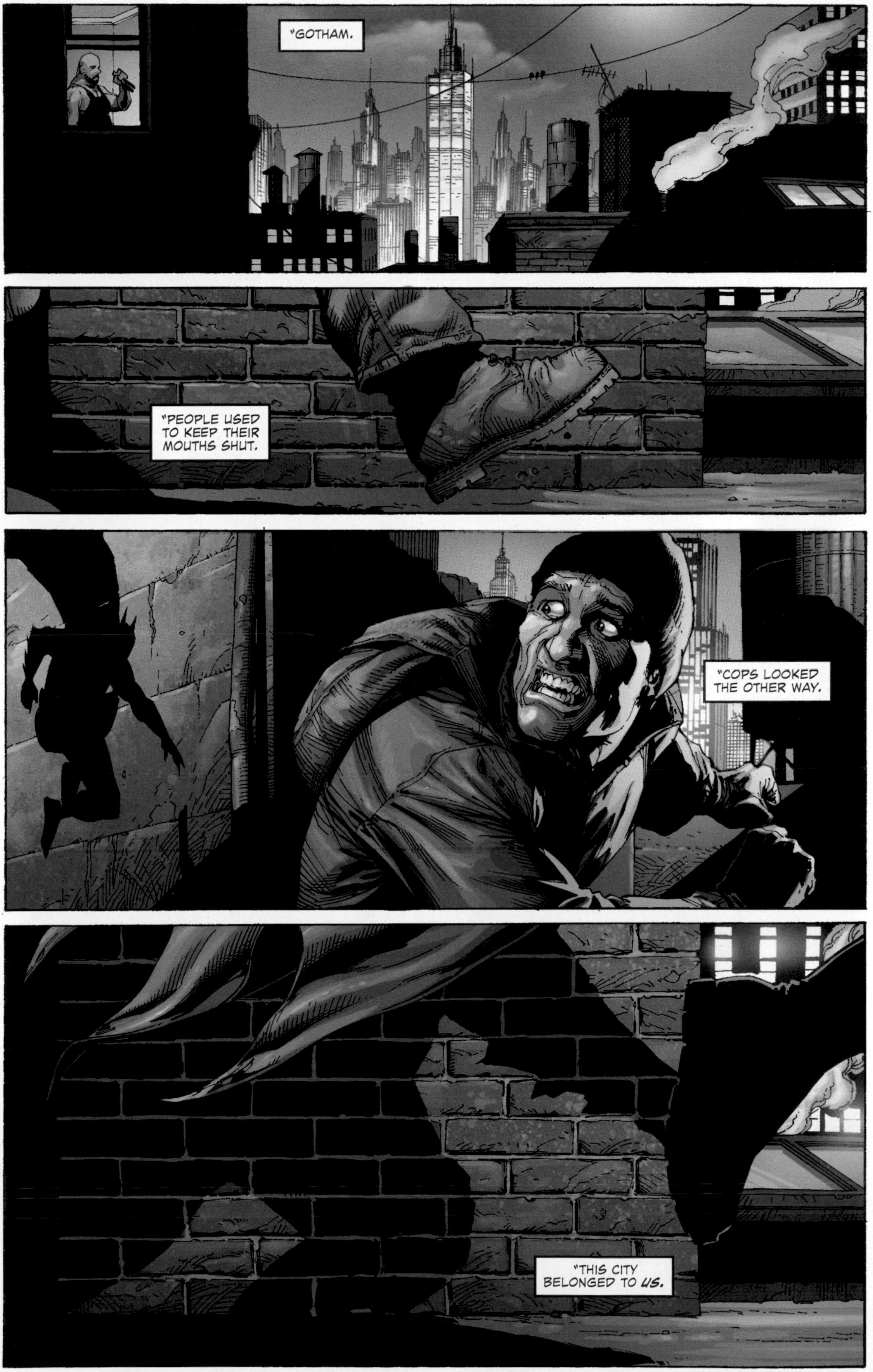
"GOTHAM.
"PEOPLE USED TO KEEP THEIR MOUTHS SHUT.
"COPS LOOKED THE OTHER WAY.
"THIS CITY BELONGED TO US.

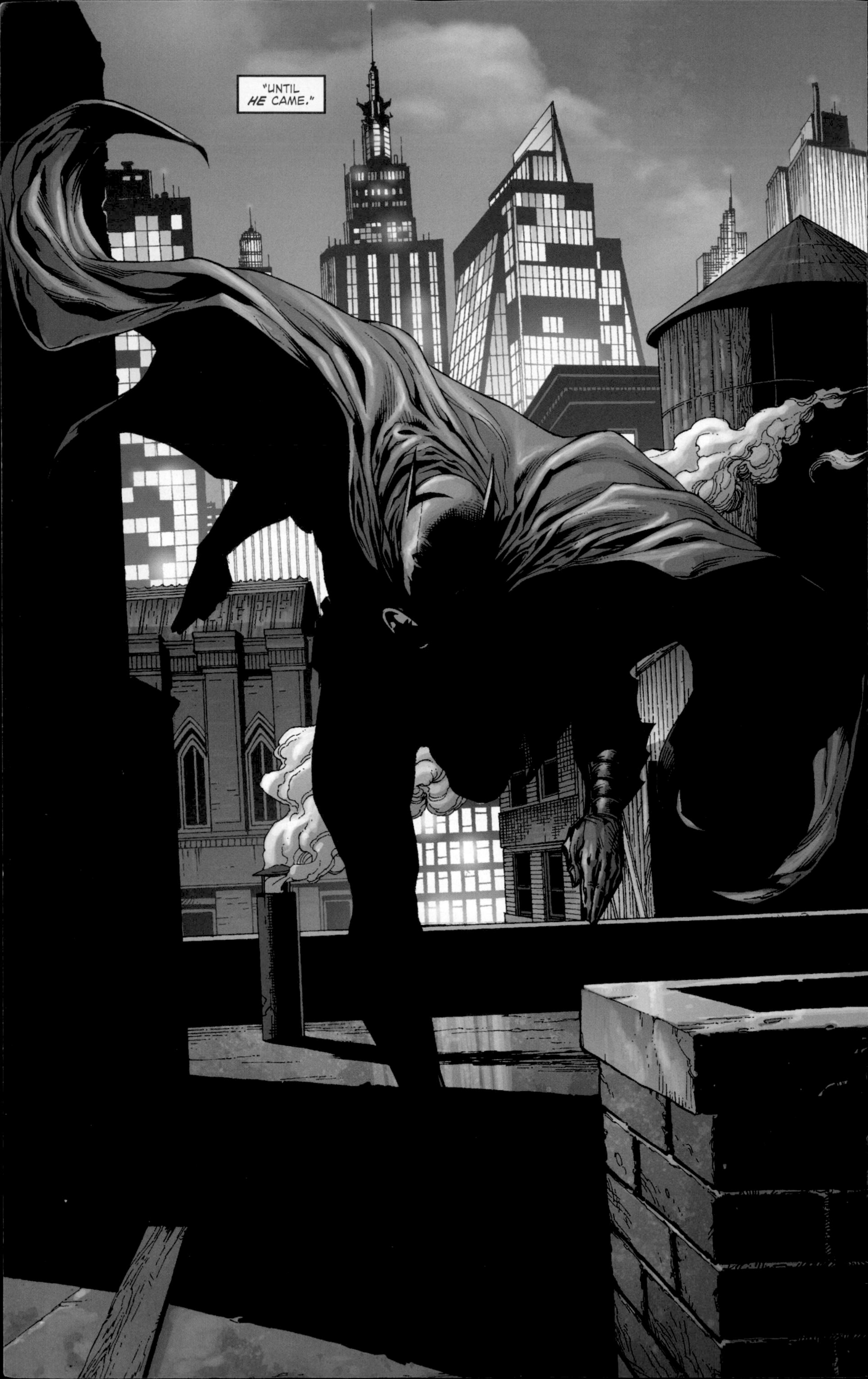
"UNTIL HE CAME."

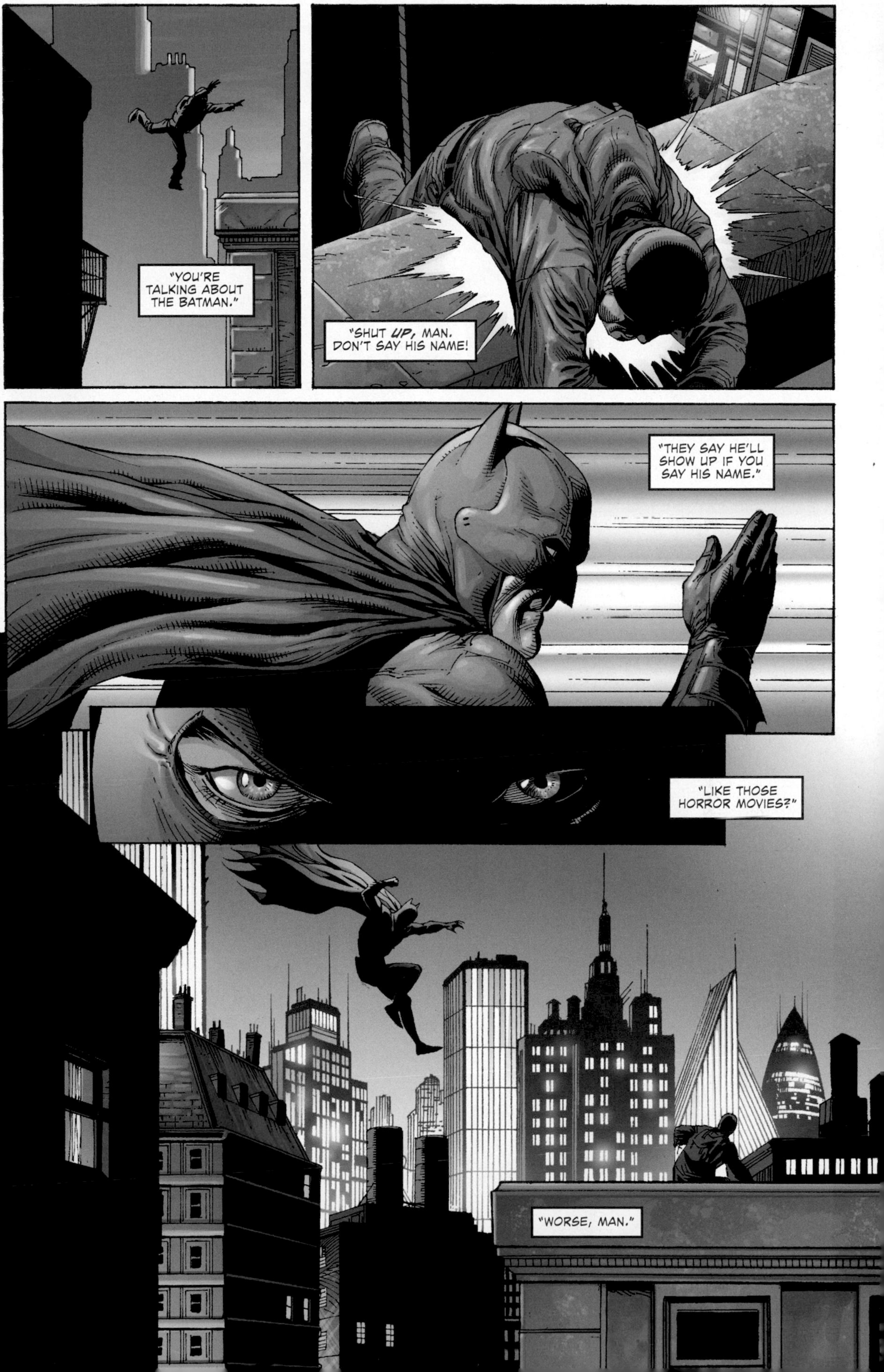
"YOU'RE TALKING ABOUT THE BATMAN."
"SHUT UP, MAN. DON'T SAY HIS NAME!
"THEY SAY HE'LL SHOW UP IF YOU SAY HIS NAME."
"LIKE THOSE HORROR MOVIES?"
"WORSE, MAN."

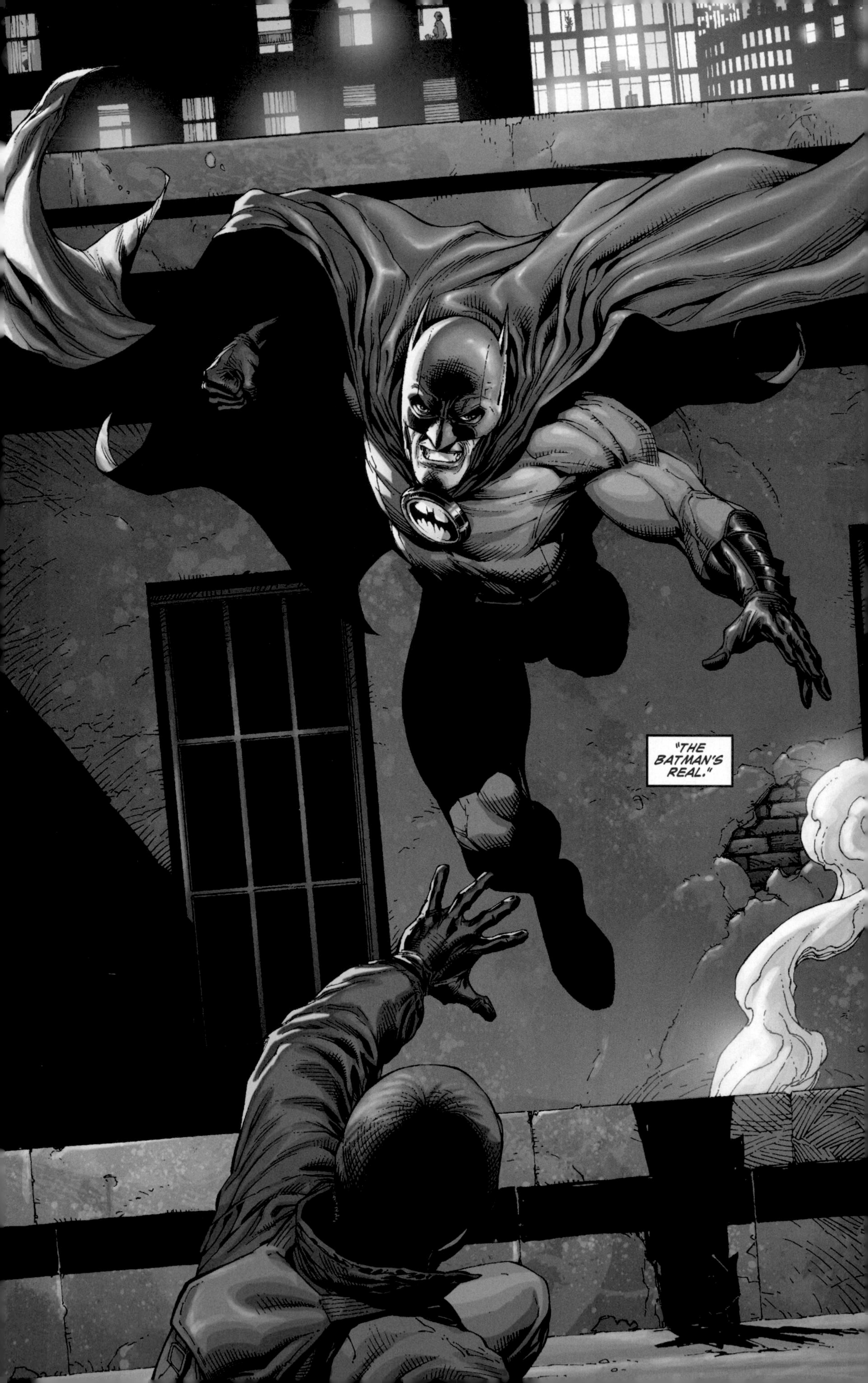
"THE BATMAN'S REAL."

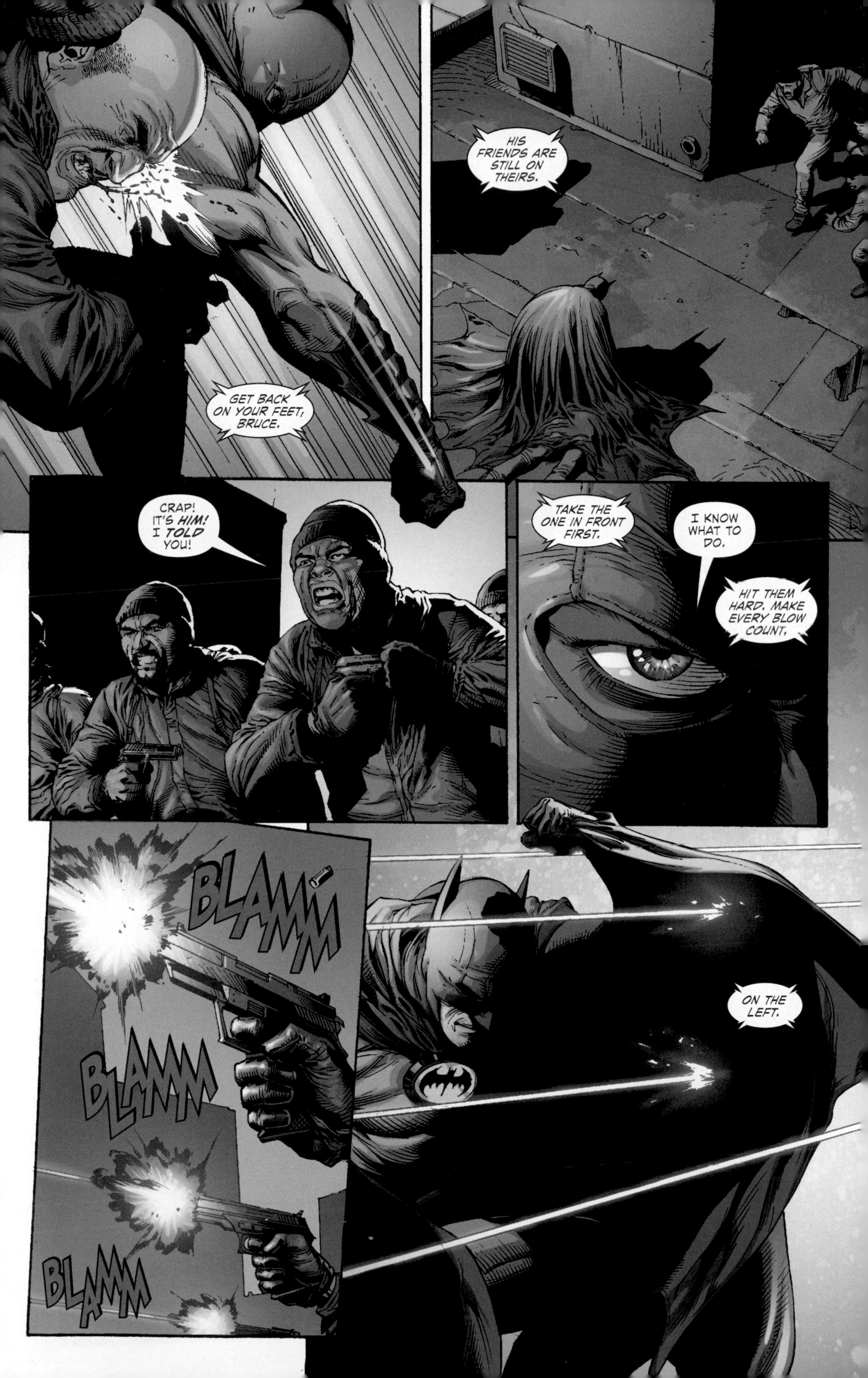
GET BACK ON YOUR FEET, BRUCE.
HIS FRIENDS ARE STILL ON THEIRS.
CRAP! IT'S HIM! I TOLD YOU!
TAKE THE ONE IN FRONT FIRST.
I KNOW WHAT TO DO.
HIT THEM HARD. MAKE EVERY BLOW COUNT.
BLAMM
BLAMM
BLAMM
ON THE LEFT.

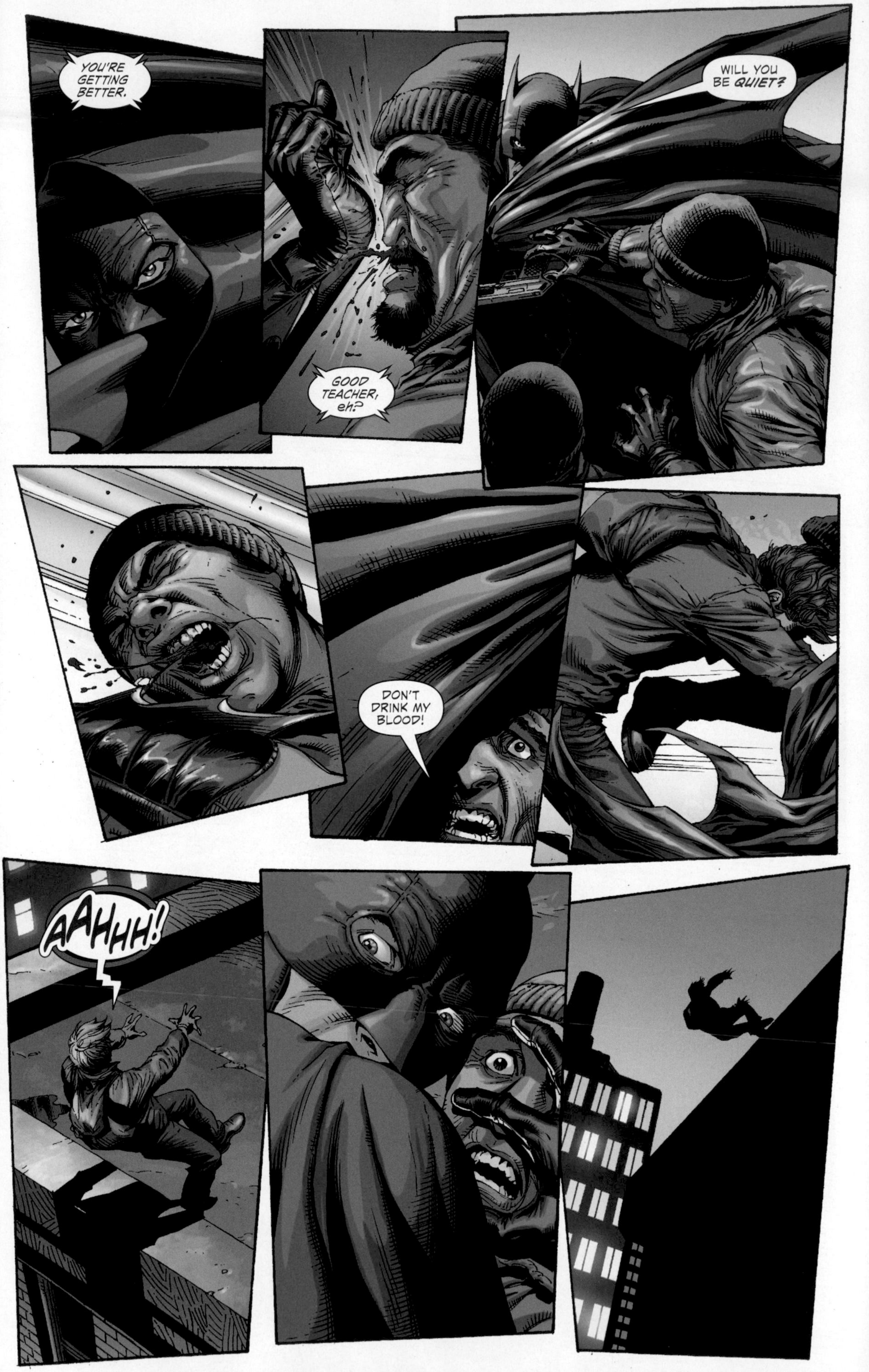
YOU'RE GETTING BETTER.
GOOD TEACHER, eh?
WILL YOU BE QUIET?
DON'T DRINK MY BLOOD!
AAHHH!

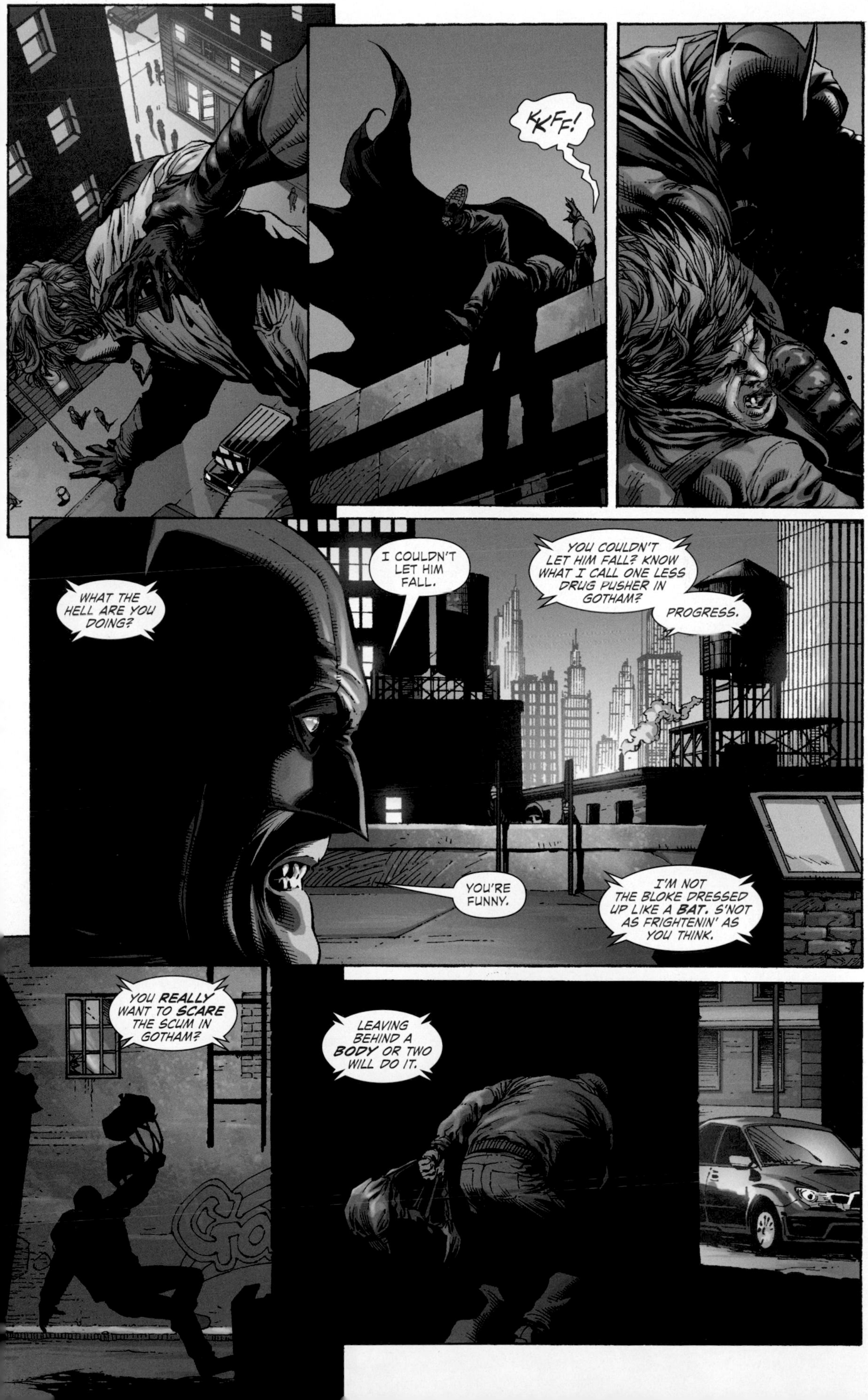
KKFF!
WHAT THE HELL ARE YOU DOING?
I COULDN'T LET HIM FALL.
YOU COULDN'T LET HIM FALL? KNOW WHAT I CALL ONE LESS DRUG PUSHER IN GOTHAM?
PROGRESS.
YOU'RE FUNNY.
I'M NOT THE BLOKE DRESSED UP LIKE A **BAT.** S'NOT AS FRIGHTENIN' AS YOU THINK.
YOU **REALLY** WANT TO **SCARE** THE SCUM IN GOTHAM?
LEAVING BEHIND A **BODY** OR TWO WILL DO IT.

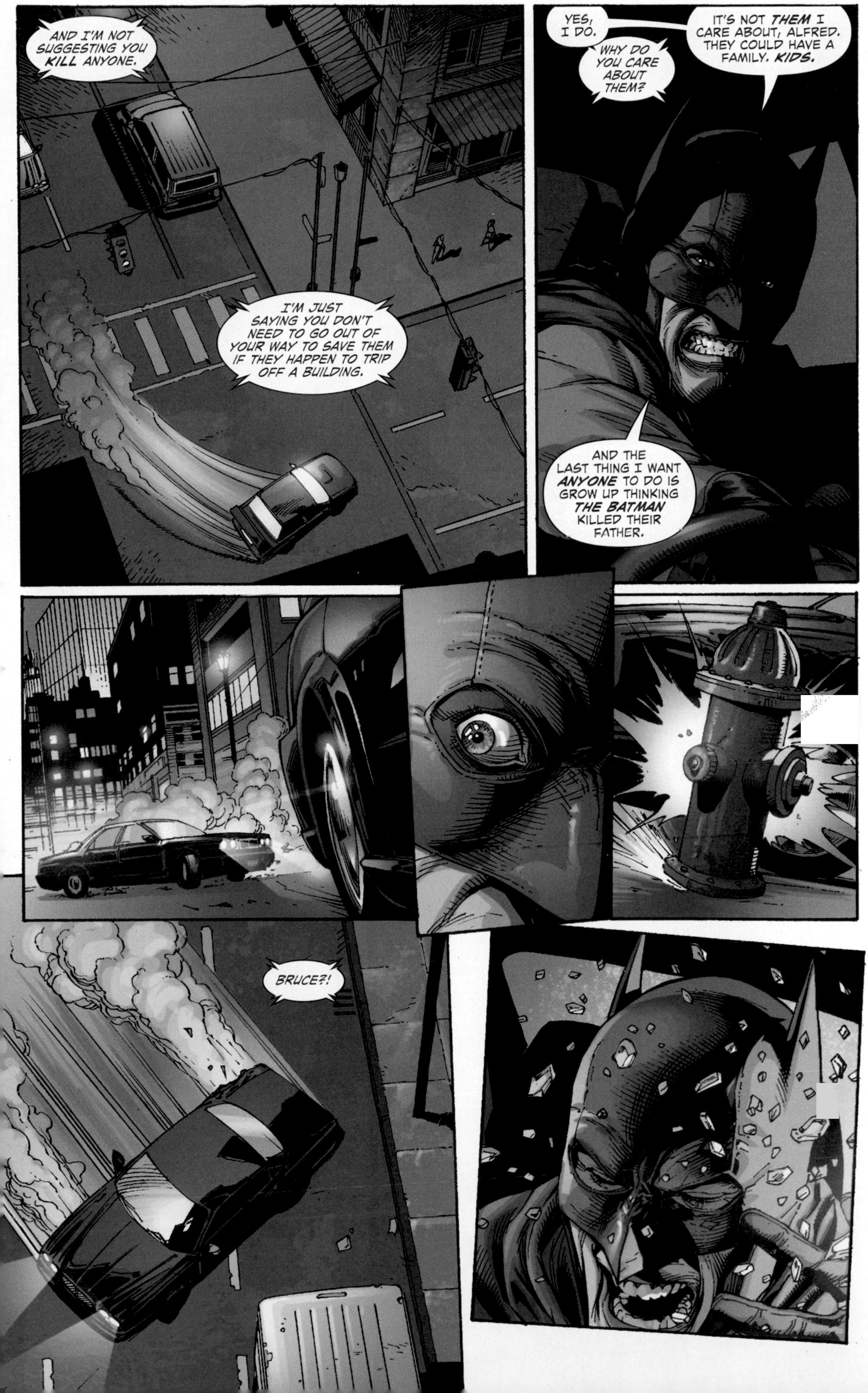
AND I'M NOT SUGGESTING YOU KILL ANYONE.
I'M JUST SAYING YOU DON'T NEED TO GO OUT OF YOUR WAY TO SAVE THEM IF THEY HAPPEN TO TRIP OFF A BUILDING.
YES, I DO.
WHY DO YOU CARE ABOUT THEM?
IT'S NOT THEM I CARE ABOUT, ALFRED. THEY COULD HAVE A FAMILY. KIDS.
AND THE LAST THING I WANT ANYONE TO DO IS GROW UP THINKING THE BATMAN KILLED THEIR FATHER.
BRUCE?!

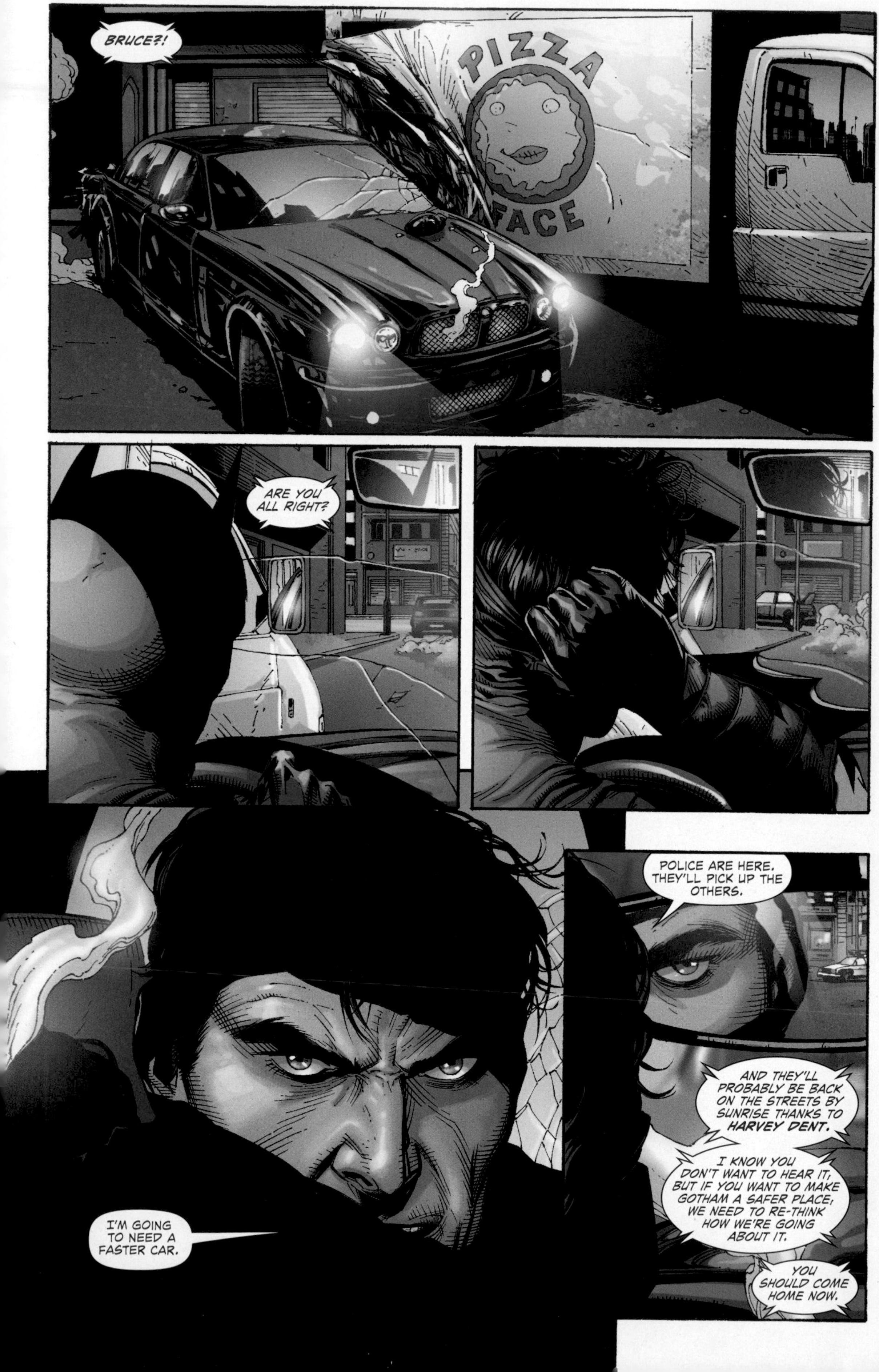
BRUCE?!
PIZZA
FACE
ARE YOU ALL RIGHT?
POLICE ARE HERE. THEY'LL PICK UP THE OTHERS.
AND THEY'LL PROBABLY BE BACK ON THE STREETS BY SUNRISE THANKS TO HARVEY DENT.
I KNOW YOU DON'T WANT TO HEAR IT, BUT IF YOU WANT TO MAKE GOTHAM A SAFER PLACE, WE NEED TO RE-THINK HOW WE'RE GOING ABOUT IT.
YOU SHOULD COME HOME NOW.
I'M GOING TO NEED A FASTER CAR.

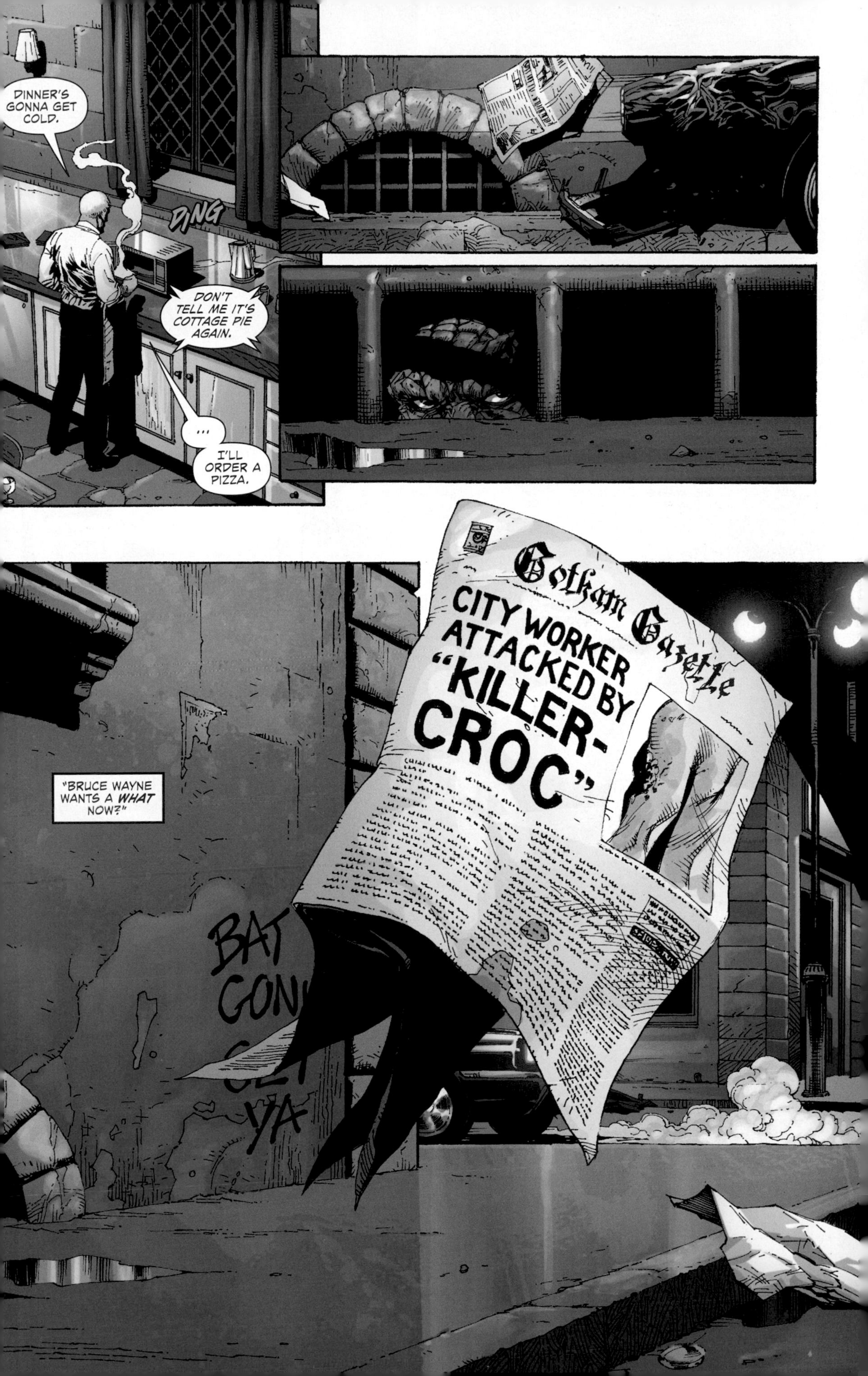
DINNER'S GONNA GET COLD.
DING
DON'T TELL ME IT'S COTTAGE PIE AGAIN.
...
I'LL ORDER A PIZZA.
Gotham Gazette
CITY WORKER ATTACKED BY "KILLER-CROC"
"BRUCE WAYNE WANTS A *WHAT* NOW?"
BAT
GON
YA

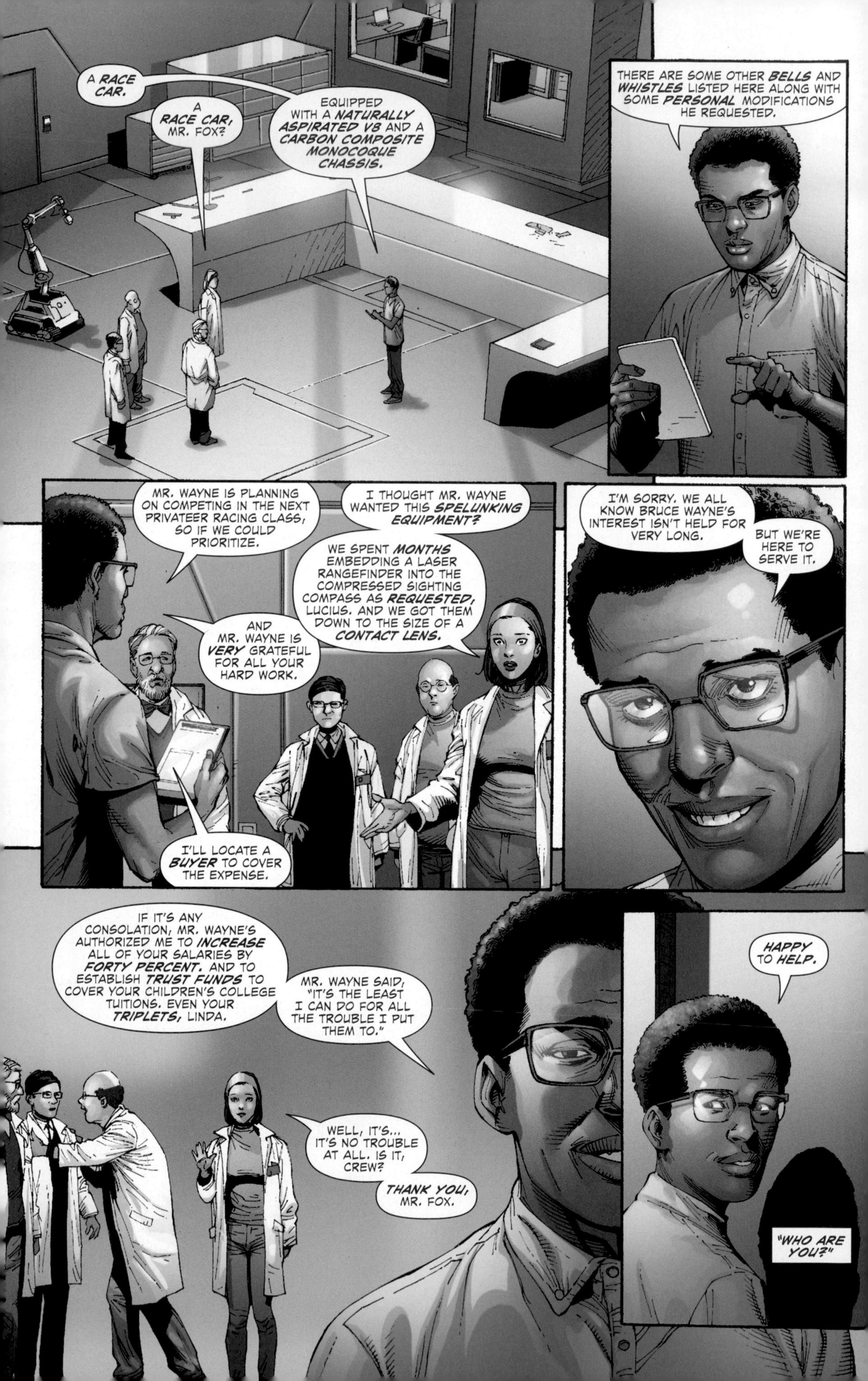
A RACE CAR.
A RACE CAR, MR. FOX?
EQUIPPED WITH A NATURALLY ASPIRATED V8 AND A CARBON COMPOSITE MONOCOQUE CHASSIS.
THERE ARE SOME OTHER BELLS AND WHISTLES LISTED HERE ALONG WITH SOME PERSONAL MODIFICATIONS HE REQUESTED.
MR. WAYNE IS PLANNING ON COMPETING IN THE NEXT PRIVATEER RACING CLASS, SO IF WE COULD PRIORITIZE.
I THOUGHT MR. WAYNE WANTED THIS SPELUNKING EQUIPMENT?
WE SPENT MONTHS EMBEDDING A LASER RANGEFINDER INTO THE COMPRESSED SIGHTING COMPASS AS REQUESTED, LUCIUS. AND WE GOT THEM DOWN TO THE SIZE OF A CONTACT LENS.
AND MR. WAYNE IS VERY GRATEFUL FOR ALL YOUR HARD WORK.
I'LL LOCATE A BUYER TO COVER THE EXPENSE.
I'M SORRY. WE ALL KNOW BRUCE WAYNE'S INTEREST ISN'T HELD FOR VERY LONG.
BUT WE'RE HERE TO SERVE IT.
IF IT'S ANY CONSOLATION, MR. WAYNE'S AUTHORIZED ME TO INCREASE ALL OF YOUR SALARIES BY FORTY PERCENT. AND TO ESTABLISH TRUST FUNDS TO COVER YOUR CHILDREN'S COLLEGE TUITIONS. EVEN YOUR TRIPLETS, LINDA.
MR. WAYNE SAID, "IT'S THE LEAST I CAN DO FOR ALL THE TROUBLE I PUT THEM TO."
WELL, IT'S... IT'S NO TROUBLE AT ALL. IS IT, CREW?
THANK YOU, MR. FOX.
HAPPY TO HELP.
"WHO ARE YOU?"

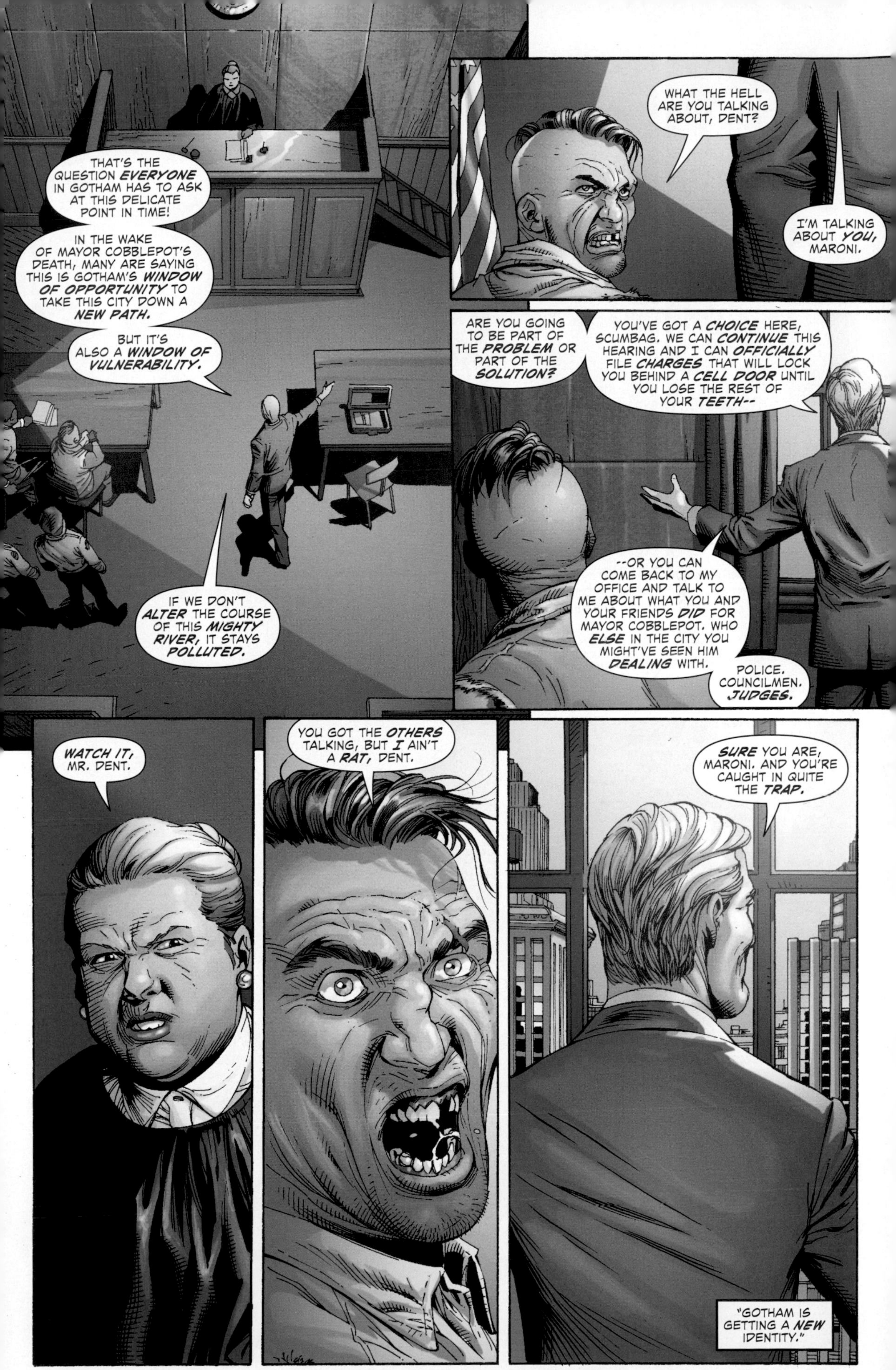
THAT'S THE QUESTION EVERYONE IN GOTHAM HAS TO ASK AT THIS DELICATE POINT IN TIME!
IN THE WAKE OF MAYOR COBBLEPOT'S DEATH, MANY ARE SAYING THIS IS GOTHAM'S WINDOW OF OPPORTUNITY TO TAKE THIS CITY DOWN A NEW PATH.
BUT IT'S ALSO A WINDOW OF VULNERABILITY.
IF WE DON'T ALTER THE COURSE OF THIS MIGHTY RIVER, IT STAYS POLLUTED.
WHAT THE HELL ARE YOU TALKING ABOUT, DENT?
I'M TALKING ABOUT YOU, MARONI.
ARE YOU GOING TO BE PART OF THE PROBLEM OR PART OF THE SOLUTION?
YOU'VE GOT A CHOICE HERE, SCUMBAG. WE CAN CONTINUE THIS HEARING AND I CAN OFFICIALLY FILE CHARGES THAT WILL LOCK YOU BEHIND A CELL DOOR UNTIL YOU LOSE THE REST OF YOUR TEETH--
--OR YOU CAN COME BACK TO MY OFFICE AND TALK TO ME ABOUT WHAT YOU AND YOUR FRIENDS DID FOR MAYOR COBBLEPOT. WHO ELSE IN THE CITY YOU MIGHT'VE SEEN HIM DEALING WITH.
POLICE. COUNCILMEN. JUDGES.
WATCH IT, MR. DENT.
YOU GOT THE OTHERS TALKING, BUT I AIN'T A RAT, DENT.
SURE YOU ARE, MARONI. AND YOU'RE CAUGHT IN QUITE THE TRAP.
"GOTHAM IS GETTING A NEW IDENTITY."

WE DON'T KNOW IF IT'S FOR GOOD OR BAD, BUT--

GOOD OR BAD?

MAYOR JESSICA DENT AND HER BROTHER ARE ON A CRUSADE TO SAVE THIS CITY FROM THE FILTH IT'S BEEN WALLOWING IN SINCE THE WAYNES WERE MURDERED.

THE SOONER THE DENTS CLEAN UP THE MESS MAYOR COBBLEPOT CREATED, THE BETTER.

BEFORE HIS DEATH AT THE HANDS OF THE BATMAN, COBBLEPOT'S EMPIRE OF CRIMINAL ACTIVITY STRETCHED DEEP INTO THE ROOTS OF OUR CITY, INCLUDING THE "ILLUSTRIOUS" GOTHAM P.D.

ASK ME, THERE'S NOTHING WORSE THAN A BAD COP.

I AGREE WITH YOU ON THAT, BUT I'M STILL NOT CONVINCED THE BATMAN KILLED MAYOR COBBLEPOT. COBBLEPOT WAS SHOT, BUT EYEWITNESSES SAY THE BATMAN DOESN'T CARRY GUNS.

THEY ALSO SAY BATMAN CAN TRAVEL THROUGH SHADOWS. LOOK, IF THE BATMAN DIDN'T KILL MAYOR COBBLEPOT--

--WHO THE HELL DID?

CLAK

BULLOCK?

HAIR OF THE DOG

LADI

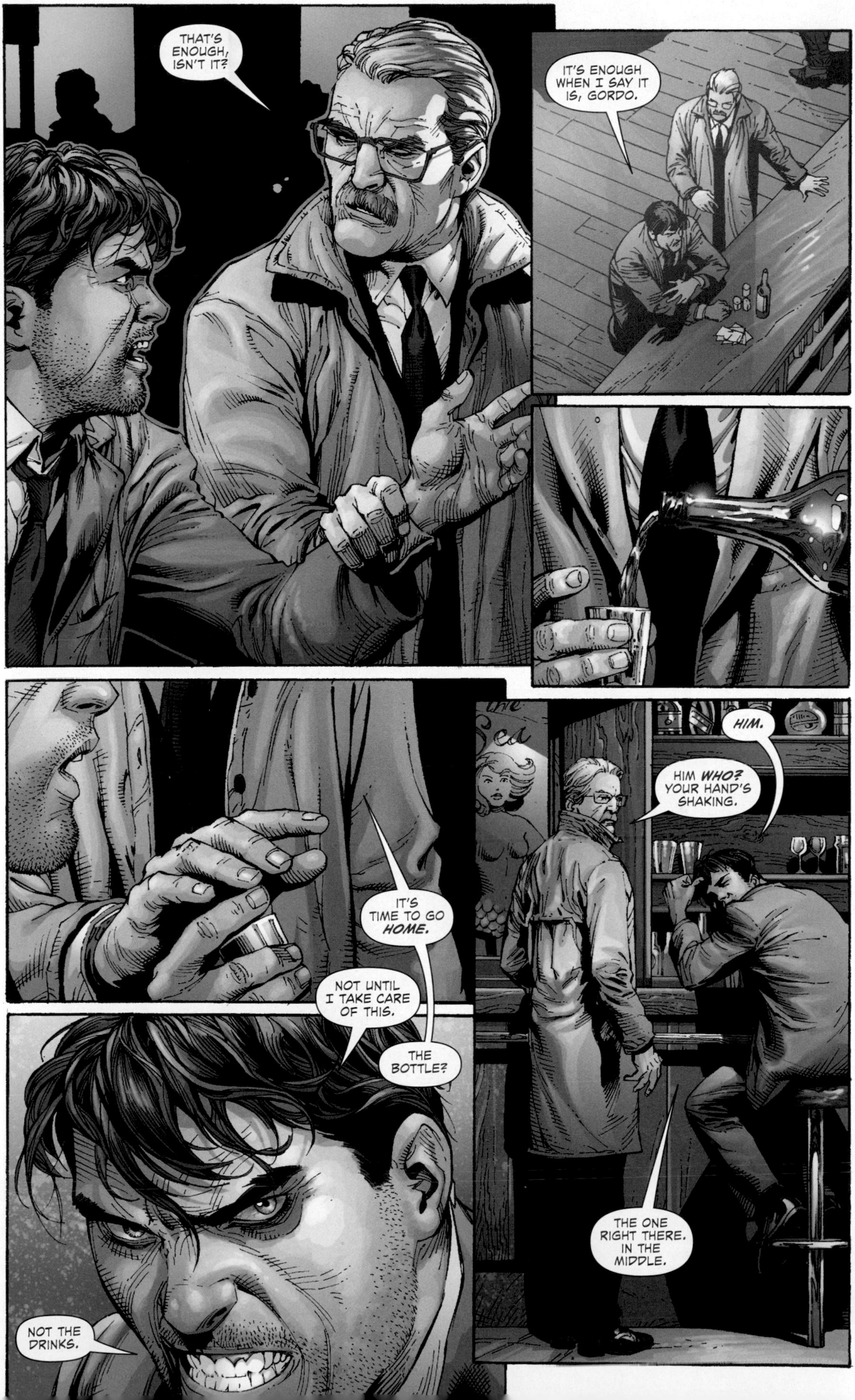
THAT'S ENOUGH, ISN'T IT?
IT'S ENOUGH WHEN I SAY IT IS, GORDO.
IT'S TIME TO GO HOME.
NOT UNTIL I TAKE CARE OF THIS.
THE BOTTLE?
NOT THE DRINKS.
HIM.
HIM WHO? YOUR HAND'S SHAKING.
THE ONE RIGHT THERE. IN THE MIDDLE.

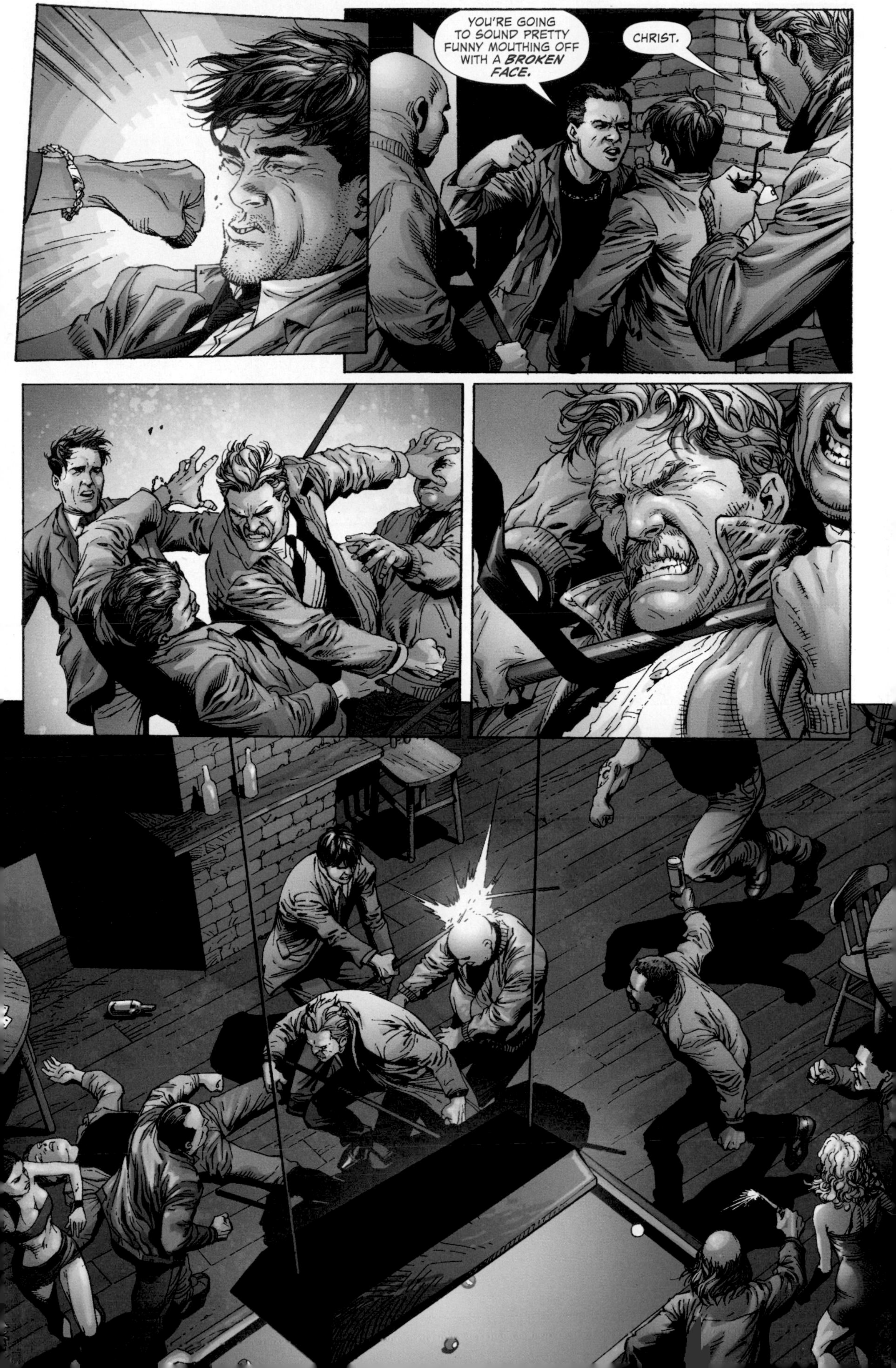
YOU'RE GOING TO SOUND PRETTY FUNNY MOUTHING OFF WITH A BROKEN FACE.
CHRIST.

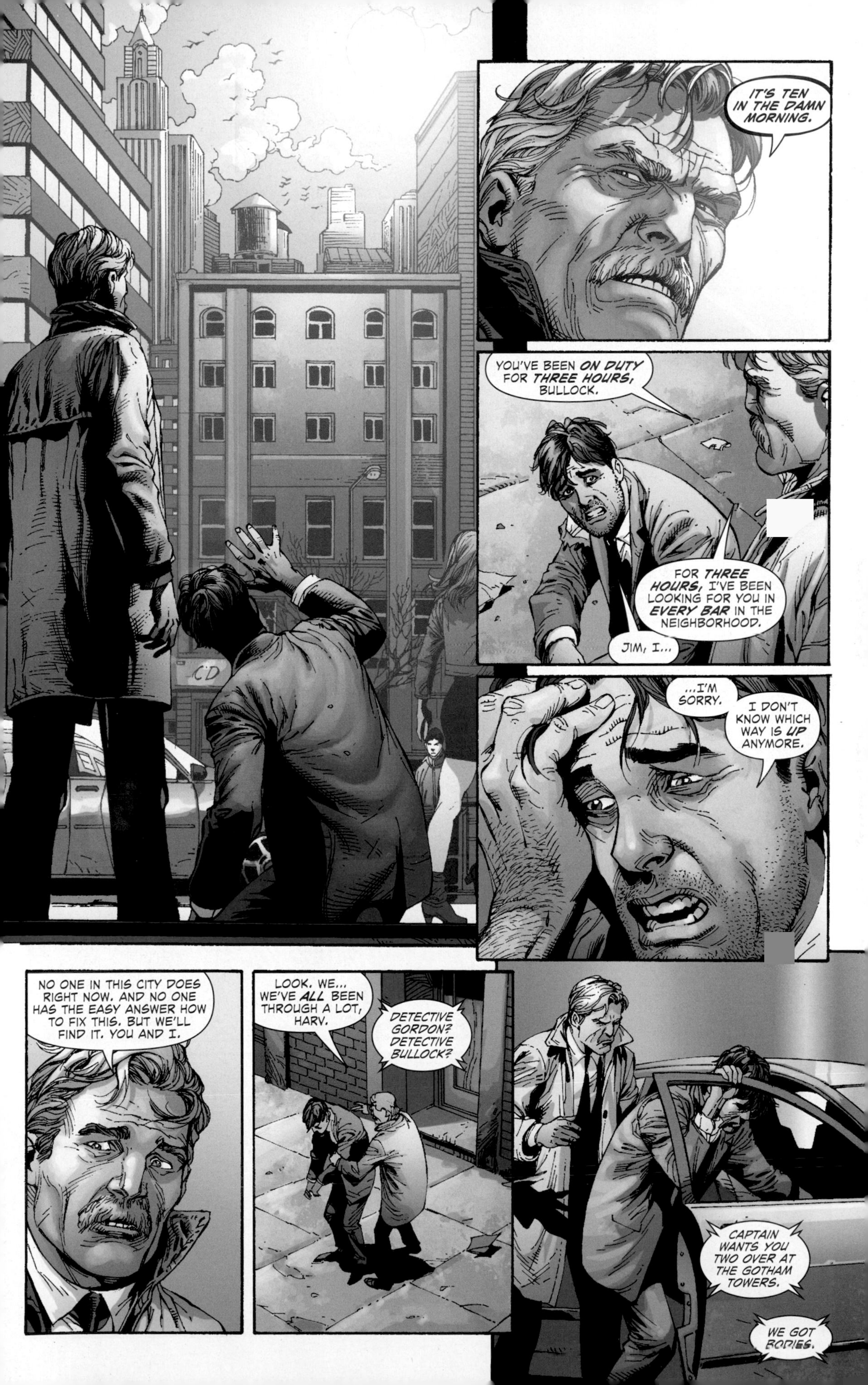
IT'S TEN IN THE DAMN MORNING.
YOU'VE BEEN ON DUTY FOR THREE HOURS, BULLOCK.
FOR THREE HOURS, I'VE BEEN LOOKING FOR YOU IN EVERY BAR IN THE NEIGHBORHOOD.
JIM, I...
...I'M SORRY.
I DON'T KNOW WHICH WAY IS UP ANYMORE.
NO ONE IN THIS CITY DOES RIGHT NOW. AND NO ONE HAS THE EASY ANSWER HOW TO FIX THIS. BUT WE'LL FIND IT. YOU AND I.
LOOK. WE... WE'VE ALL BEEN THROUGH A LOT, HARV.
DETECTIVE GORDON? DETECTIVE BULLOCK?
CAPTAIN WANTS YOU TWO OVER AT THE GOTHAM TOWERS.
WE GOT BODIES.

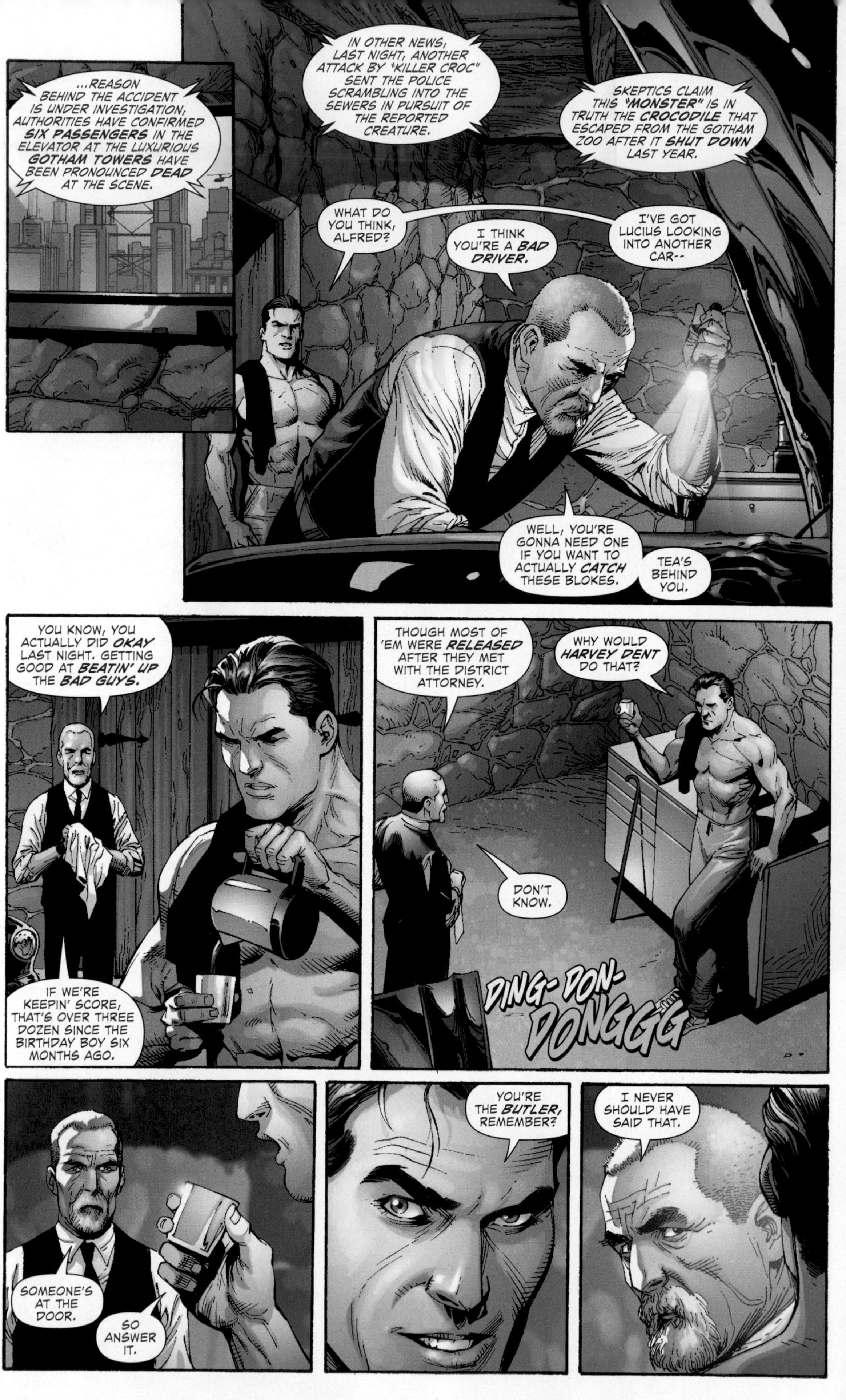
...REASON BEHIND THE ACCIDENT IS UNDER INVESTIGATION, AUTHORITIES HAVE CONFIRMED SIX PASSENGERS IN THE ELEVATOR AT THE LUXURIOUS GOTHAM TOWERS HAVE BEEN PRONOUNCED DEAD AT THE SCENE.
IN OTHER NEWS, LAST NIGHT, ANOTHER ATTACK BY "KILLER CROC" SENT THE POLICE SCRAMBLING INTO THE SEWERS IN PURSUIT OF THE REPORTED CREATURE.
SKEPTICS CLAIM THIS "MONSTER" IS IN TRUTH THE CROCODILE THAT ESCAPED FROM THE GOTHAM ZOO AFTER IT SHUT DOWN LAST YEAR.
WHAT DO YOU THINK, ALFRED?
I'VE GOT LUCIUS LOOKING INTO ANOTHER CAR--
I THINK YOU'RE A BAD DRIVER.
WELL, YOU'RE GONNA NEED ONE IF YOU WANT TO ACTUALLY CATCH THESE BLOKES.
TEA'S BEHIND YOU.
YOU KNOW, YOU ACTUALLY DID OKAY LAST NIGHT. GETTING GOOD AT BEATIN' UP THE BAD GUYS.
IF WE'RE KEEPIN' SCORE, THAT'S OVER THREE DOZEN SINCE THE BIRTHDAY BOY SIX MONTHS AGO.
THOUGH MOST OF 'EM WERE RELEASED AFTER THEY MET WITH THE DISTRICT ATTORNEY.
WHY WOULD HARVEY DENT DO THAT?
DON'T KNOW.
DING-DON-DONGGG
SOMEONE'S AT THE DOOR.
SO ANSWER IT.
YOU'RE THE BUTLER, REMEMBER?
I NEVER SHOULD HAVE SAID THAT.

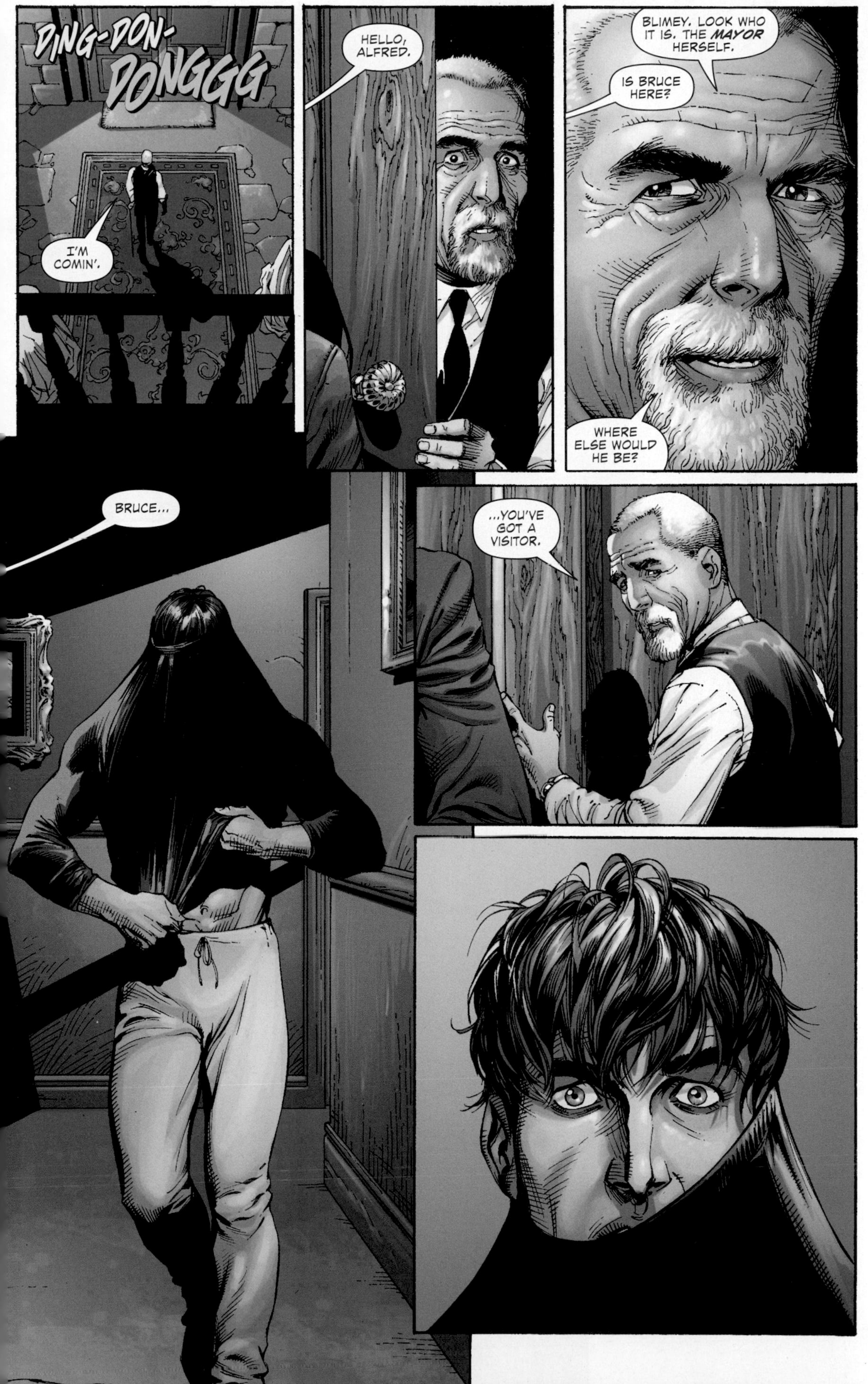
DING-DON-DONGGG
I'M COMIN'.
HELLO, ALFRED.
BLIMEY. LOOK WHO IT IS. THE MAYOR HERSELF.
IS BRUCE HERE?
WHERE ELSE WOULD HE BE?
BRUCE...
...YOU'VE GOT A VISITOR.

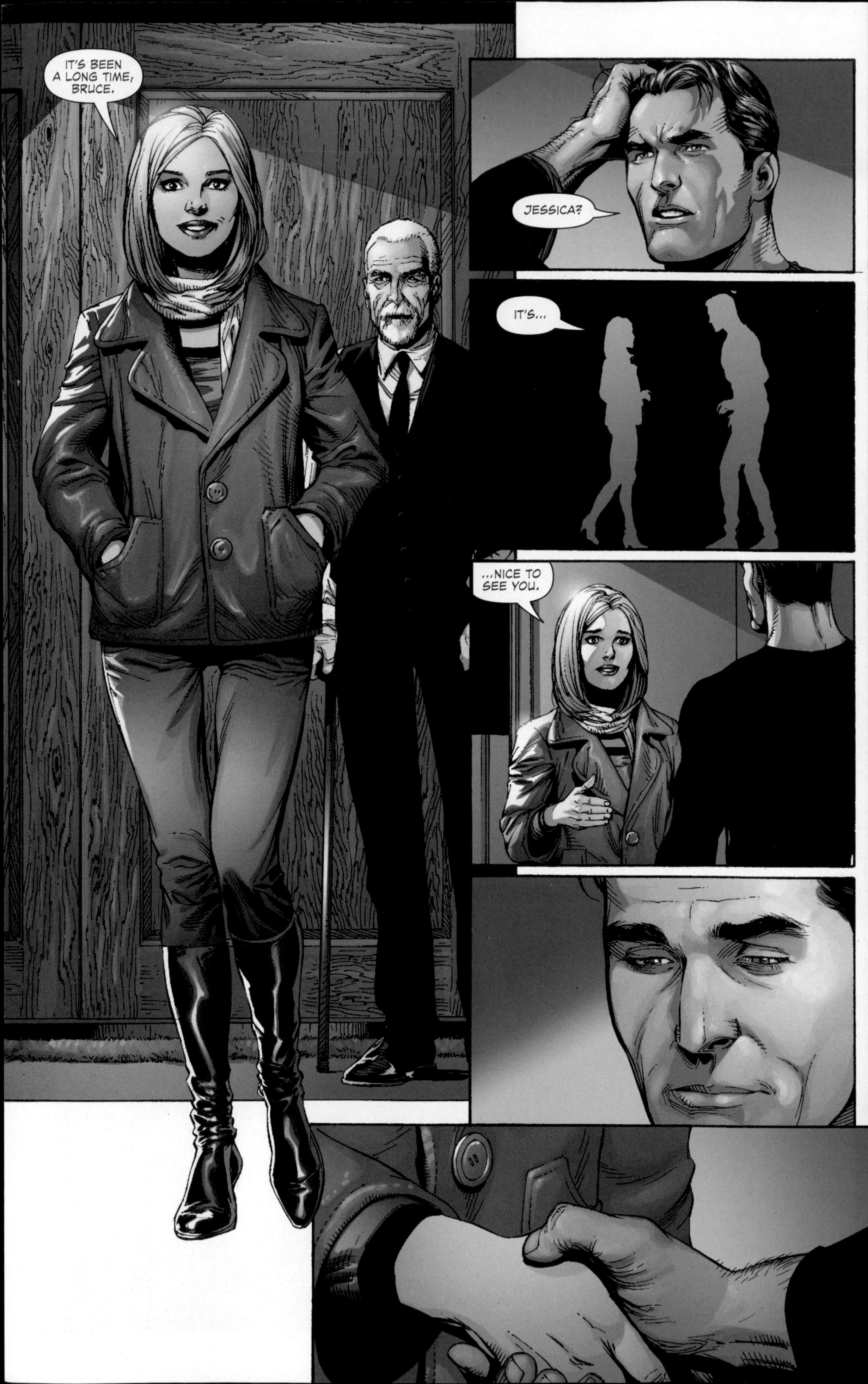
IT'S BEEN A LONG TIME, BRUCE.
JESSICA?
IT'S...
...NICE TO SEE YOU.

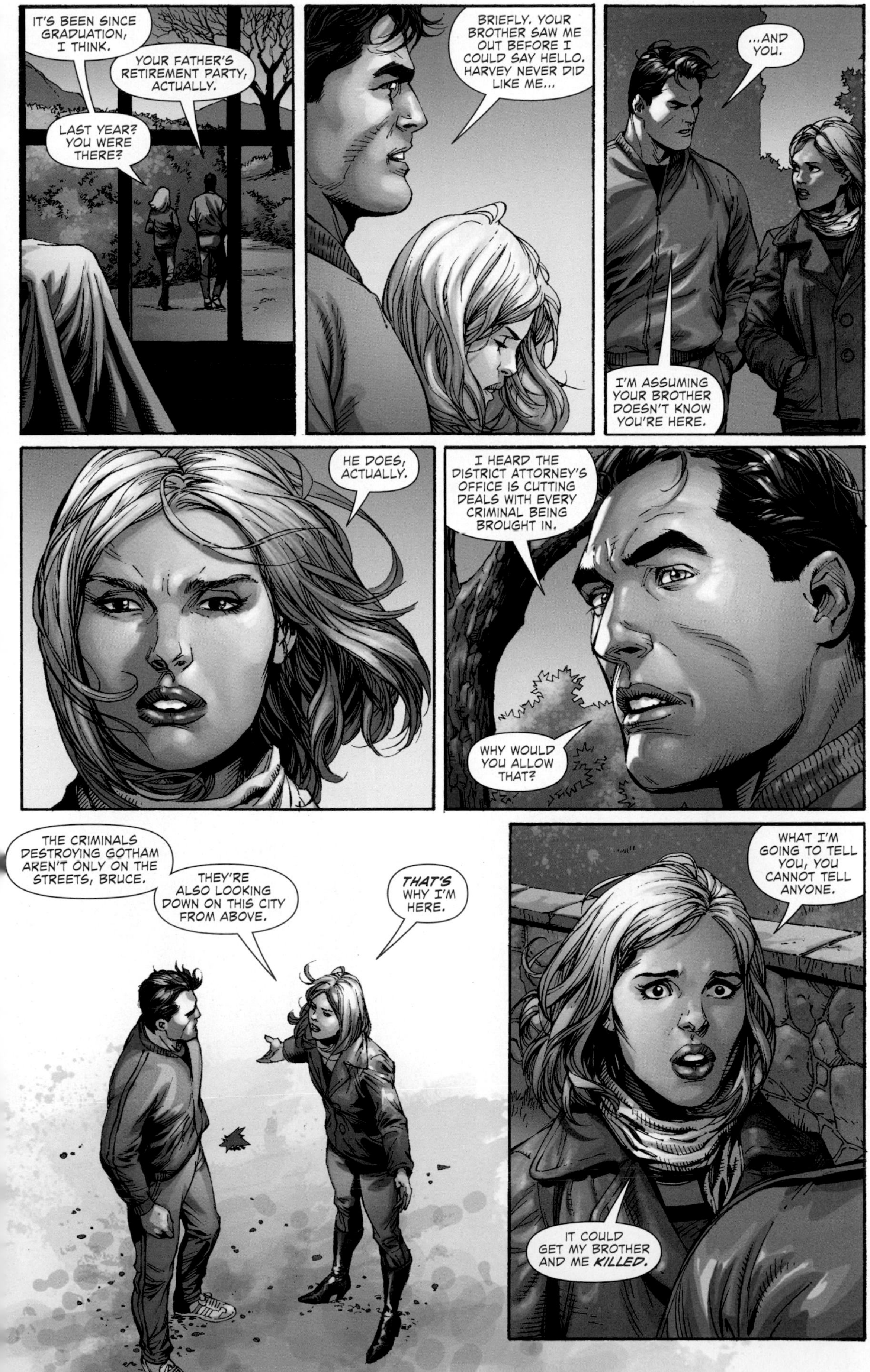
IT'S BEEN SINCE GRADUATION, I THINK.
YOUR FATHER'S RETIREMENT PARTY, ACTUALLY.
LAST YEAR? YOU WERE THERE?
BRIEFLY. YOUR BROTHER SAW ME OUT BEFORE I COULD SAY HELLO. HARVEY NEVER DID LIKE ME...
...AND YOU.
I'M ASSUMING YOUR BROTHER DOESN'T KNOW YOU'RE HERE.
HE DOES, ACTUALLY.
I HEARD THE DISTRICT ATTORNEY'S OFFICE IS CUTTING DEALS WITH EVERY CRIMINAL BEING BROUGHT IN.
WHY WOULD YOU ALLOW THAT?
THE CRIMINALS DESTROYING GOTHAM AREN'T ONLY ON THE STREETS, BRUCE.
THEY'RE ALSO LOOKING DOWN ON THIS CITY FROM ABOVE.
THAT'S WHY I'M HERE.
WHAT I'M GOING TO TELL YOU, YOU CANNOT TELL ANYONE.
IT COULD GET MY BROTHER AND ME KILLED.

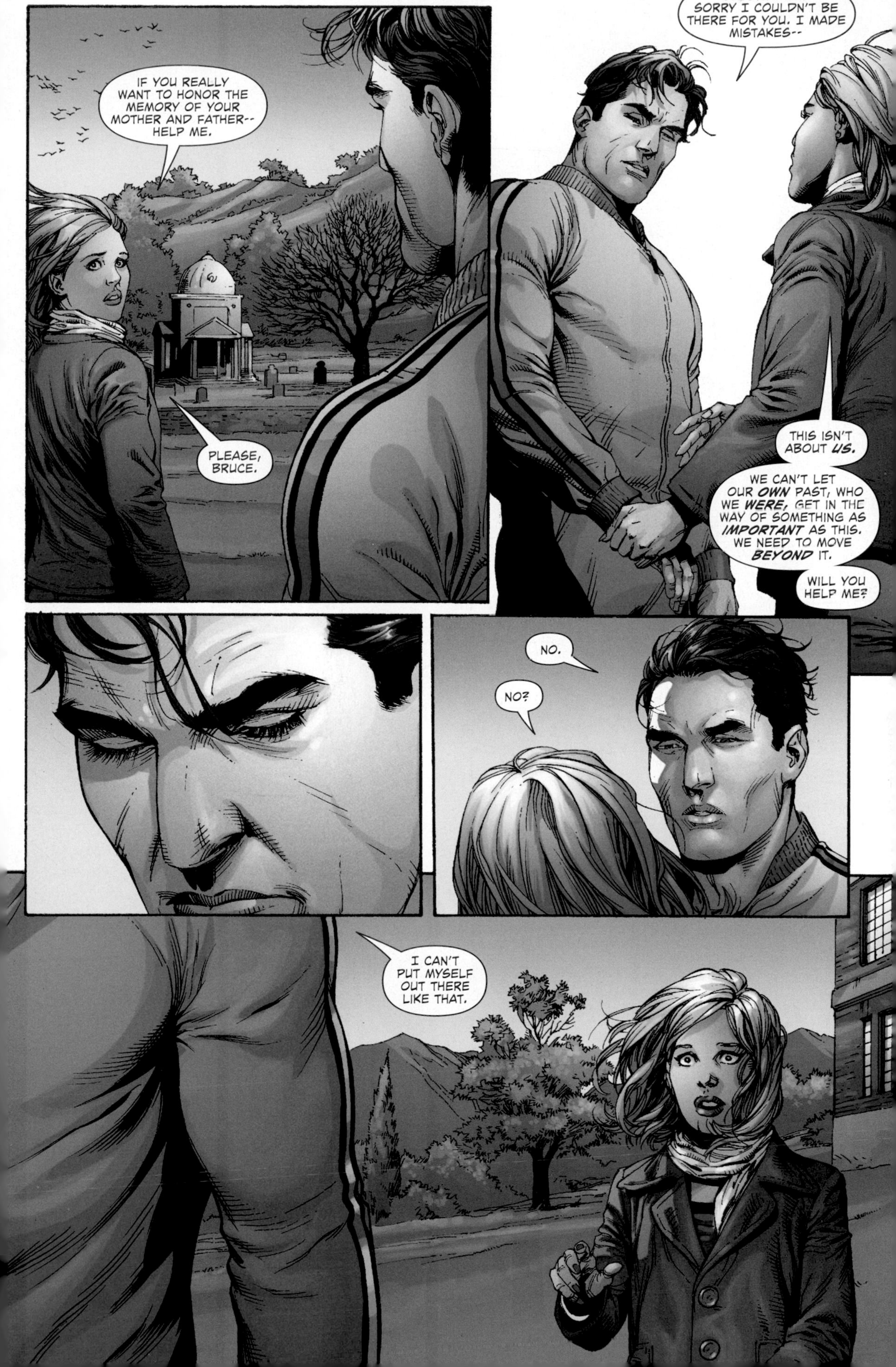
IF YOU REALLY WANT TO HONOR THE MEMORY OF YOUR MOTHER AND FATHER--HELP ME.
PLEASE, BRUCE.
JESSICA...I'M SORRY I COULDN'T BE THERE FOR YOU. I MADE MISTAKES--
THIS ISN'T ABOUT *US.*
WE CAN'T LET OUR *OWN* PAST, WHO WE *WERE,* GET IN THE WAY OF SOMETHING AS *IMPORTANT* AS THIS. WE NEED TO MOVE *BEYOND* IT.
WILL YOU HELP ME?
NO.
NO?
I CAN'T PUT MYSELF OUT THERE LIKE THAT.

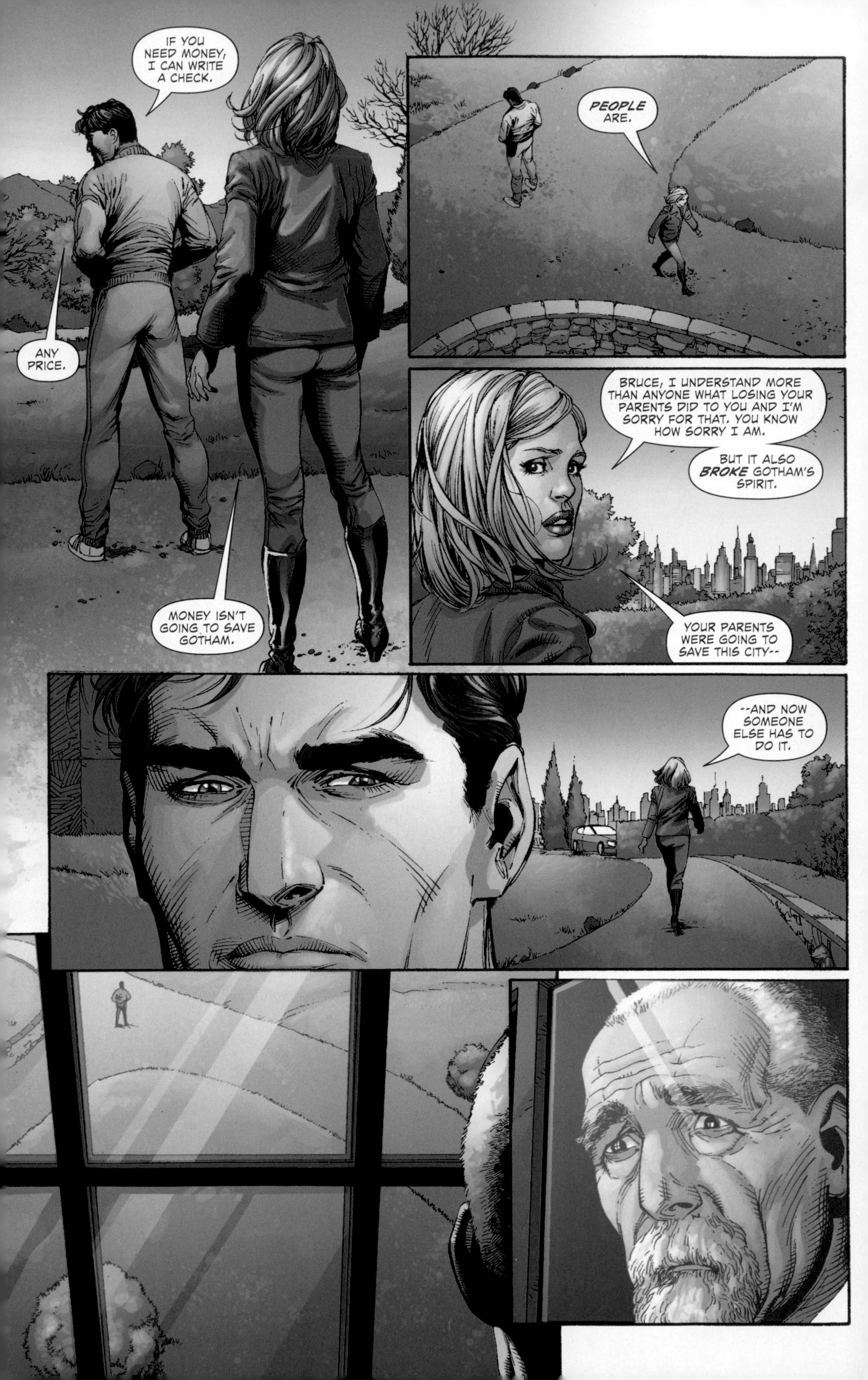
IF YOU NEED MONEY, I CAN WRITE A CHECK.
ANY PRICE.
MONEY ISN'T GOING TO SAVE GOTHAM.
PEOPLE ARE.
BRUCE, I UNDERSTAND MORE THAN ANYONE WHAT LOSING YOUR PARENTS DID TO YOU AND I'M SORRY FOR THAT. YOU KNOW HOW SORRY I AM.
BUT IT ALSO BROKE GOTHAM'S SPIRIT.
YOUR PARENTS WERE GOING TO SAVE THIS CITY--
--AND NOW SOMEONE ELSE HAS TO DO IT.

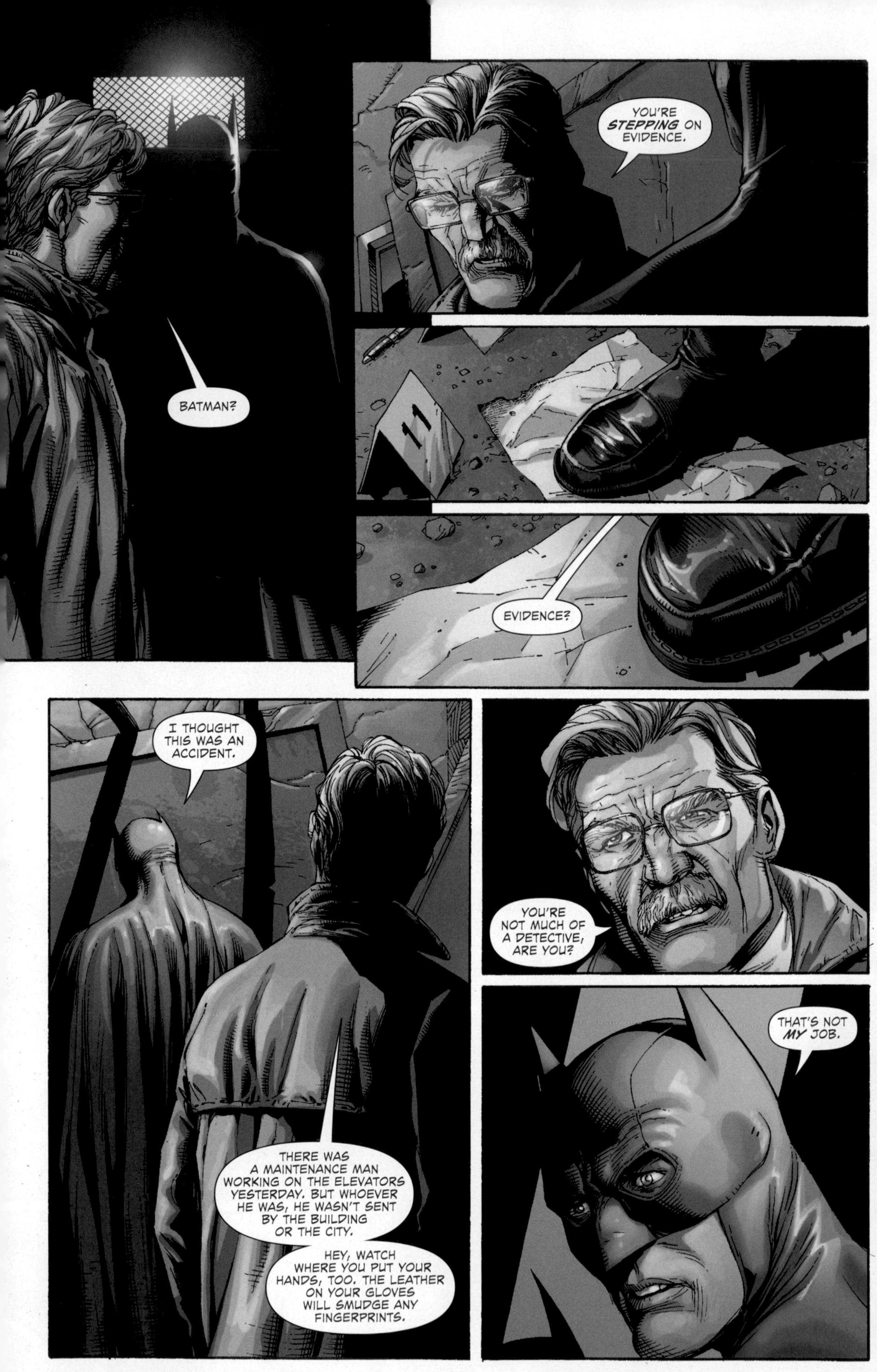
BATMAN?
YOU'RE STEPPING ON EVIDENCE.
EVIDENCE?
I THOUGHT THIS WAS AN ACCIDENT.
THERE WAS A MAINTENANCE MAN WORKING ON THE ELEVATORS YESTERDAY. BUT WHOEVER HE WAS, HE WASN'T SENT BY THE BUILDING OR THE CITY.
HEY, WATCH WHERE YOU PUT YOUR HANDS, TOO. THE LEATHER ON YOUR GLOVES WILL SMUDGE ANY FINGERPRINTS.
YOU'RE NOT MUCH OF A DETECTIVE, ARE YOU?
THAT'S NOT MY JOB.

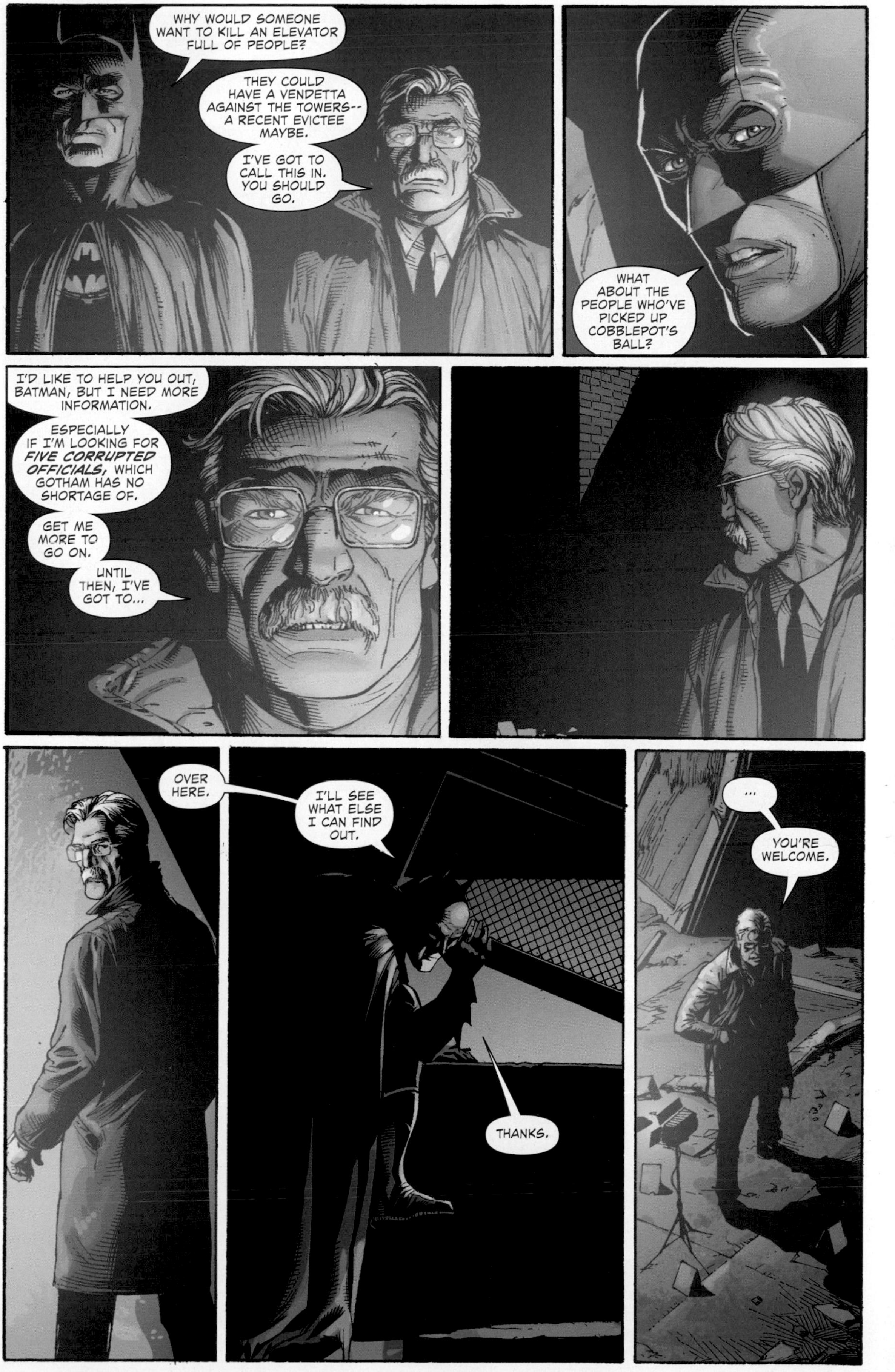
WHY WOULD SOMEONE WANT TO KILL AN ELEVATOR FULL OF PEOPLE?
THEY COULD HAVE A VENDETTA AGAINST THE TOWERS-- A RECENT EVICTEE MAYBE.
I'VE GOT TO CALL THIS IN. YOU SHOULD GO.
WHAT ABOUT THE PEOPLE WHO'VE PICKED UP COBBLEPOT'S BALL?
I'D LIKE TO HELP YOU OUT, BATMAN, BUT I NEED MORE INFORMATION.
ESPECIALLY IF I'M LOOKING FOR FIVE CORRUPTED OFFICIALS, WHICH GOTHAM HAS NO SHORTAGE OF.
GET ME MORE TO GO ON.
UNTIL THEN, I'VE GOT TO...
OVER HERE.
I'LL SEE WHAT ELSE I CAN FIND OUT.
THANKS.
...
YOU'RE WELCOME.

A *QUESTION MARK?*

YOU SURE THIS IS CONNECTED TO THE ELEVATOR CRASH, GORDO? MAYBE IT WAS JUST SOME KIDS.

FORENSICS FOUND TRACES OF THE SAME PAINT IN THE ELEVATOR SHAFT AND IN THE CALL BOX.

THE CALL BOX?

WHOEVER BLEW THE CABLE WAS TALKING TO THEM FOR SOME REASON.

WE WOULD'VE FOUND HIM BY NOW IF HE HACKED INTO THE PHONE LINE. HE REPLACED THE WHOLE CALL BOX WITH AN *SRD,* DIDN'T HE? A *SHORT-RANGE DEVICE?*

A *TWO-WAY RADIO* BROADCASTING AT *LESS* THAN A *SINGLE WATT.* HOW DID YOU KNOW THAT?

THERE WAS AN EPISODE OF *"HOLLYWOOD DETECTIVES"* I CONSULTED ON ABOUT THIS GUY AND HIS MISTRESS. THEY FAKED THE MAN'S KIDNAPPING TO HIDE HIS MONEY FROM HIS EX.

GUY USED A SHORT-RANGE DEVICE SO THEY COULDN'T TRACE THE CALL BACK TO THE HOUSE...AND SO HE COULD KEEP AN EYE ON THINGS.

BUT IT ALSO MEANT HE HAD TO BE NEARBY.

WHOEVER *OUR* GUY IS, HE PROBABLY TRIGGERED THE EXPLOSION WITH THE SAME RADIO.

BUT WHY THE QUESTION MARK?

BLKKF!

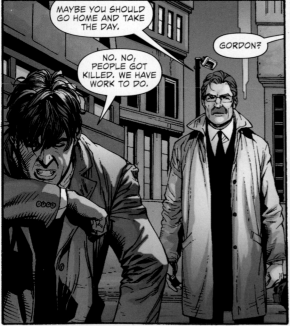

MAYBE YOU SHOULD GO HOME AND TAKE THE DAY.

GORDON?

NO. NO, PEOPLE GOT KILLED. WE HAVE WORK TO DO.

ALLEN? MONTOYA? WHAT IS IT?

CAPTAIN WANTS TO SEE YOU BOTH.

AND HE'S GOT A *GUEST.*

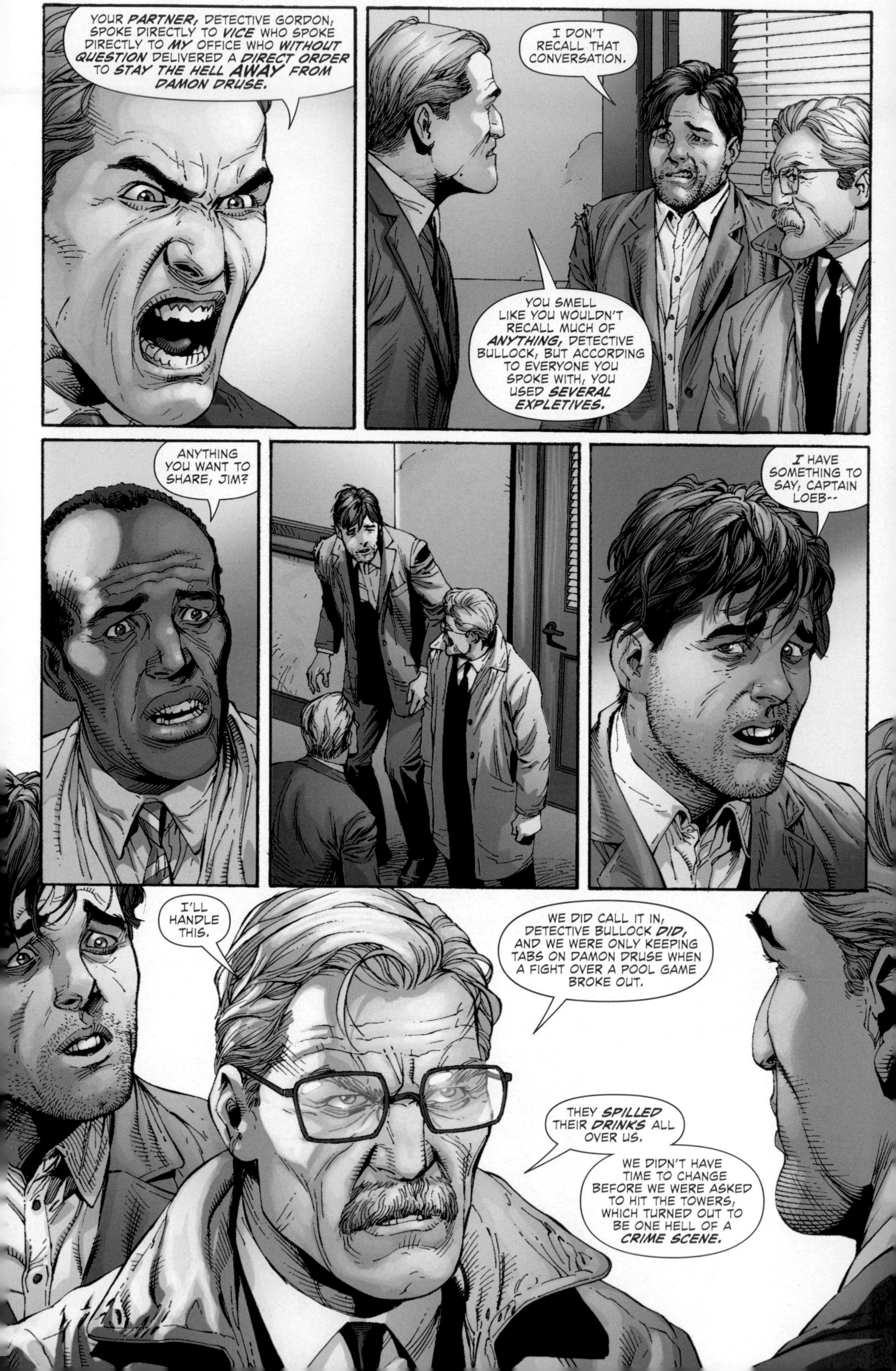
YOUR PARTNER, DETECTIVE GORDON, SPOKE DIRECTLY TO VICE WHO SPOKE DIRECTLY TO MY OFFICE WHO WITHOUT QUESTION DELIVERED A DIRECT ORDER TO STAY THE HELL AWAY FROM DAMON DRUSE.
I DON'T RECALL THAT CONVERSATION.
YOU SMELL LIKE YOU WOULDN'T RECALL MUCH OF ANYTHING, DETECTIVE BULLOCK, BUT ACCORDING TO EVERYONE YOU SPOKE WITH, YOU USED SEVERAL EXPLETIVES.
ANYTHING YOU WANT TO SHARE, JIM?
I HAVE SOMETHING TO SAY, CAPTAIN LOEB--
I'LL HANDLE THIS.
WE DID CALL IT IN, DETECTIVE BULLOCK DID, AND WE WERE ONLY KEEPING TABS ON DAMON DRUSE WHEN A FIGHT OVER A POOL GAME BROKE OUT.
THEY SPILLED THEIR DRINKS ALL OVER US.
WE DIDN'T HAVE TIME TO CHANGE BEFORE WE WERE ASKED TO HIT THE TOWERS, WHICH TURNED OUT TO BE ONE HELL OF A CRIME SCENE.

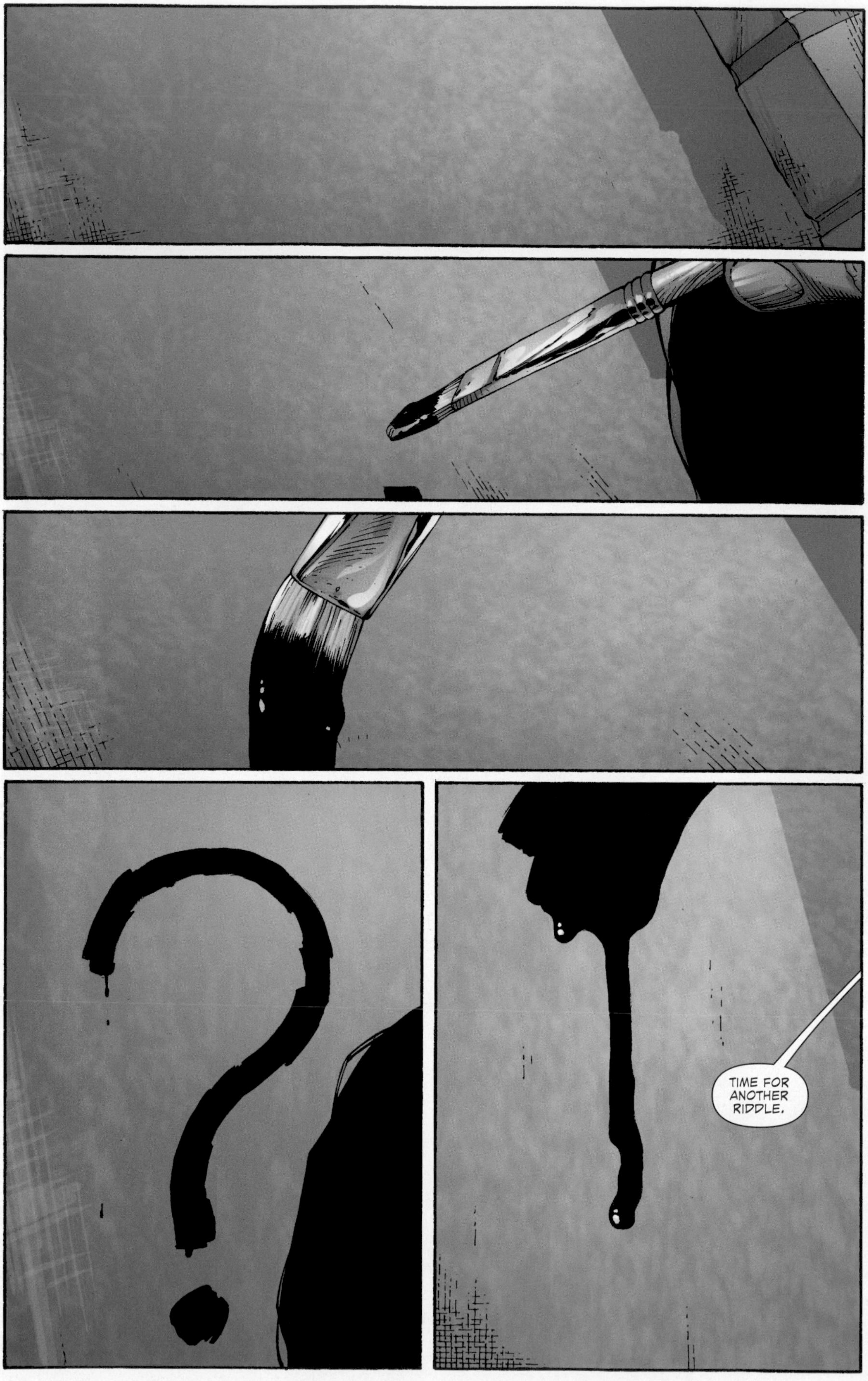
TIME FOR ANOTHER RIDDLE.

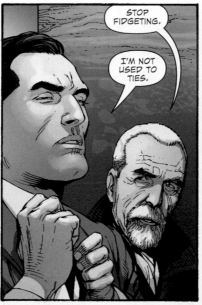

STOP FIDGETING.

I'M NOT USED TO TIES.

YOU'RE WAY OUT OF PRACTICE, BOY.

THIS ISN'T A SOCIAL CALL.

I'M ONLY HERE FOR MORE INFORMATION ON THESE FIVE OFFICIALS. AND ONCE I GET IT, I'LL TALK TO DETECTIVE GORDON--

ENOUGH WITH HIM. DETECTIVE GORDON DOESN'T KNOW YOU OR WHAT YOU'RE DOING OR WHY.

I CAN TRUST HIM.

I WOULDN'T TRUST ANY COP IN GOTHAM.

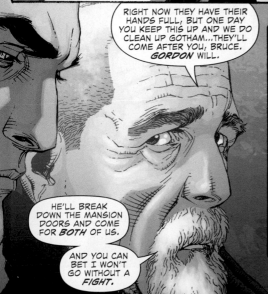

RIGHT NOW THEY HAVE THEIR HANDS FULL, BUT ONE DAY YOU KEEP THIS UP AND WE DO CLEAN UP GOTHAM...THEY'LL COME AFTER YOU, BRUCE. GORDON WILL.

HE'LL BREAK DOWN THE MANSION DOORS AND COME FOR BOTH OF US.

AND YOU CAN BET I WON'T GO WITHOUT A FIGHT.

28

DING

CAREFUL ABOUT GETTING JESSICA TOO INVOLVED.

I KNOW, ALFRED.

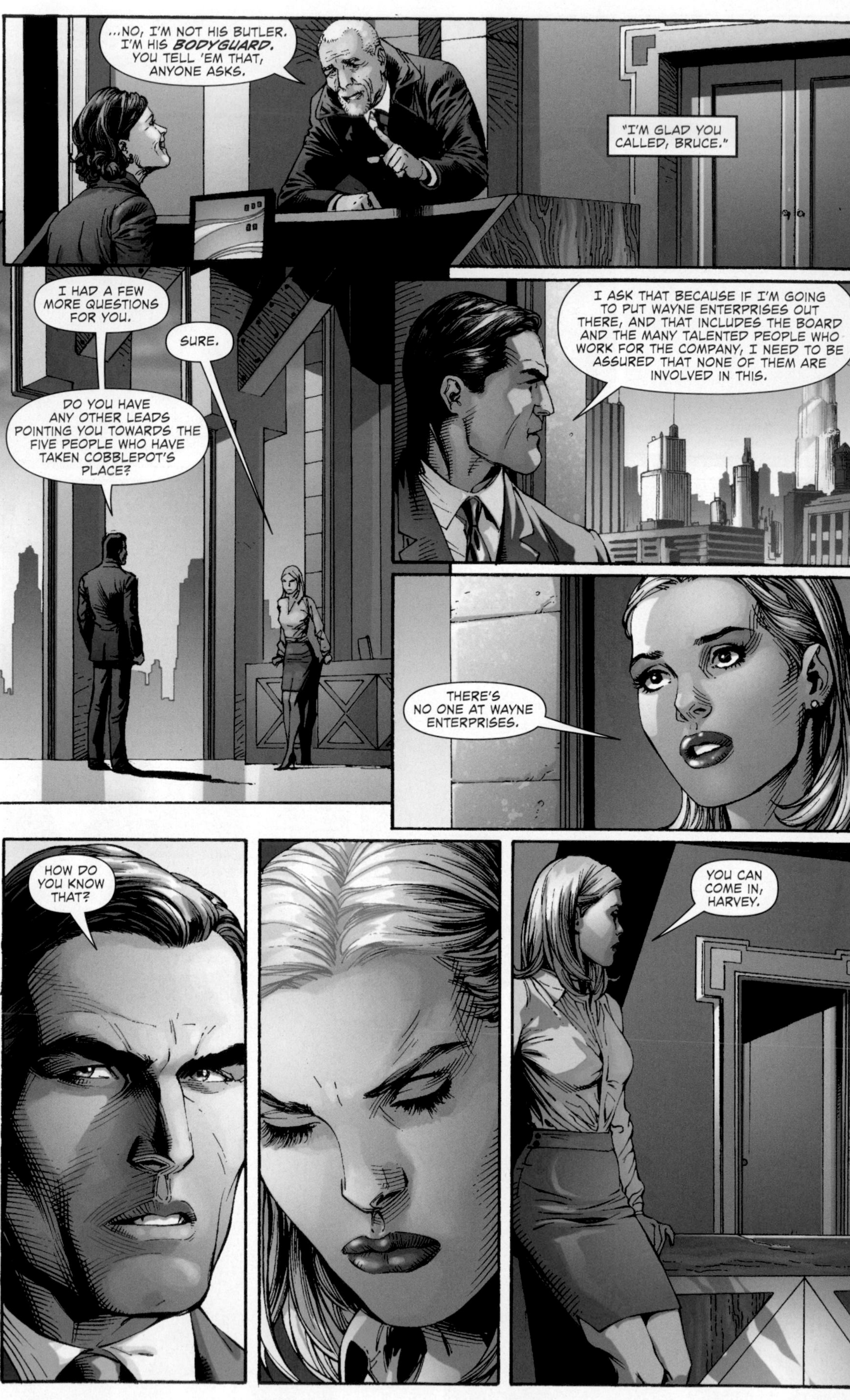
...NO, I'M NOT HIS BUTLER. I'M HIS *BODYGUARD.* YOU TELL 'EM THAT, ANYONE ASKS.
"I'M GLAD YOU CALLED, BRUCE."
I HAD A FEW MORE QUESTIONS FOR YOU.
SURE.
DO YOU HAVE ANY OTHER LEADS POINTING YOU TOWARDS THE FIVE PEOPLE WHO HAVE TAKEN COBBLEPOT'S PLACE?
I ASK THAT BECAUSE IF I'M GOING TO PUT WAYNE ENTERPRISES OUT THERE, AND THAT INCLUDES THE BOARD AND THE MANY TALENTED PEOPLE WHO WORK FOR THE COMPANY, I NEED TO BE ASSURED THAT NONE OF THEM ARE INVOLVED IN THIS.
THERE'S NO ONE AT WAYNE ENTERPRISES.
HOW DO YOU KNOW THAT?
YOU CAN COME IN, HARVEY.

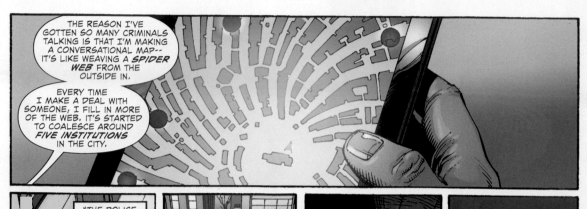

THE REASON I'VE GOTTEN SO MANY CRIMINALS TALKING IS THAT I'M MAKING A CONVERSATIONAL MAP-- IT'S LIKE WEAVING A *SPIDER WEB* FROM THE OUTSIDE IN.

EVERY TIME I MAKE A DEAL WITH SOMEONE, I FILL IN MORE OF THE WEB. IT'S STARTED TO COALESCE AROUND *FIVE INSTITUTIONS* IN THE CITY.

"THE POLICE DEPARTMENT.

"THE HOUSING COMMISSION.

"PUBLIC WORKS.

YOU HEAR THAT? I THINK SOMETHIN'S DOWN HERE.

"THE CITY COUNCIL."

AND THE STATE COURT. SOMEONE I PROBABLY SEE EVERY SINGLE DAY.

THIS IS BAD, WAYNE...

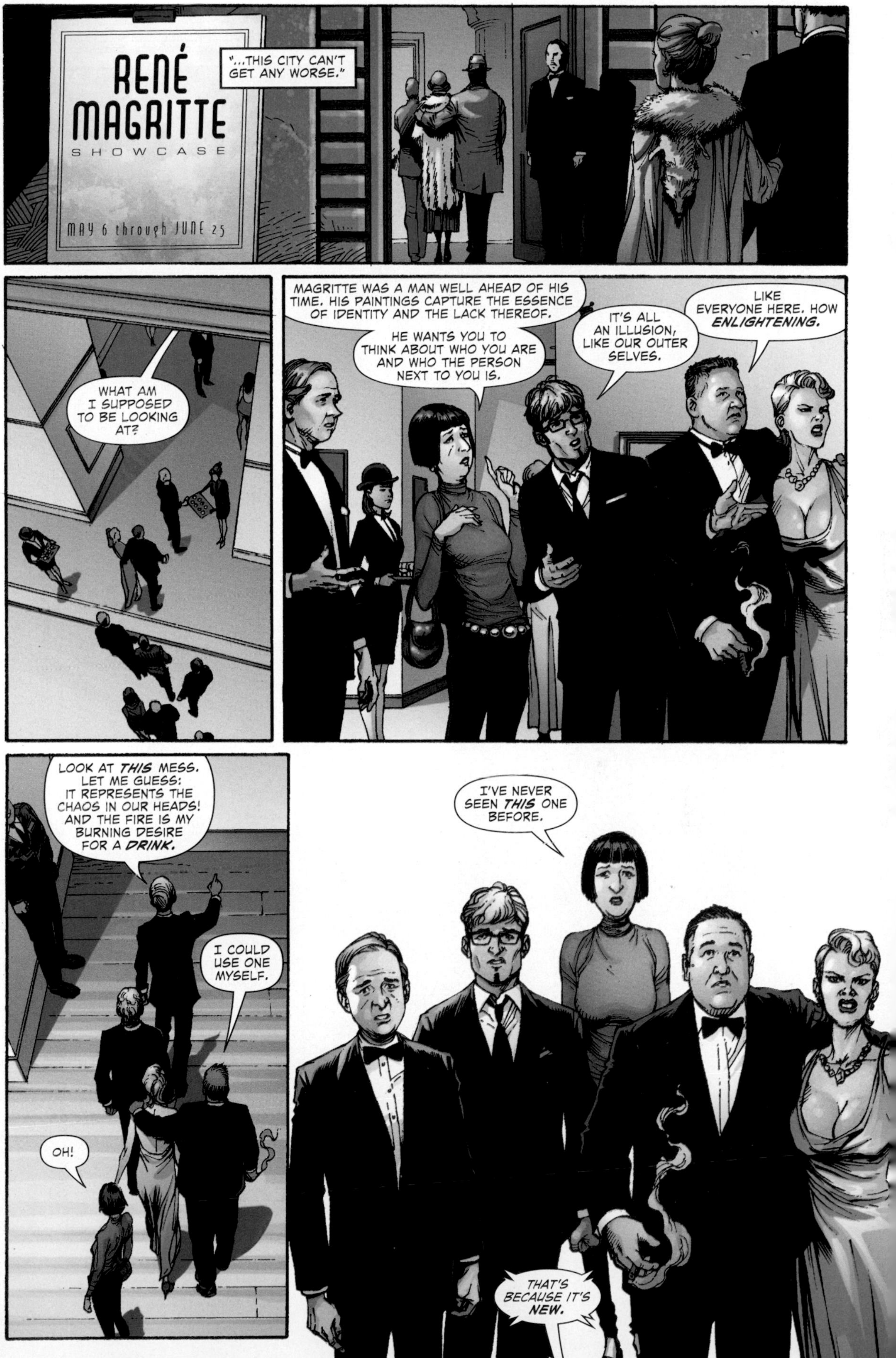
RENÉ MAGRITTE
SHOWCASE
MAY 6 through JUNE 25
"...THIS CITY CAN'T GET ANY WORSE."
WHAT AM I SUPPOSED TO BE LOOKING AT?
MAGRITTE WAS A MAN WELL AHEAD OF HIS TIME. HIS PAINTINGS CAPTURE THE ESSENCE OF IDENTITY AND THE LACK THEREOF.
HE WANTS YOU TO THINK ABOUT WHO YOU ARE AND WHO THE PERSON NEXT TO YOU IS.
IT'S ALL AN ILLUSION, LIKE OUR OUTER SELVES.
LIKE EVERYONE HERE. HOW ENLIGHTENING.
LOOK AT THIS MESS. LET ME GUESS: IT REPRESENTS THE CHAOS IN OUR HEADS! AND THE FIRE IS MY BURNING DESIRE FOR A DRINK.
I COULD USE ONE MYSELF.
OH!
I'VE NEVER SEEN THIS ONE BEFORE.
THAT'S BECAUSE IT'S NEW.

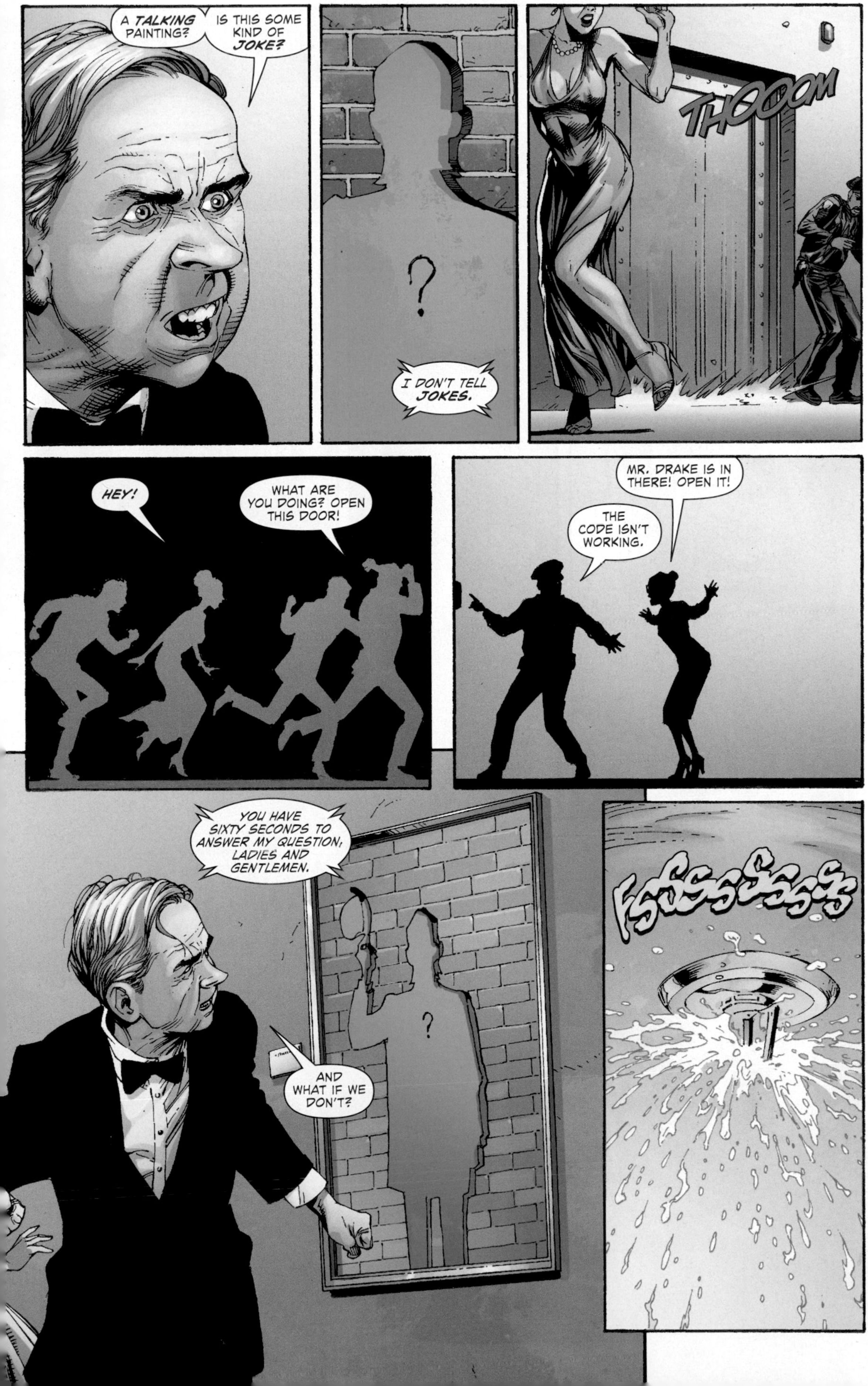

A TALKING PAINTING?
IS THIS SOME KIND OF JOKE?
I DON'T TELL JOKES.
THOOOM
HEY!
WHAT ARE YOU DOING? OPEN THIS DOOR!
MR. DRAKE IS IN THERE! OPEN IT!
THE CODE ISN'T WORKING.
YOU HAVE SIXTY SECONDS TO ANSWER MY QUESTION, LADIES AND GENTLEMEN.
AND WHAT IF WE DON'T?
FSSSSSSSSS

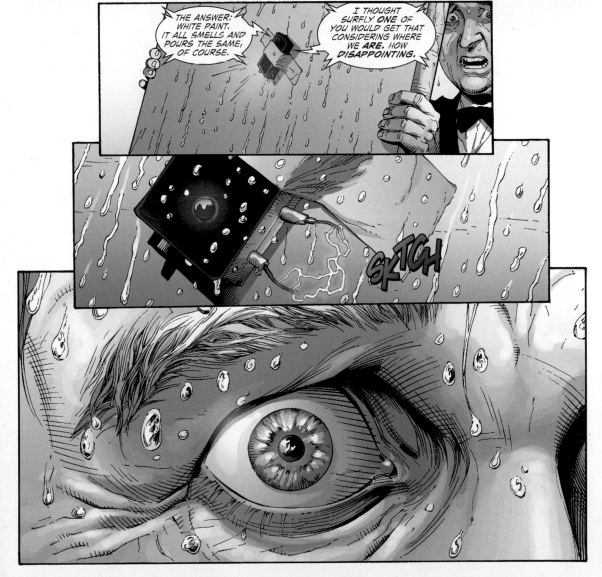

"THERE'S BEEN AN EXPLOSION AT THE MUSEUM OF ART."

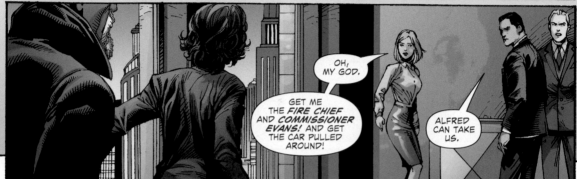

OH, MY GOD.

GET ME THE *FIRE CHIEF* AND *COMMISSIONER EVANS!* AND GET THE CAR PULLED AROUND!

ALFRED CAN TAKE US.

I WANT *ALL* UNITS THERE *NOW!*

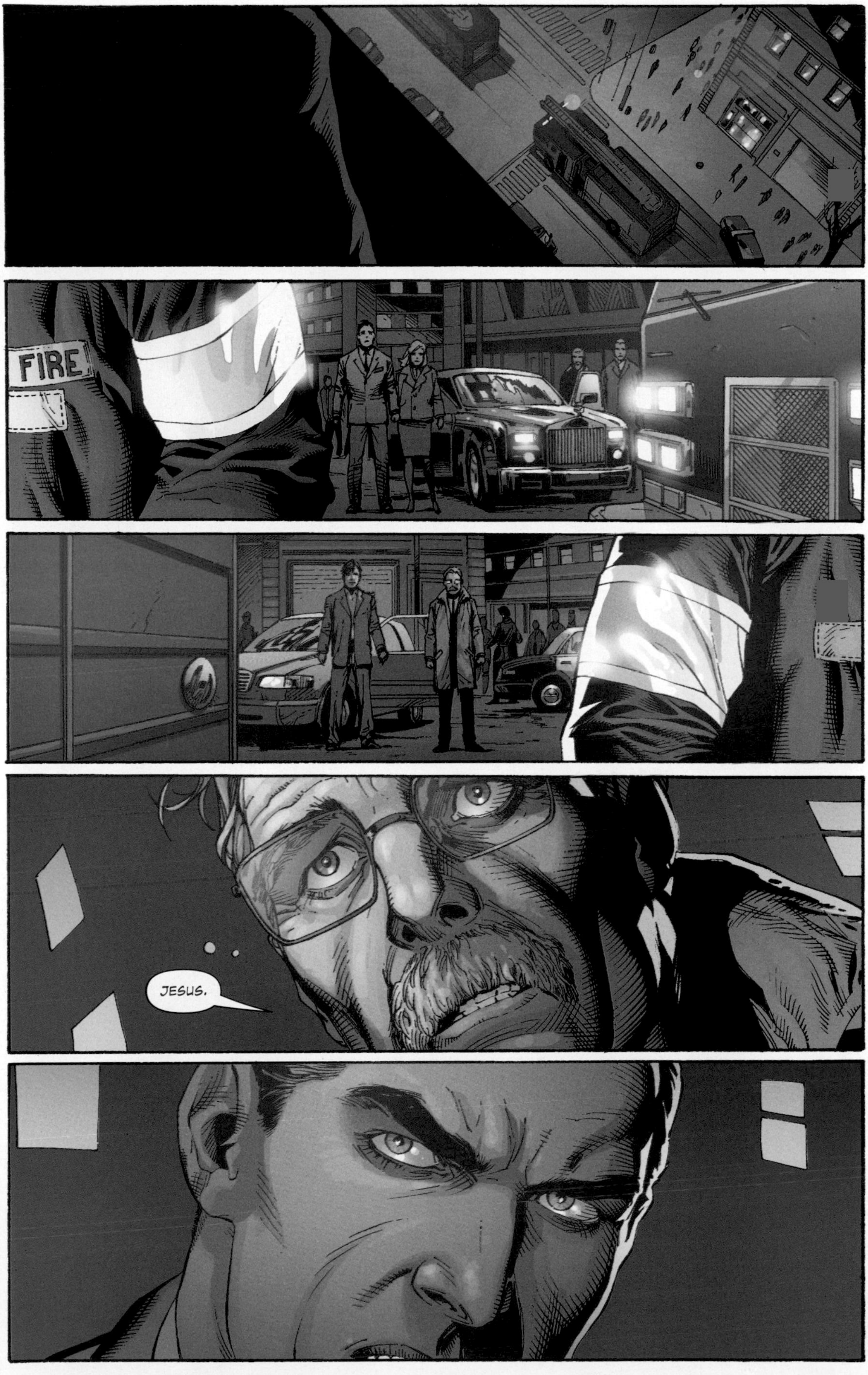
FIRE
JESUS.

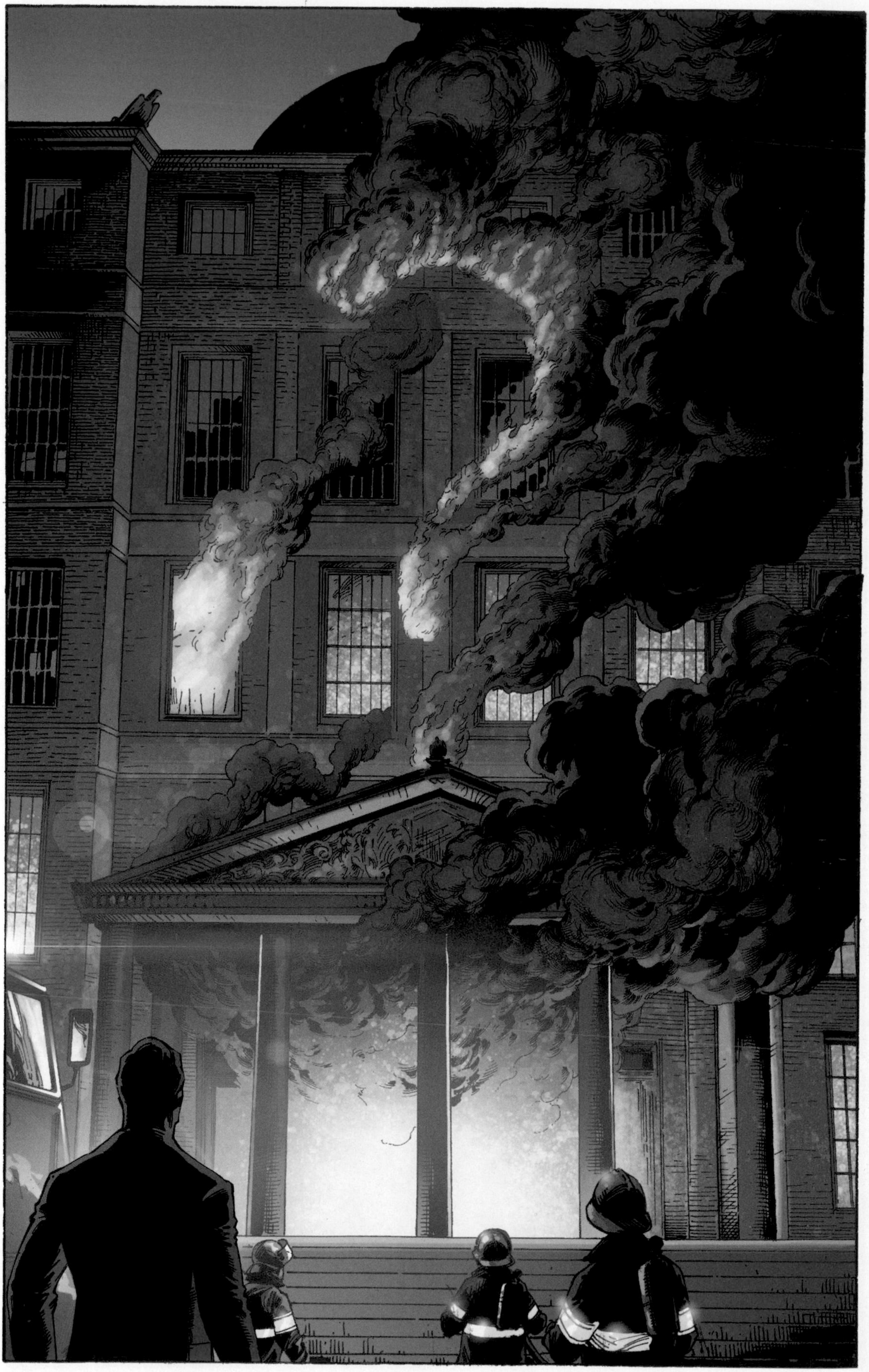

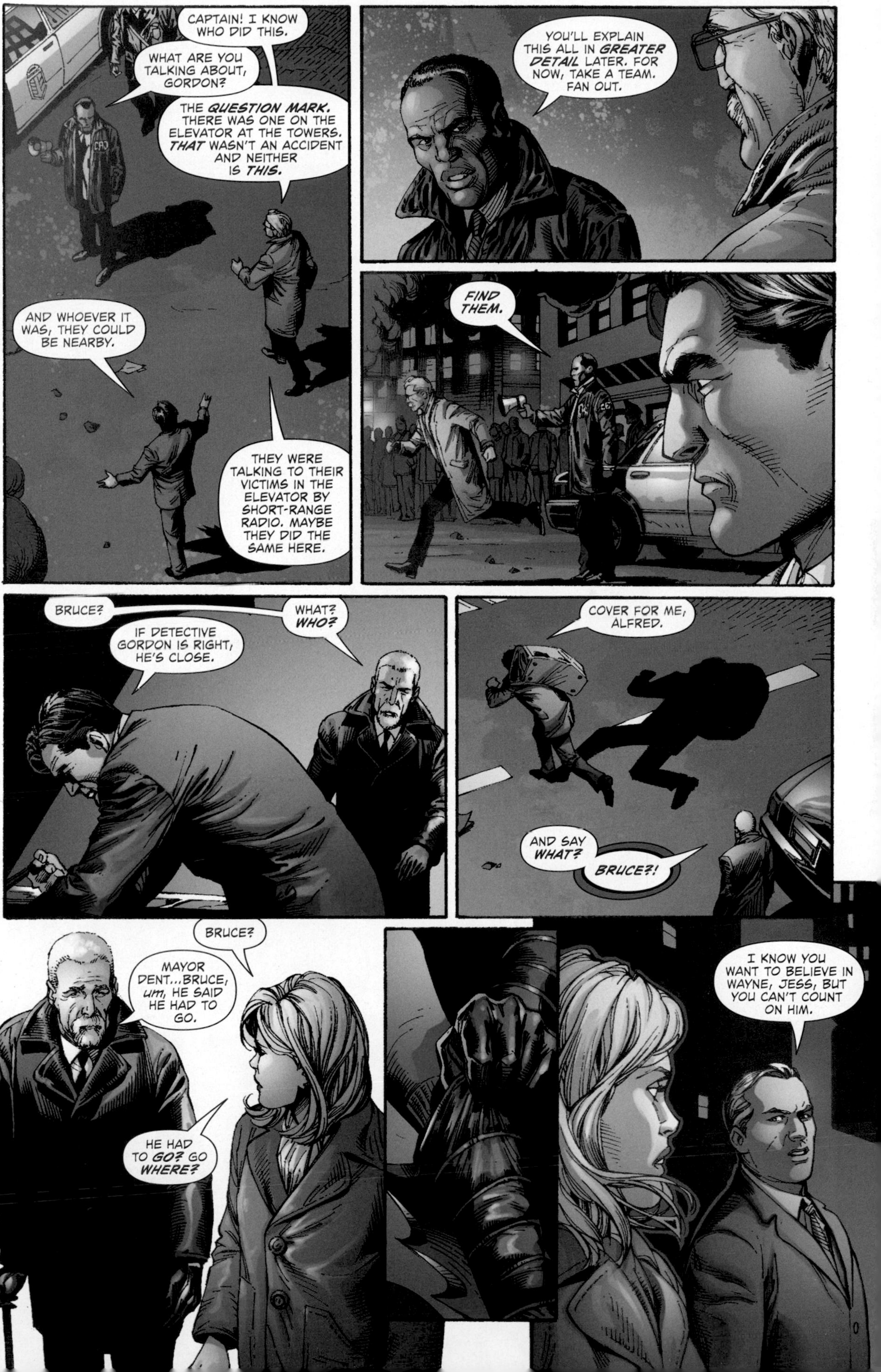
CAPTAIN! I KNOW WHO DID THIS.
WHAT ARE YOU TALKING ABOUT, GORDON?
THE QUESTION MARK. THERE WAS ONE ON THE ELEVATOR AT THE TOWERS. THAT WASN'T AN ACCIDENT AND NEITHER IS THIS.
AND WHOEVER IT WAS, THEY COULD BE NEARBY.
THEY WERE TALKING TO THEIR VICTIMS IN THE ELEVATOR BY SHORT-RANGE RADIO. MAYBE THEY DID THE SAME HERE.
YOU'LL EXPLAIN THIS ALL IN GREATER DETAIL LATER. FOR NOW, TAKE A TEAM. FAN OUT.
FIND THEM.
BRUCE?
IF DETECTIVE GORDON IS RIGHT, HE'S CLOSE.
WHAT? WHO?
COVER FOR ME, ALFRED.
AND SAY WHAT?
BRUCE?!
BRUCE?
MAYOR DENT...BRUCE, um, HE SAID HE HAD TO GO.
HE HAD TO GO? GO WHERE?
I KNOW YOU WANT TO BELIEVE IN WAYNE, JESS, BUT YOU CAN'T COUNT ON HIM.

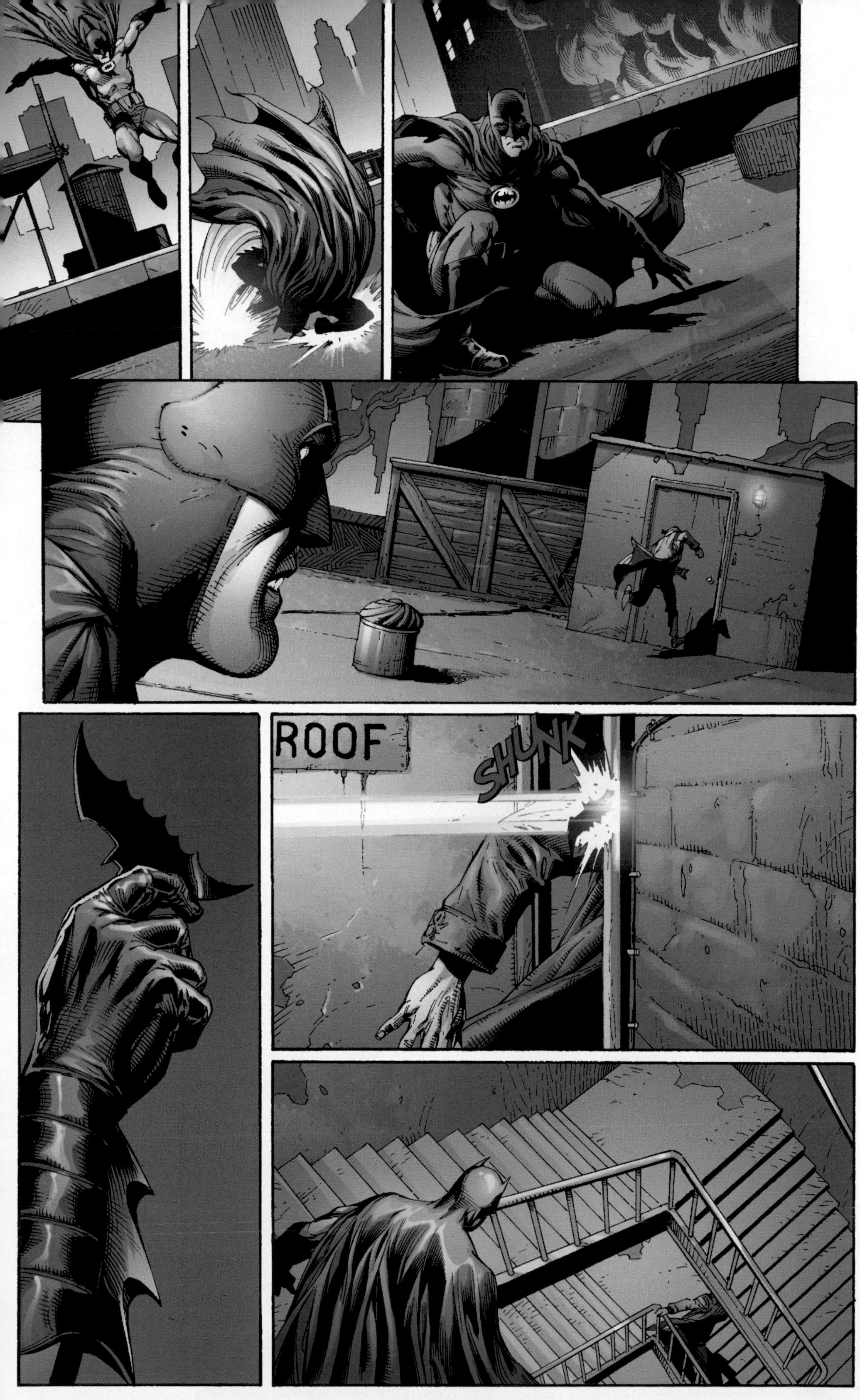
ROOF
SHUNK

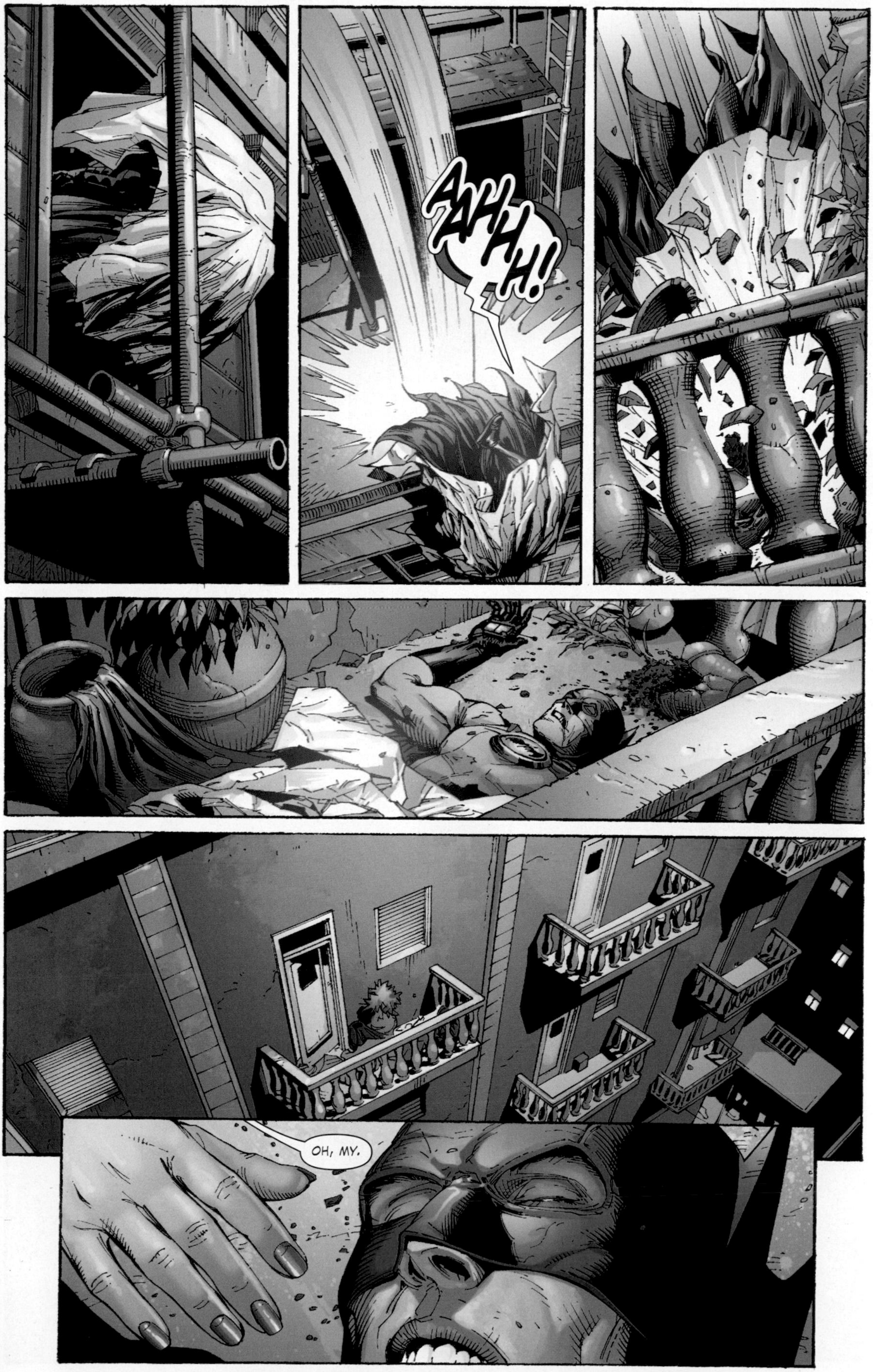
AAHHHH!
OH, MY.

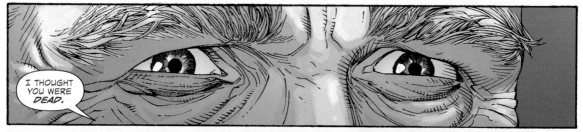

I THOUGHT YOU WERE *DEAD.*

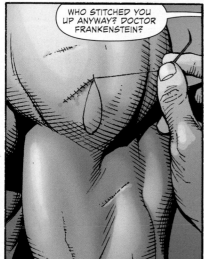

WHO STITCHED YOU UP ANYWAY? DOCTOR FRANKENSTEIN?

SHE DID THE BEST SHE COULD.

SHE?

A WOMAN. I CRASHED INTO HER GARDEN AFTER THE BOMBER PUSHED ME OFF THE BUILDING.

BUT I DID GET SOMETHING FOR MY TROUBLE.

A *SHORT-RANGE RADIO.*

THAT DOESN'T SEEM LIKE A GREAT CONSOLATION PRIZE.

I'M HOPING DETECTIVE GORDON CAN PULL SOME FINGERPRINTS OR TRACE THE SERIAL NUMBER.

DETECTIVE GORDON? YOU'RE GOING TO HIM AGAIN?

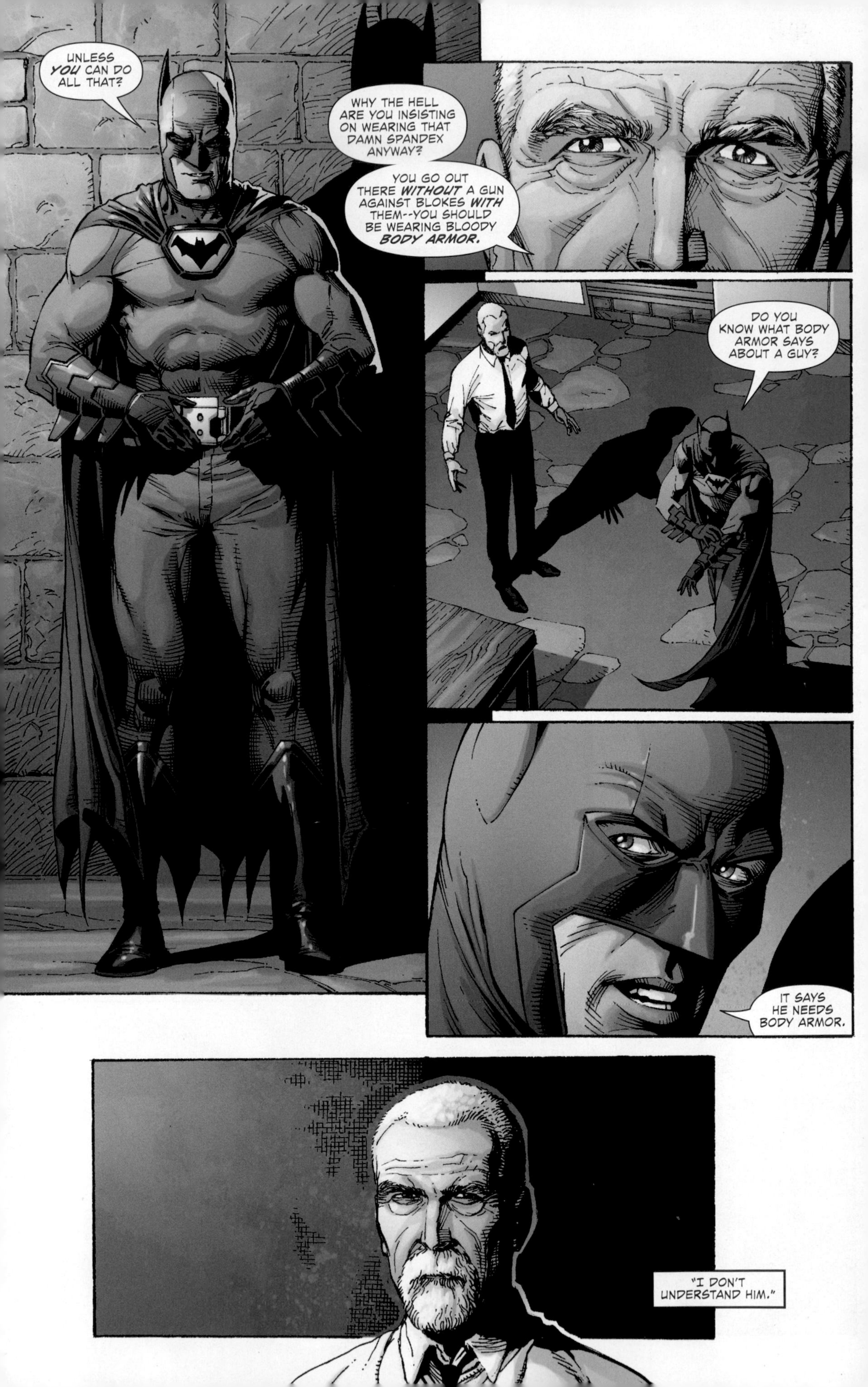
UNLESS YOU CAN DO ALL THAT?
WHY THE HELL ARE YOU INSISTING ON WEARING THAT DAMN SPANDEX ANYWAY?
YOU GO OUT THERE WITHOUT A GUN AGAINST BLOKES WITH THEM--YOU SHOULD BE WEARING BLOODY BODY ARMOR.
DO YOU KNOW WHAT BODY ARMOR SAYS ABOUT A GUY?
IT SAYS HE NEEDS BODY ARMOR.
"I DON'T UNDERSTAND HIM."

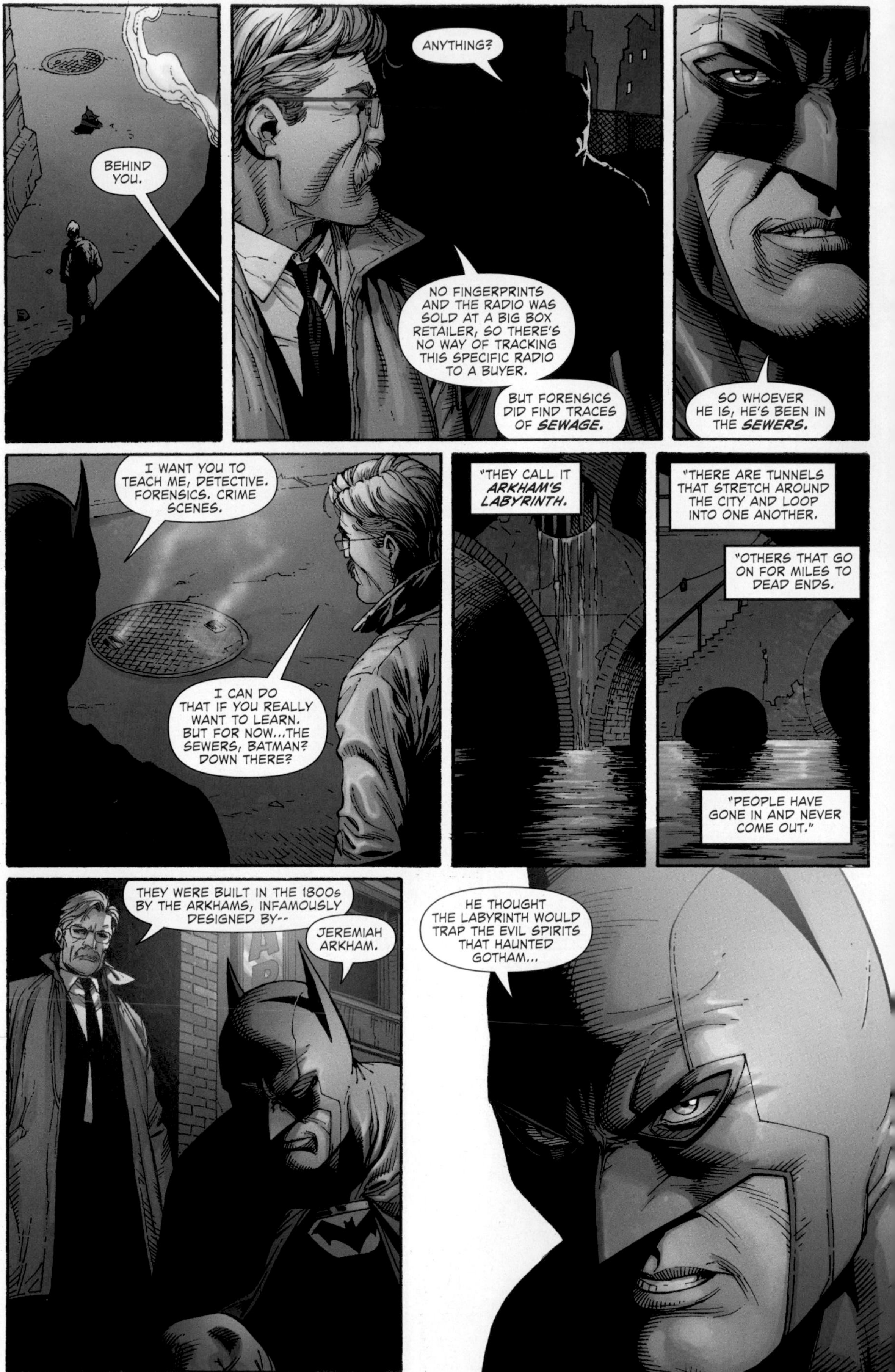
BEHIND YOU.
ANYTHING?
NO FINGERPRINTS AND THE RADIO WAS SOLD AT A BIG BOX RETAILER, SO THERE'S NO WAY OF TRACKING THIS SPECIFIC RADIO TO A BUYER.
BUT FORENSICS DID FIND TRACES OF SEWAGE.
SO WHOEVER HE IS, HE'S BEEN IN THE SEWERS.
I WANT YOU TO TEACH ME, DETECTIVE. FORENSICS. CRIME SCENES.
I CAN DO THAT IF YOU REALLY WANT TO LEARN. BUT FOR NOW...THE SEWERS, BATMAN? DOWN THERE?
"THEY CALL IT ARKHAM'S LABYRINTH.
"THERE ARE TUNNELS THAT STRETCH AROUND THE CITY AND LOOP INTO ONE ANOTHER.
"OTHERS THAT GO ON FOR MILES TO DEAD ENDS.
"PEOPLE HAVE GONE IN AND NEVER COME OUT."
THEY WERE BUILT IN THE 1800s BY THE ARKHAMS, INFAMOUSLY DESIGNED BY--
JEREMIAH ARKHAM.
HE THOUGHT THE LABYRINTH WOULD TRAP THE EVIL SPIRITS THAT HAUNTED GOTHAM...

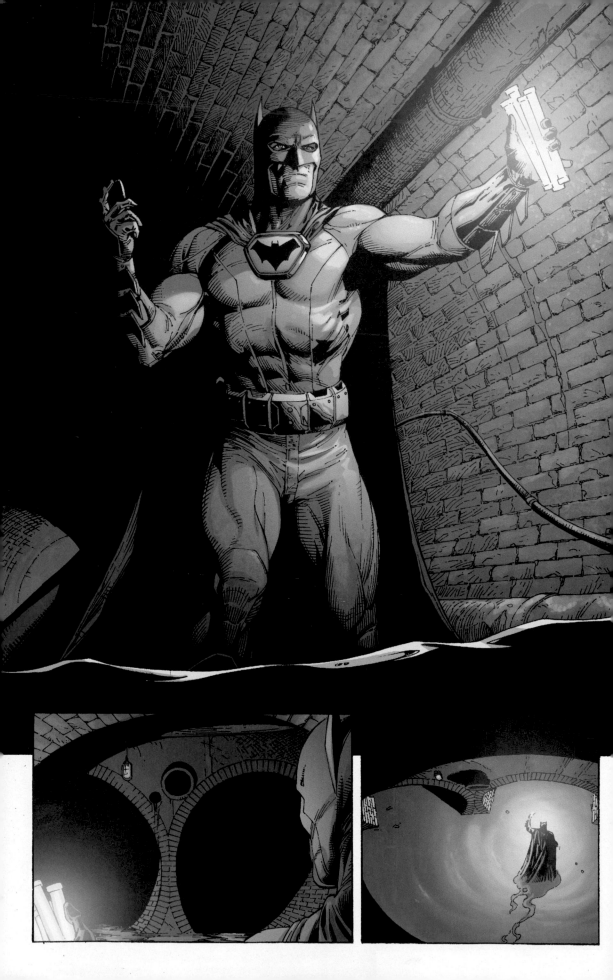

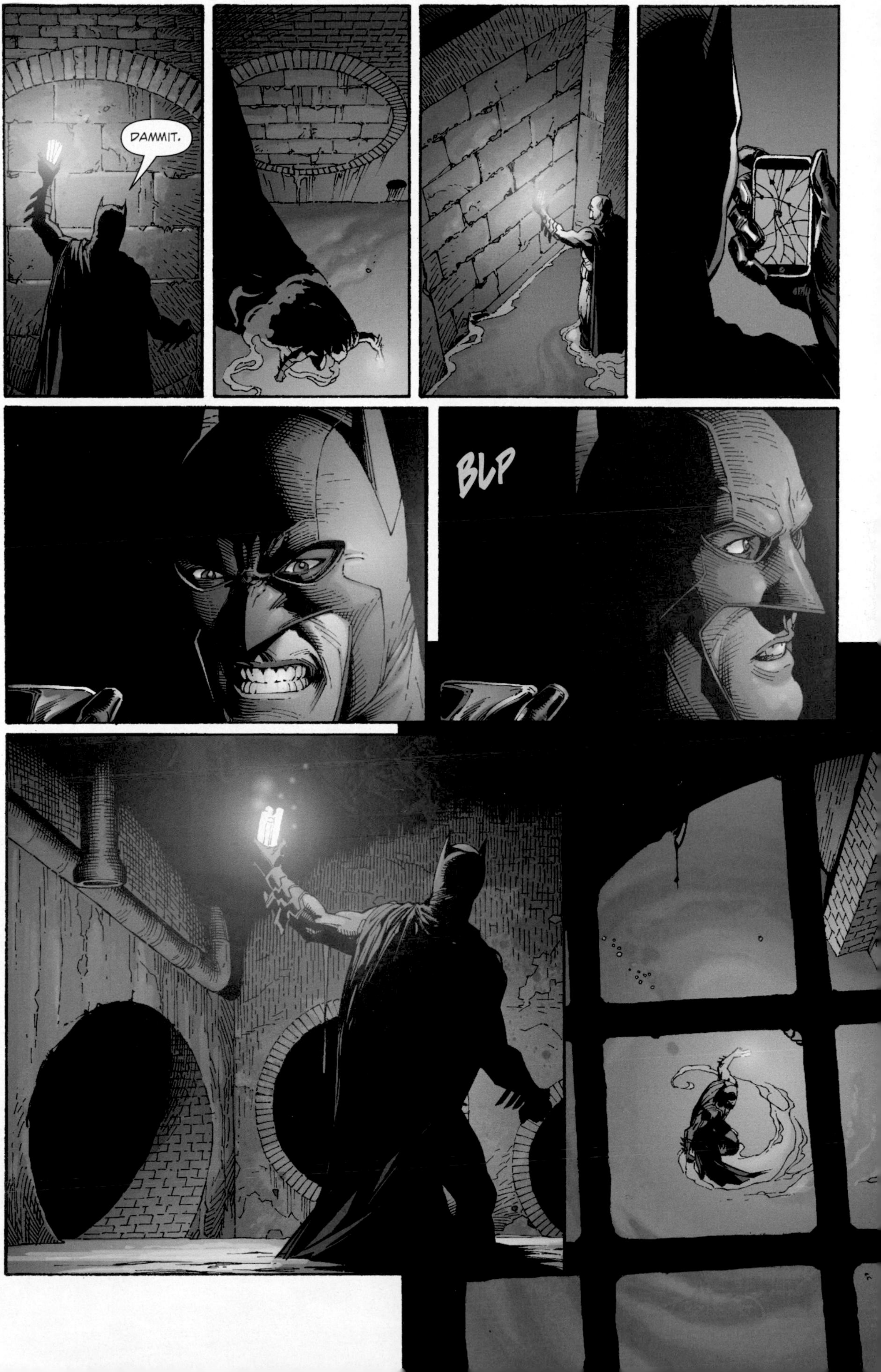
DAMMIT.
BLP

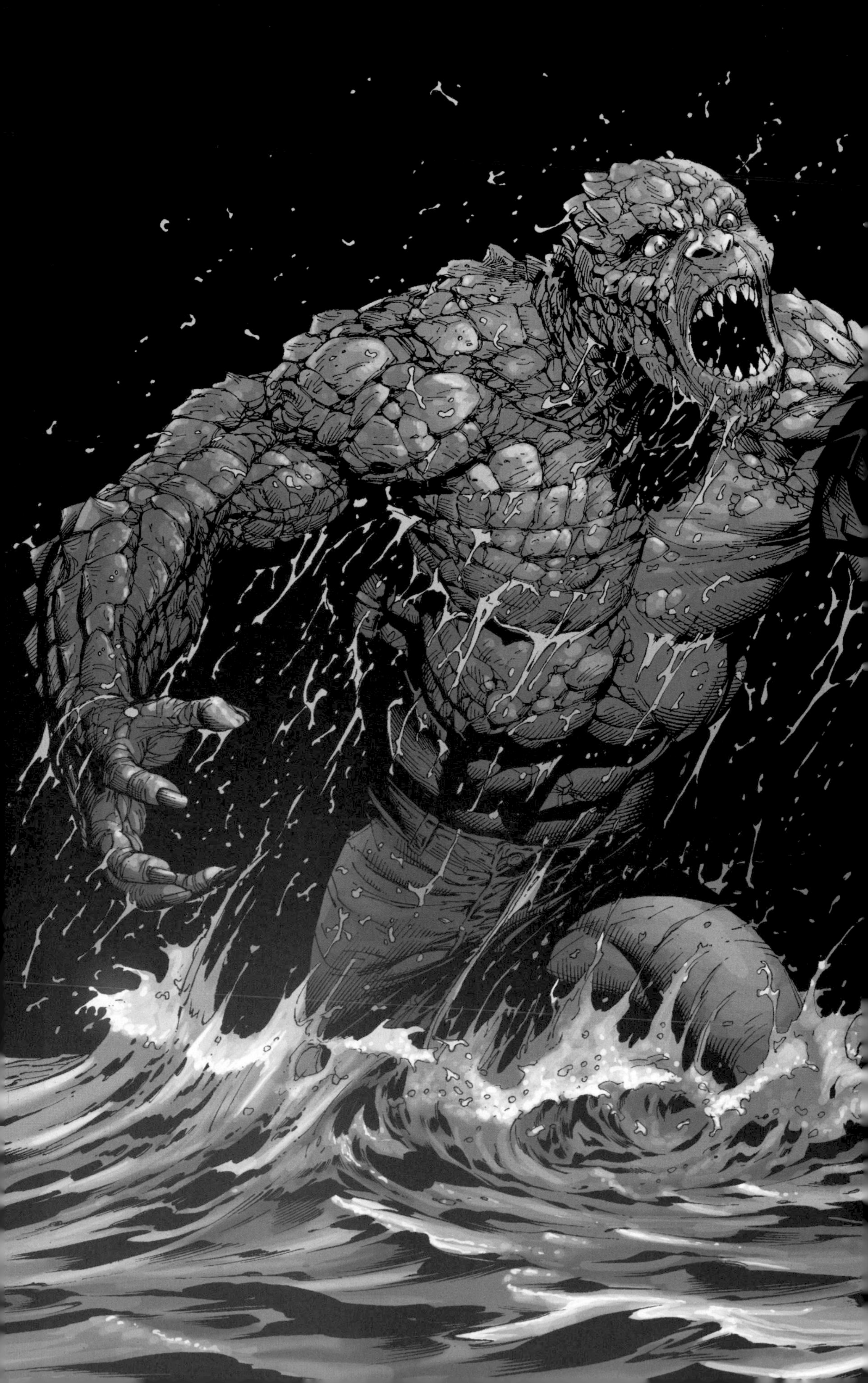

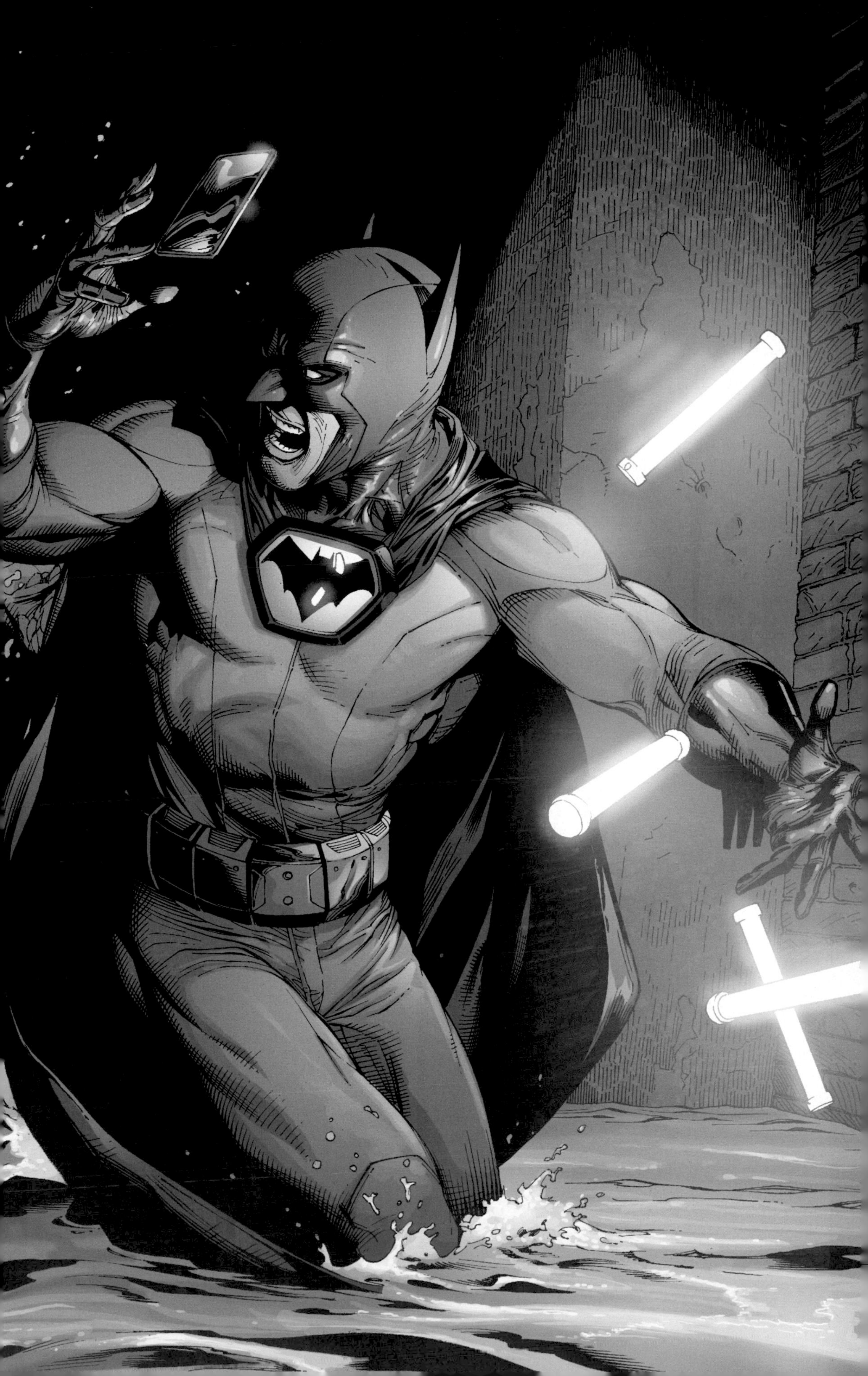

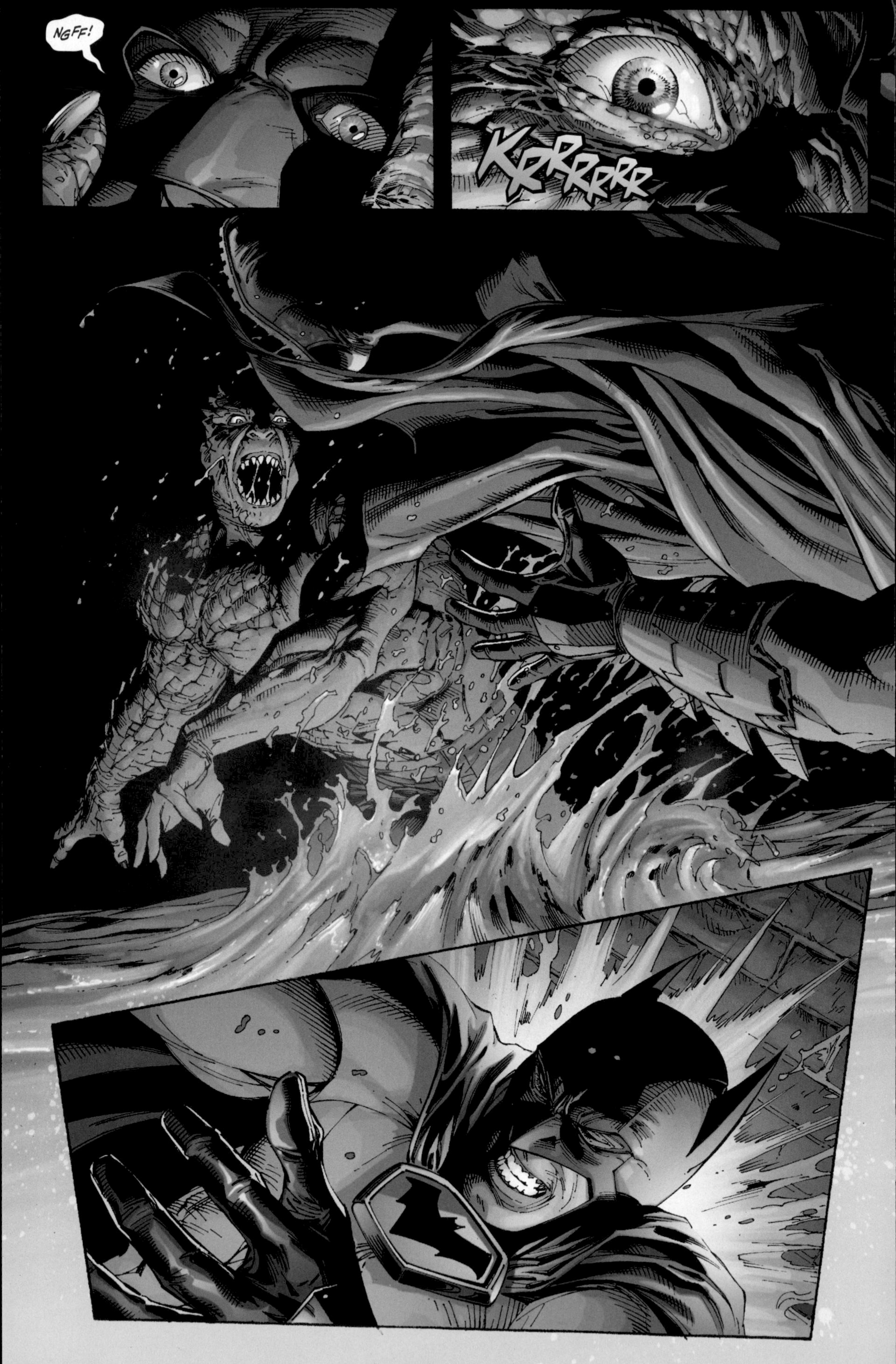
NGFF!
KRRRRRR

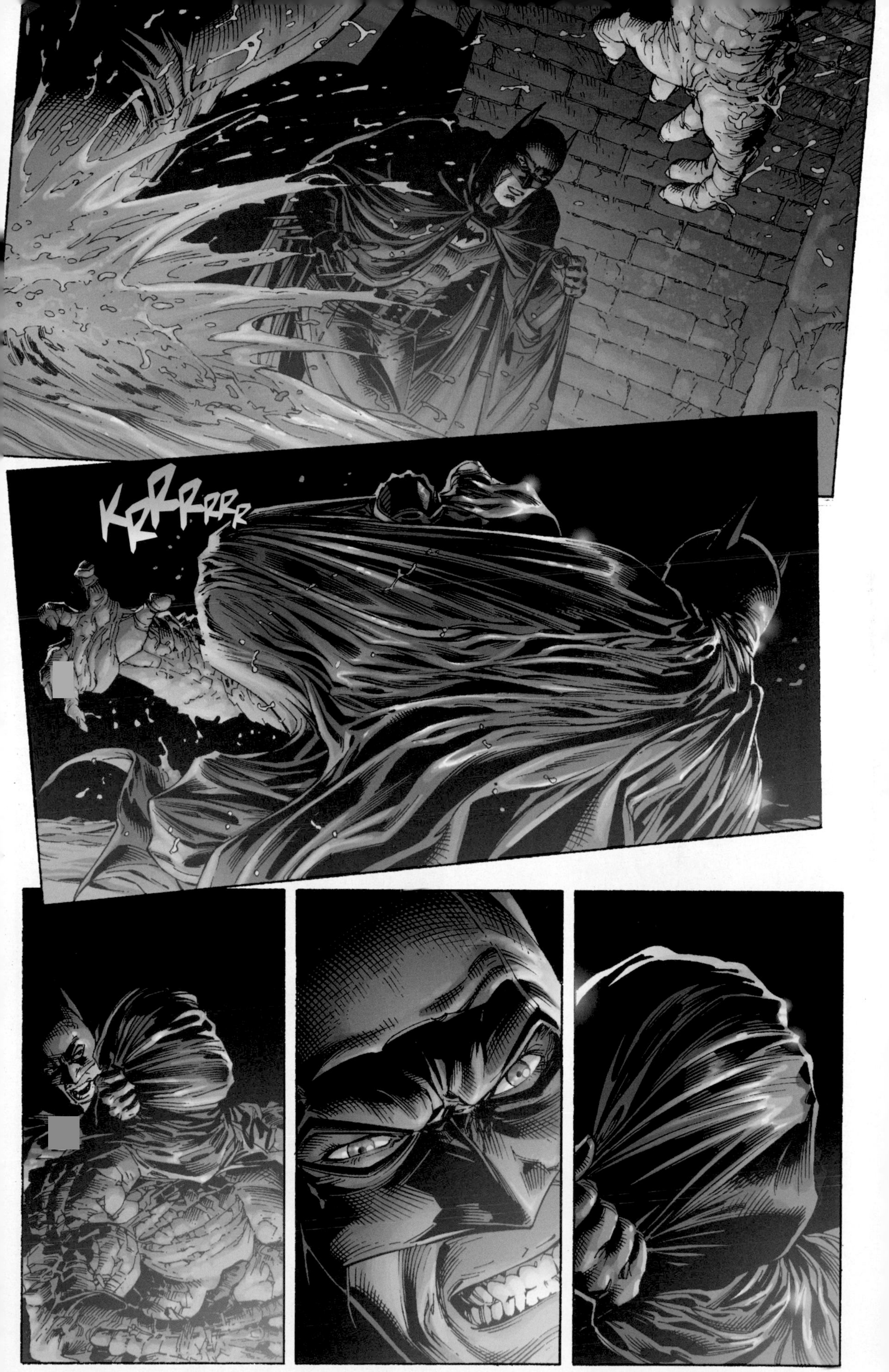
KRRRrrrr

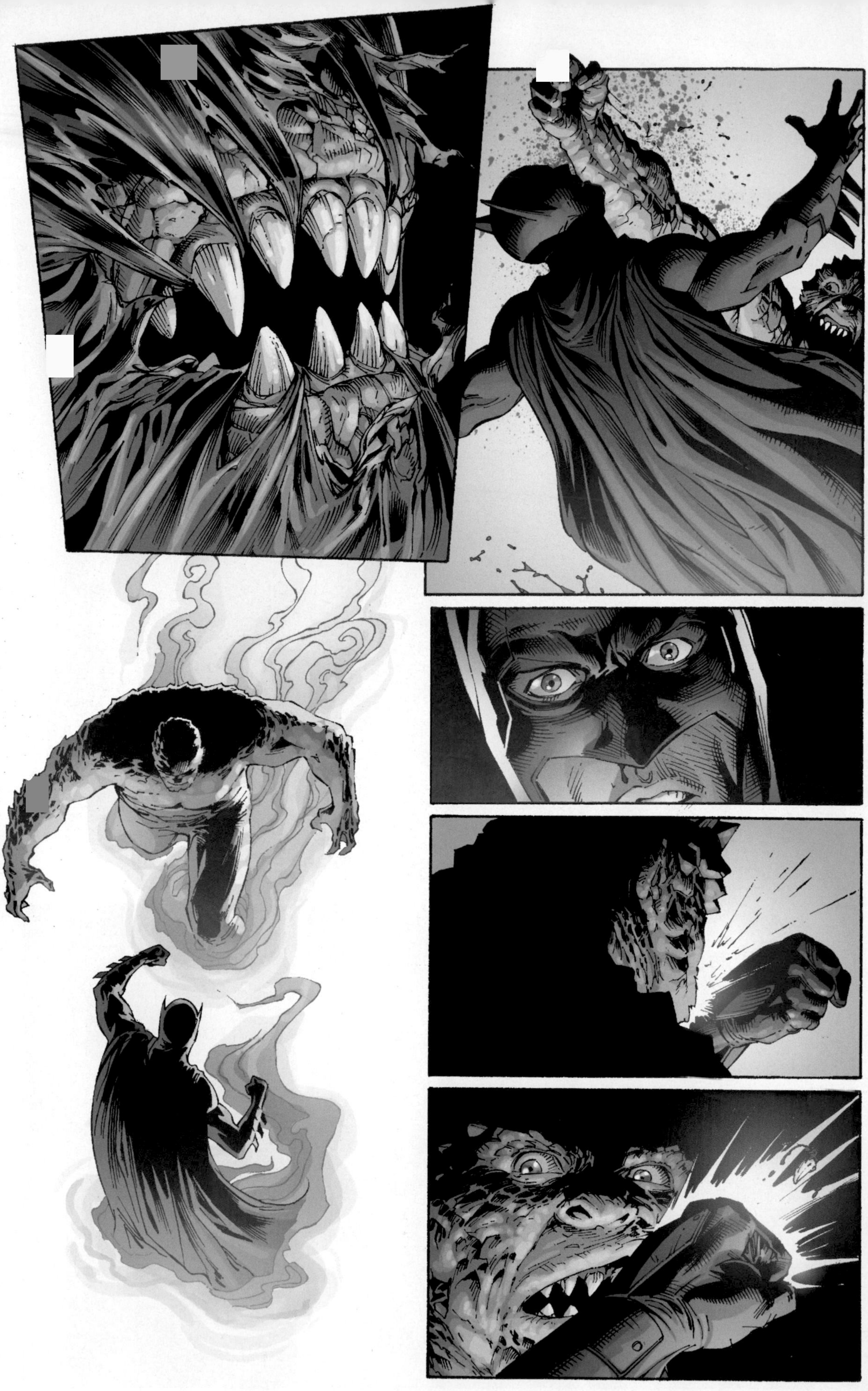

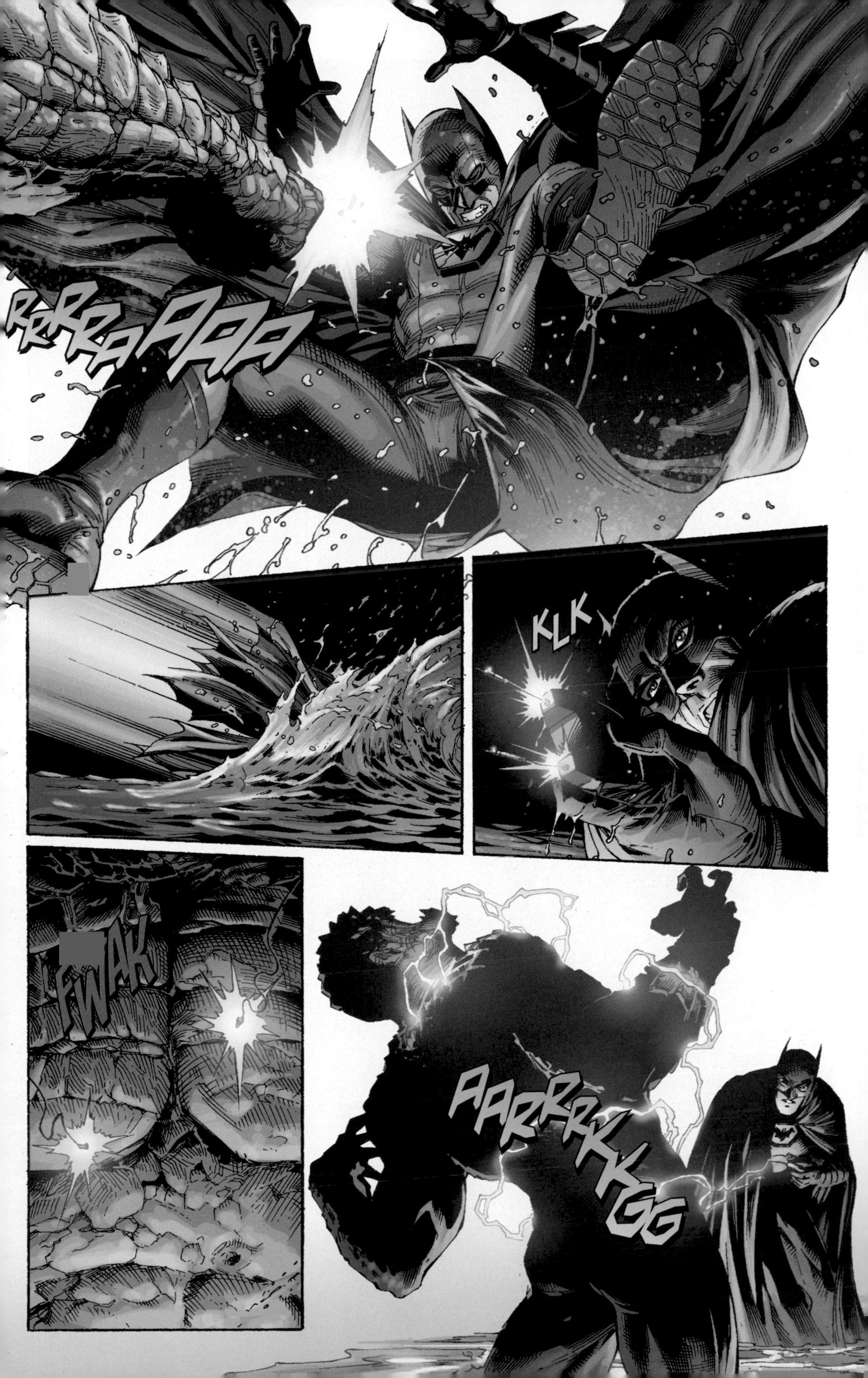
RRRAAAA
KLK
FWAK
AARRRKKGG

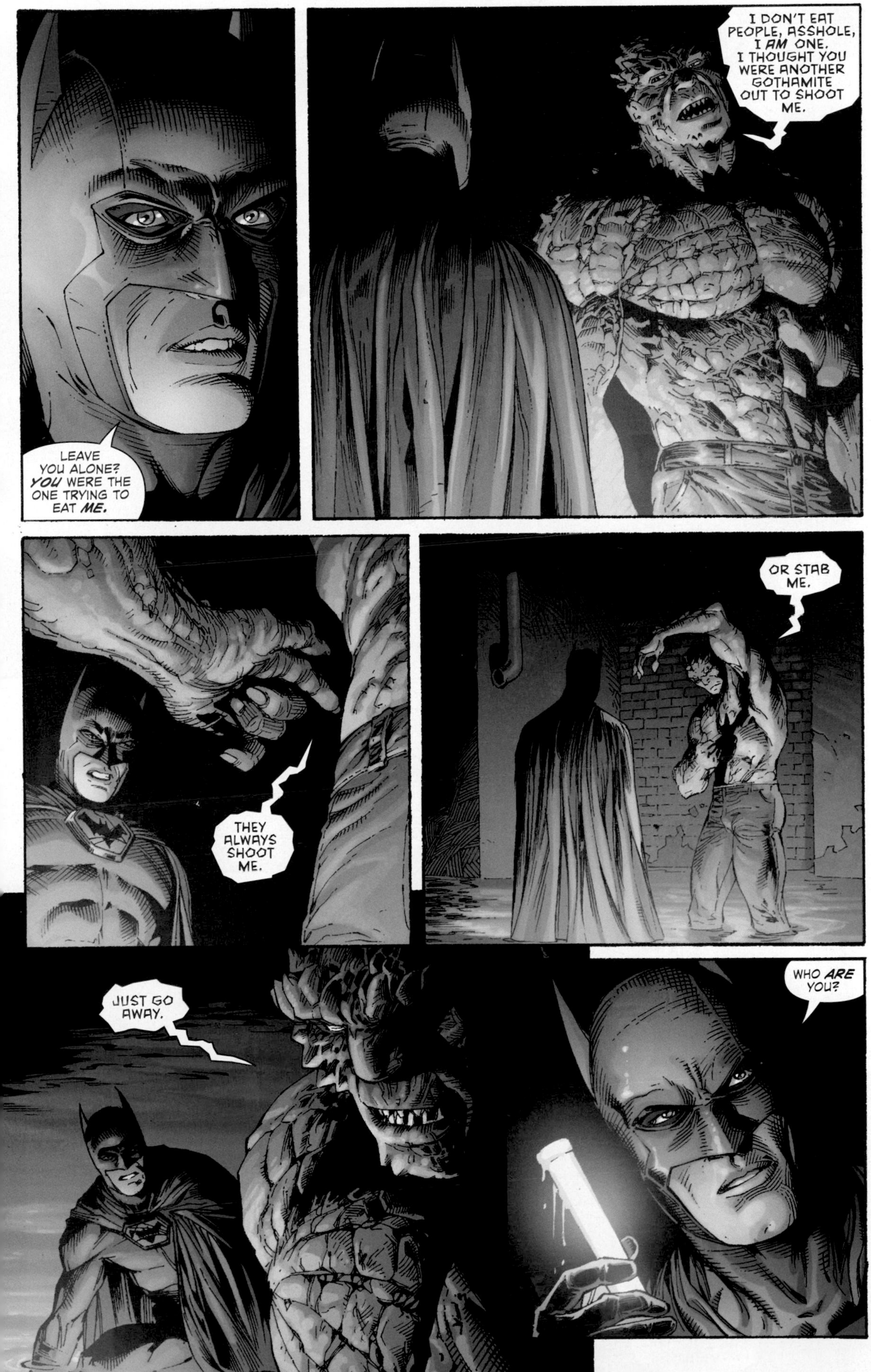
LEAVE YOU ALONE? *YOU* WERE THE ONE TRYING TO EAT *ME.*
I DON'T EAT PEOPLE, ASSHOLE, I *AM* ONE. I THOUGHT YOU WERE ANOTHER GOTHAMITE OUT TO SHOOT ME.
THEY ALWAYS SHOOT ME.
OR STAB ME.
JUST GO AWAY.
WHO *ARE* YOU?

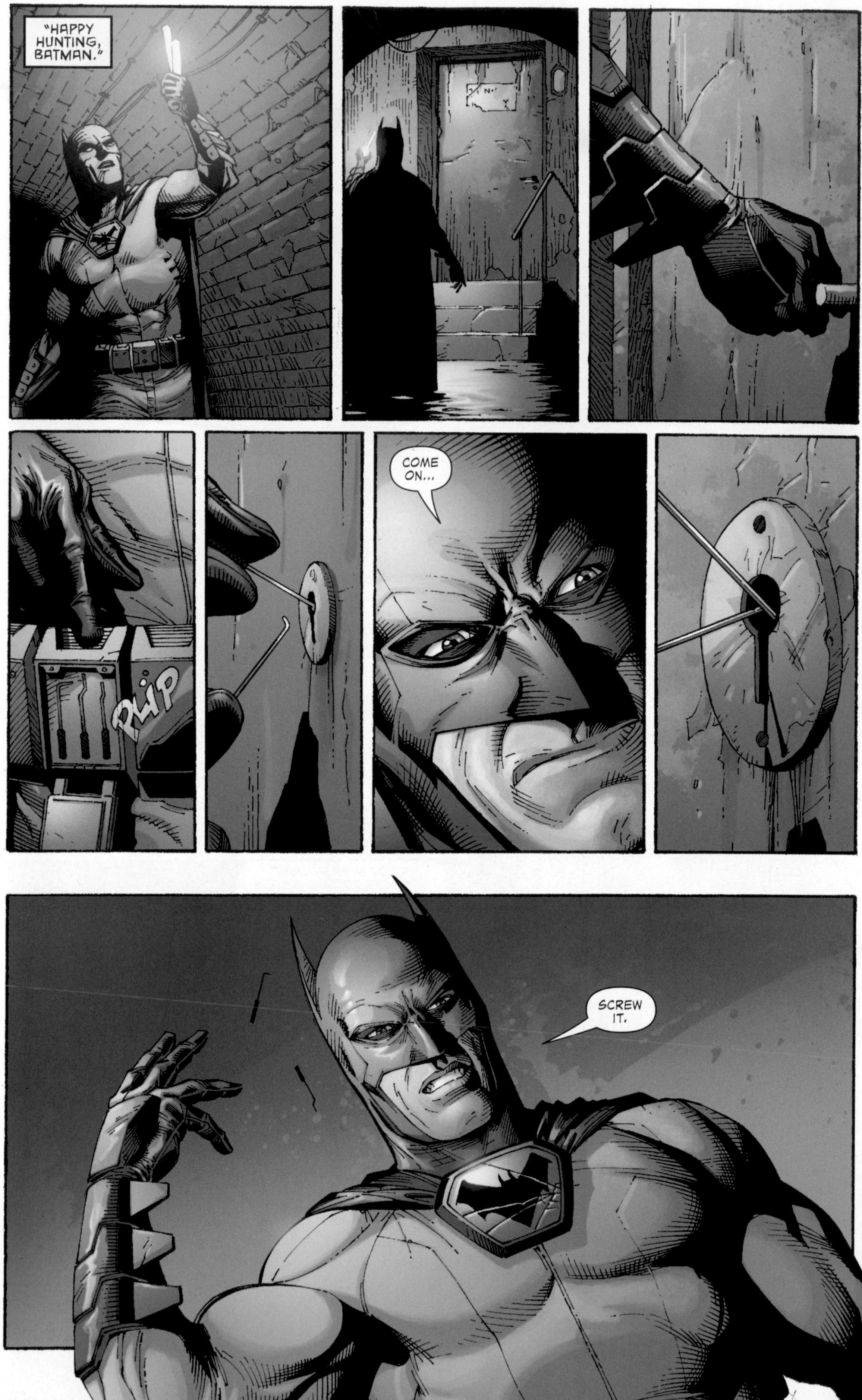
"HAPPY HUNTING, BATMAN."
RIIP
COME ON...
SCREW IT.

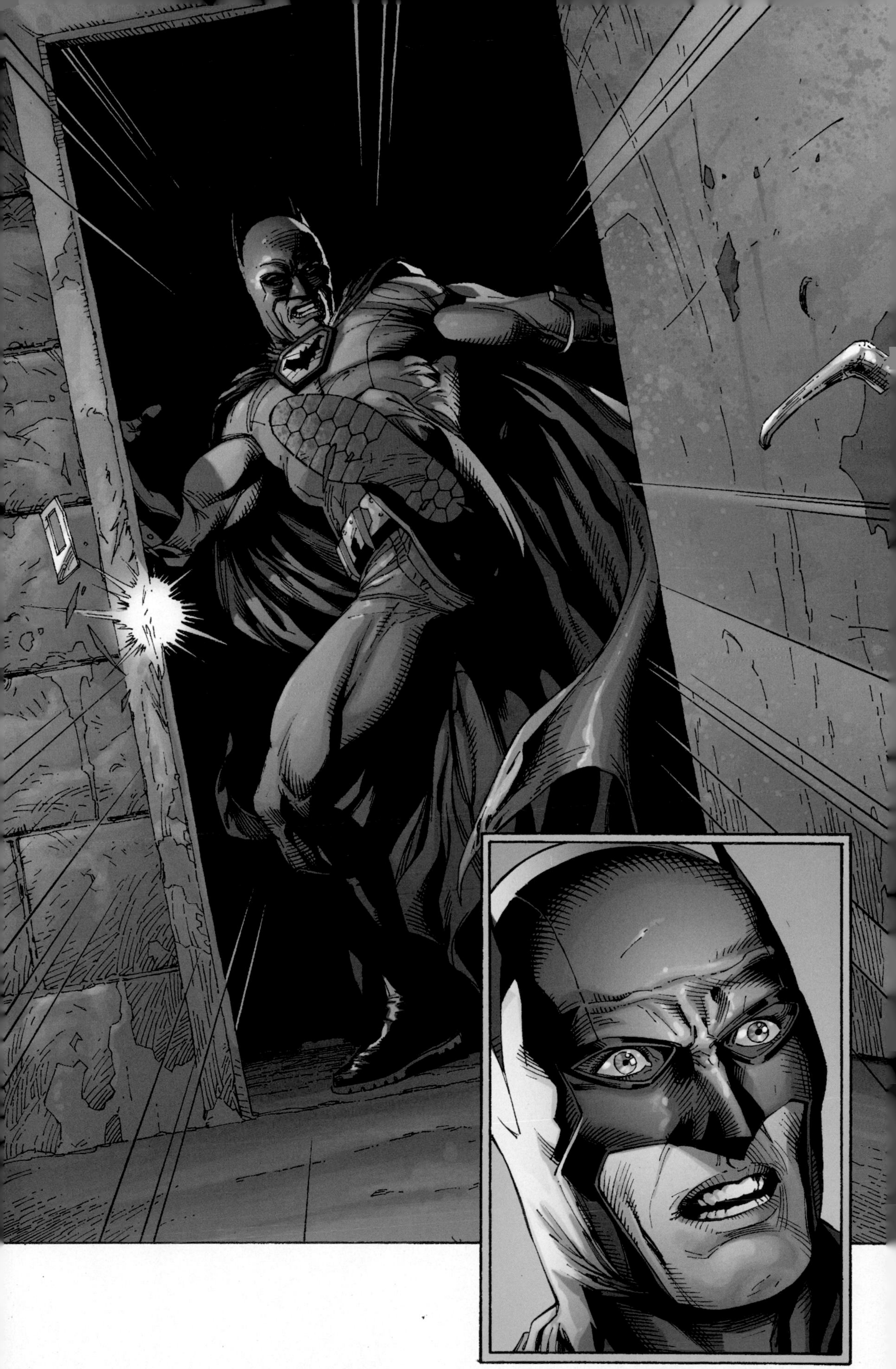

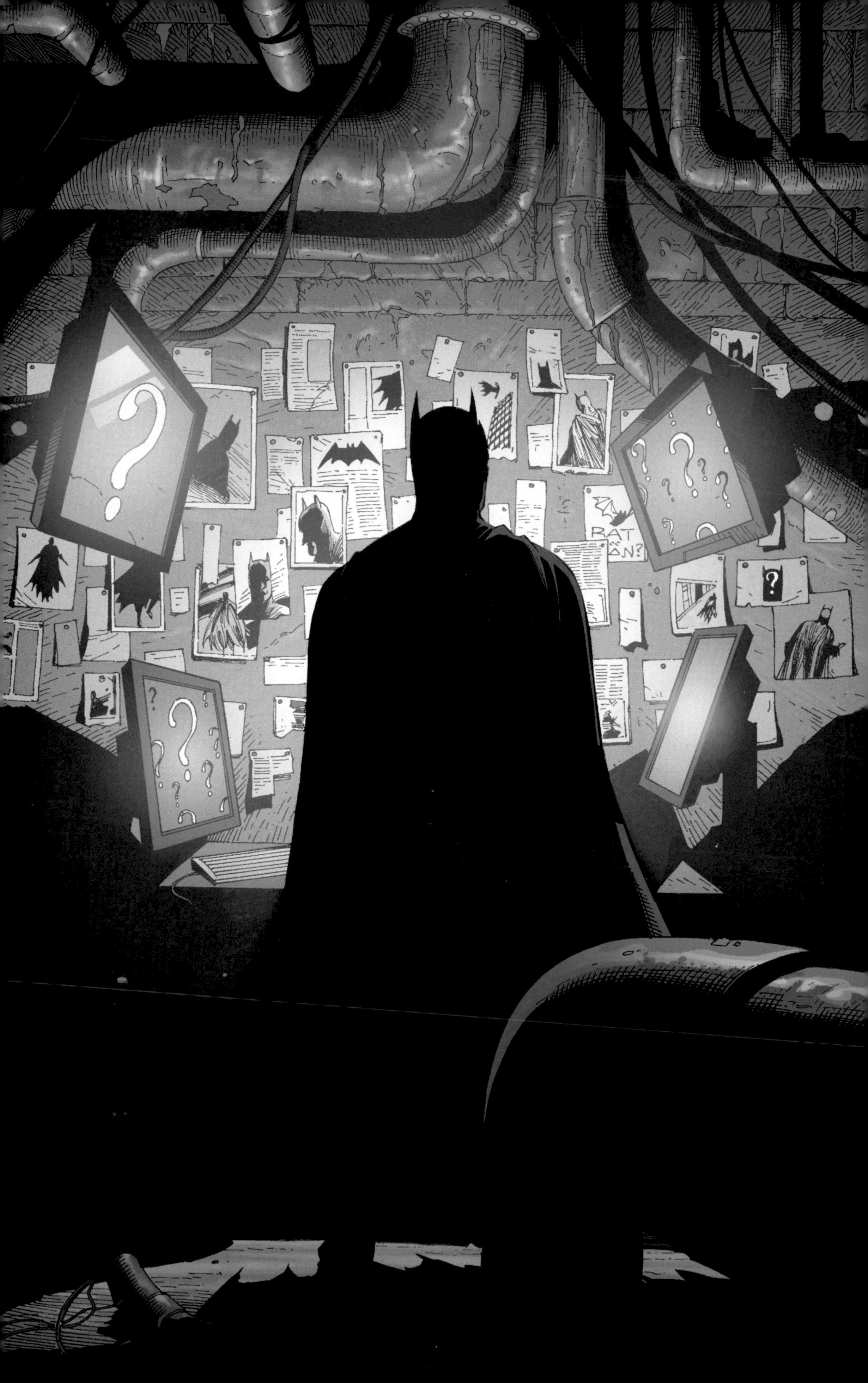

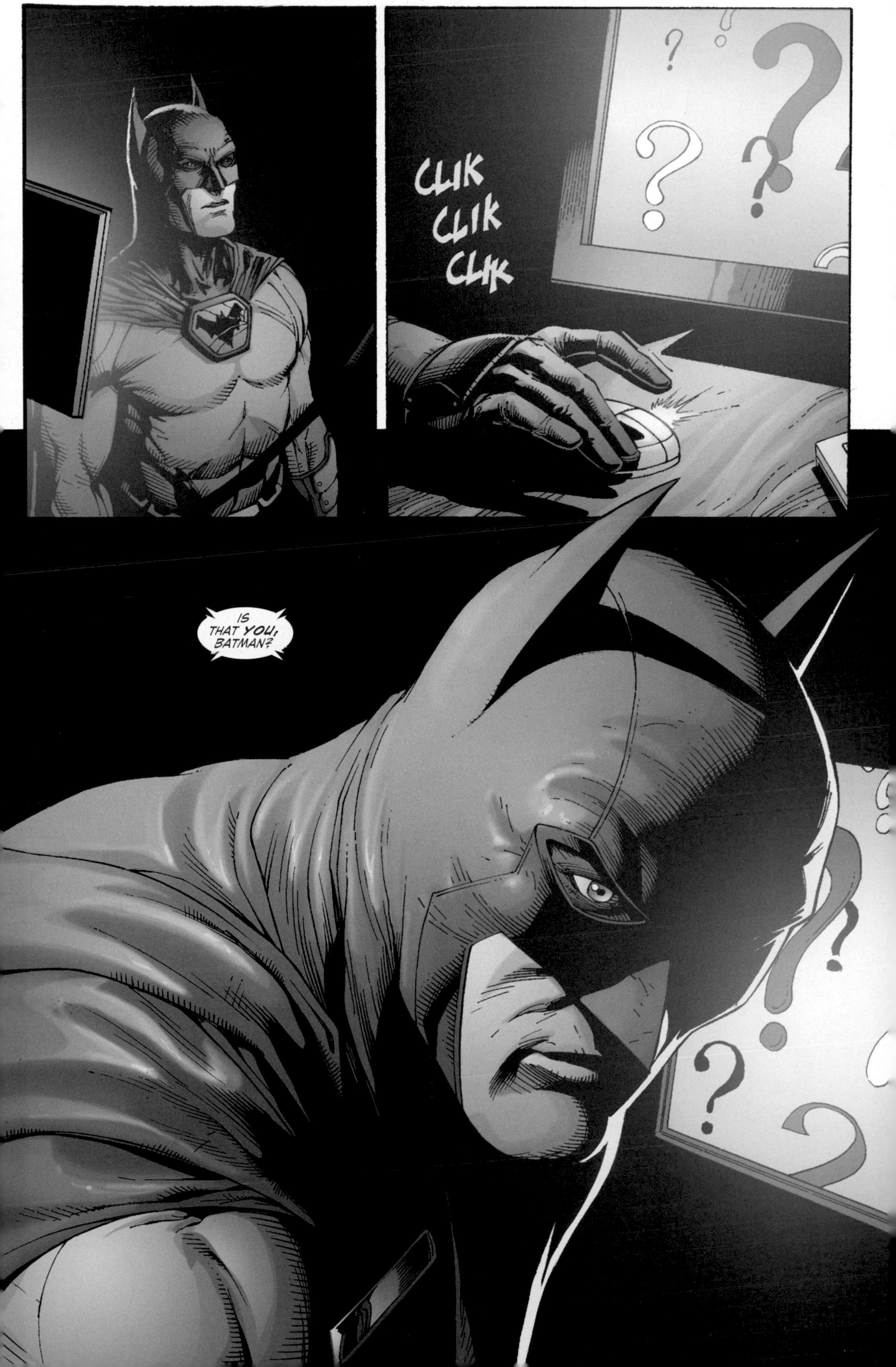
CLIK
CLIK
CLIK
IS THAT YOU, BATMAN?

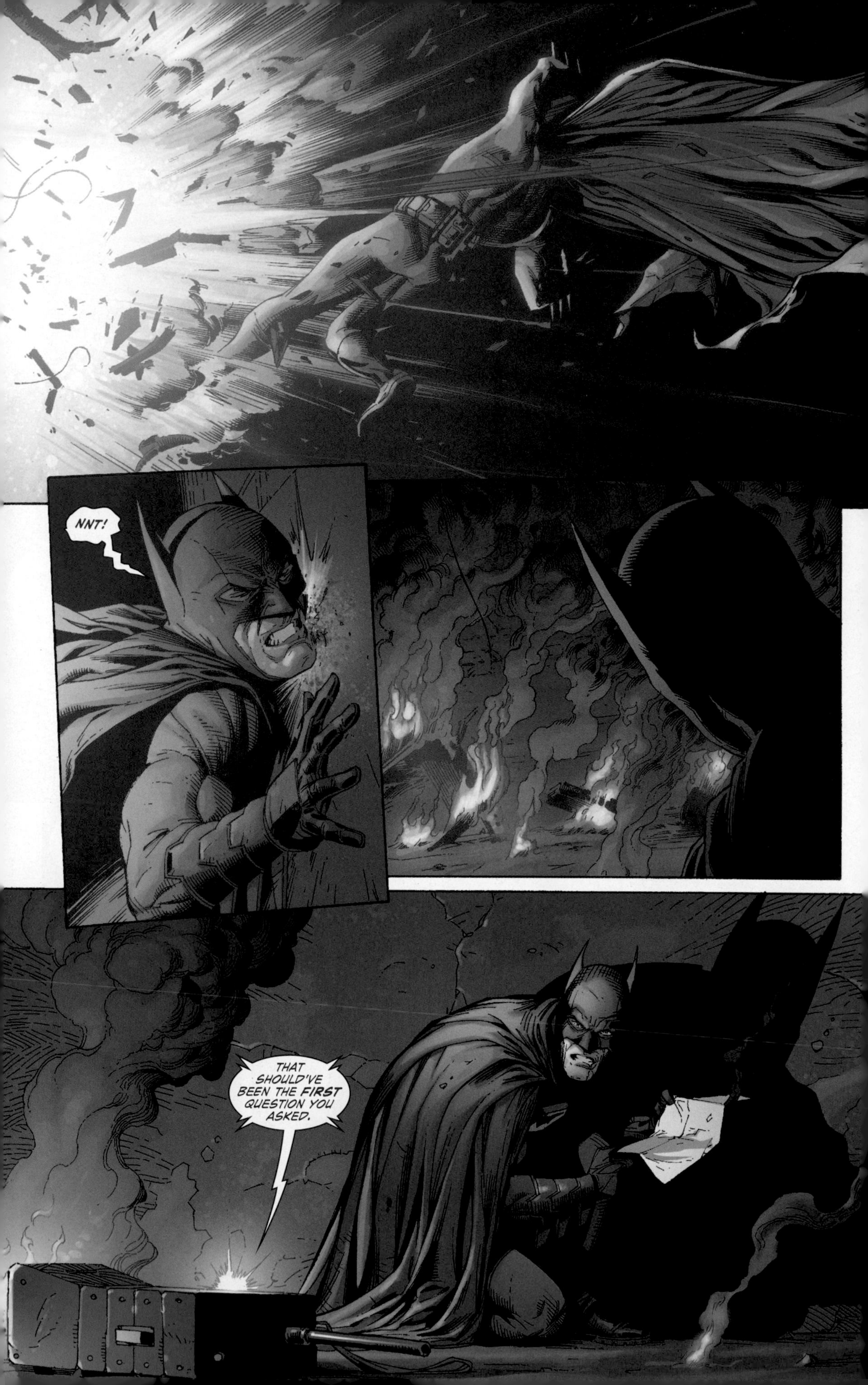
NNT!
THAT SHOULD'VE BEEN THE FIRST QUESTION YOU ASKED.

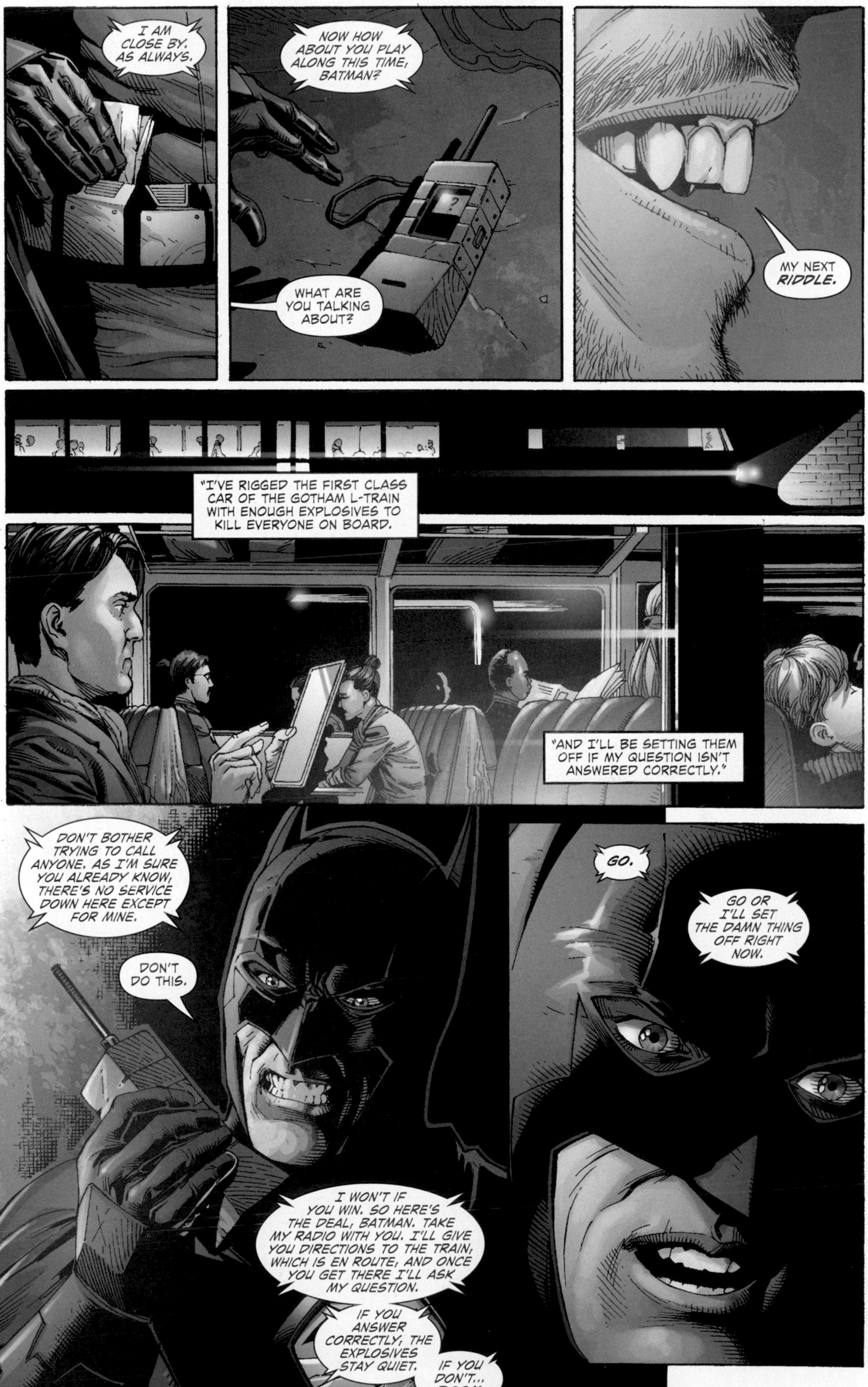
I AM CLOSE BY. AS ALWAYS.
NOW HOW ABOUT YOU PLAY ALONG THIS TIME, BATMAN?
WHAT ARE YOU TALKING ABOUT?
MY NEXT RIDDLE.
"I'VE RIGGED THE FIRST CLASS CAR OF THE GOTHAM L-TRAIN WITH ENOUGH EXPLOSIVES TO KILL EVERYONE ON BOARD.
"AND I'LL BE SETTING THEM OFF IF MY QUESTION ISN'T ANSWERED CORRECTLY."
DON'T BOTHER TRYING TO CALL ANYONE. AS I'M SURE YOU ALREADY KNOW, THERE'S NO SERVICE DOWN HERE EXCEPT FOR MINE.
DON'T DO THIS.
GO.
GO OR I'LL SET THE DAMN THING OFF RIGHT NOW.
I WON'T IF YOU WIN. SO HERE'S THE DEAL, BATMAN. TAKE MY RADIO WITH YOU. I'LL GIVE YOU DIRECTIONS TO THE TRAIN, WHICH IS EN ROUTE, AND ONCE YOU GET THERE I'LL ASK MY QUESTION.
IF YOU ANSWER CORRECTLY, THE EXPLOSIVES STAY QUIET.
IF YOU DON'T... BOOM.

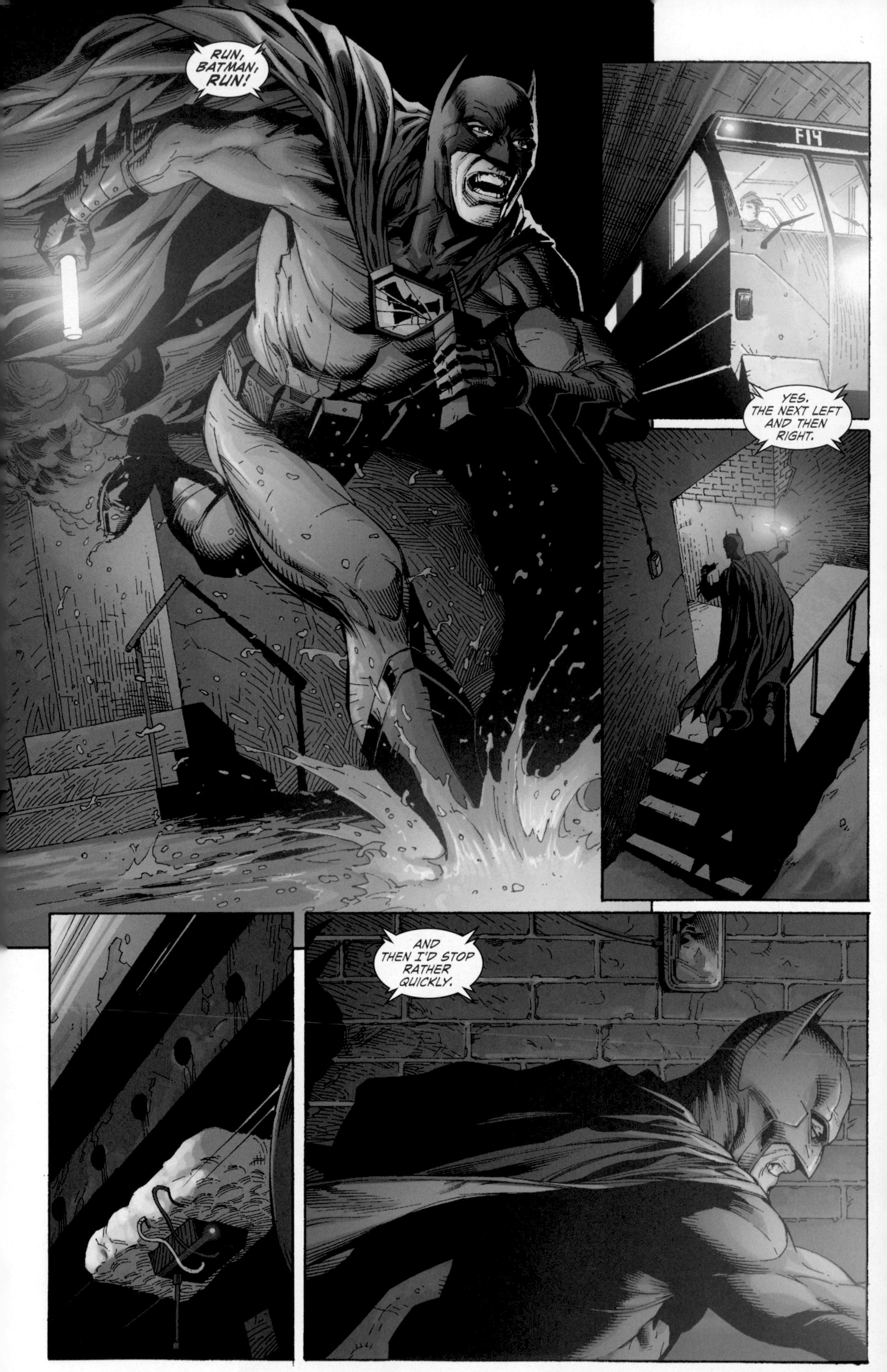
RUN, BATMAN, RUN!
YES. THE NEXT LEFT AND THEN RIGHT.
AND THEN I'D STOP RATHER QUICKLY.

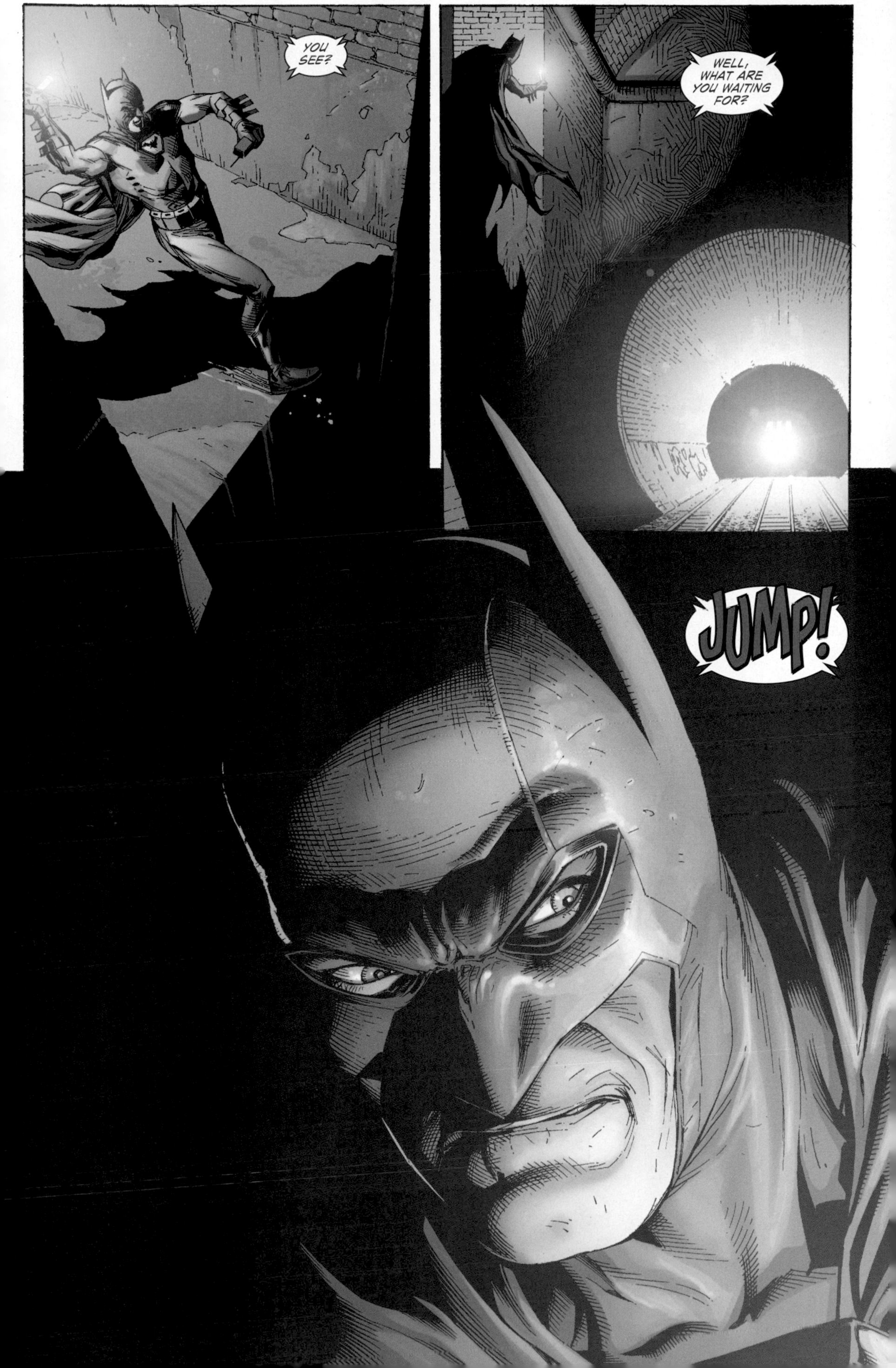
YOU SEE?
WELL, WHAT ARE YOU WAITING FOR?
JUMP!

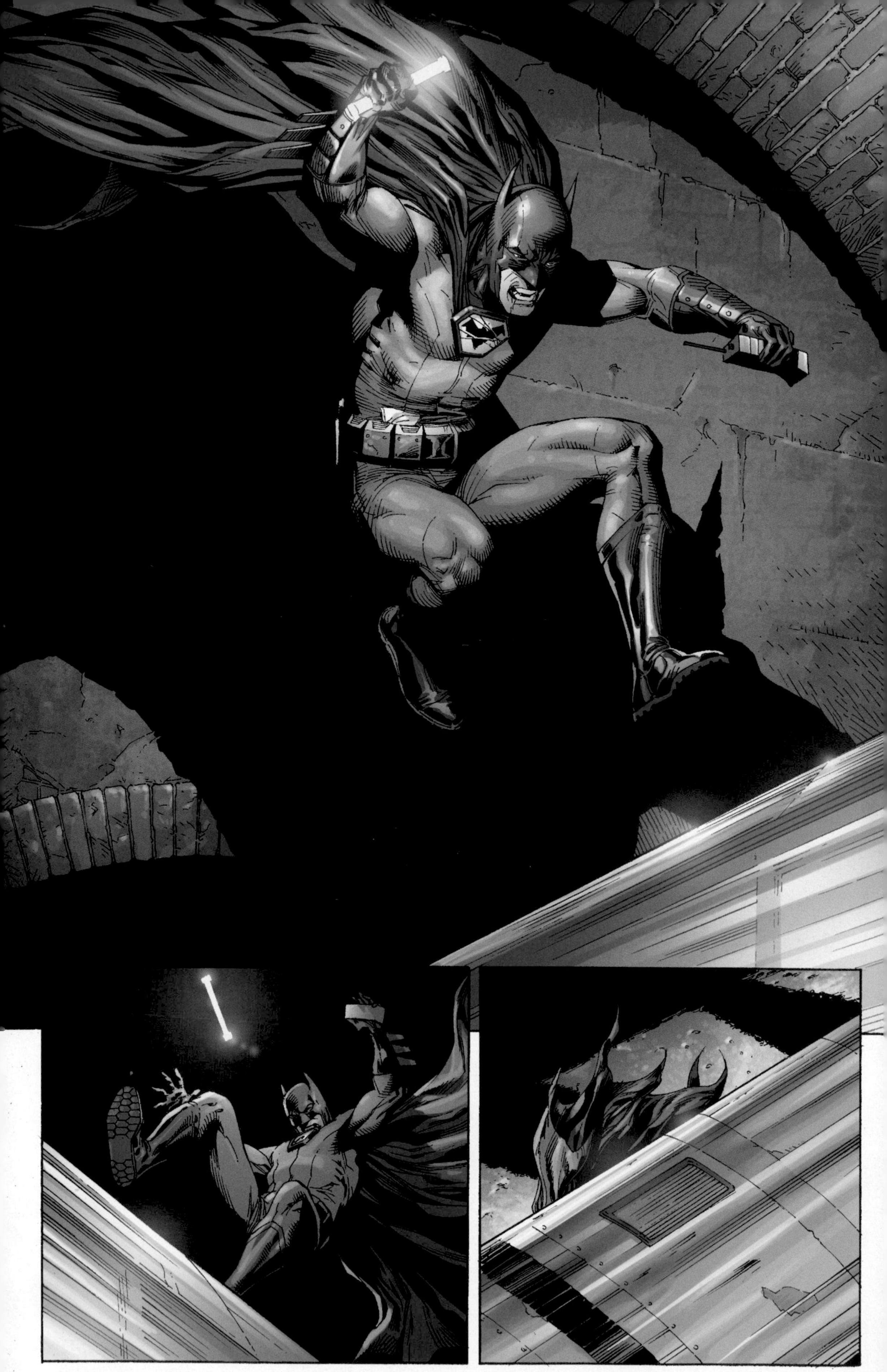

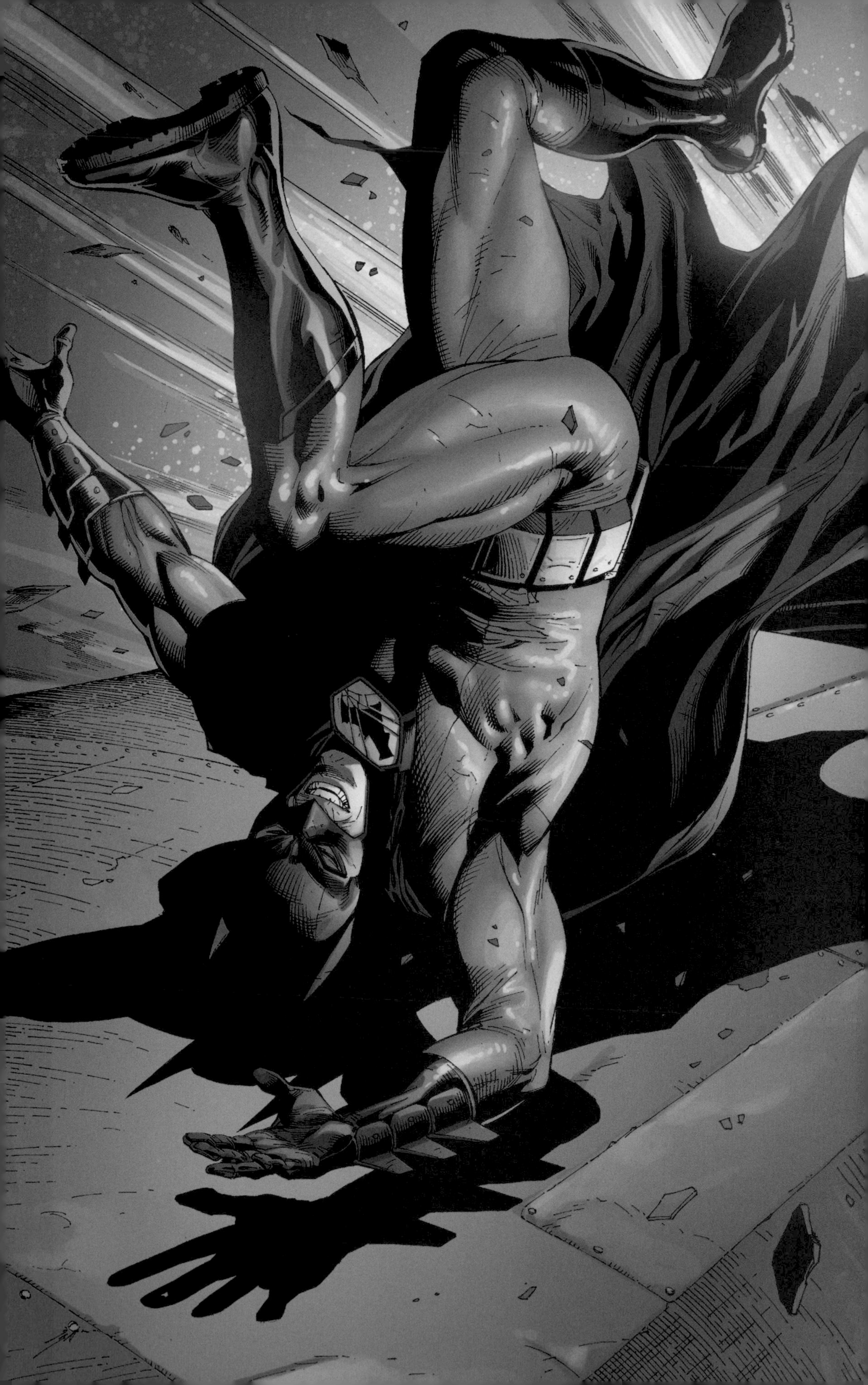

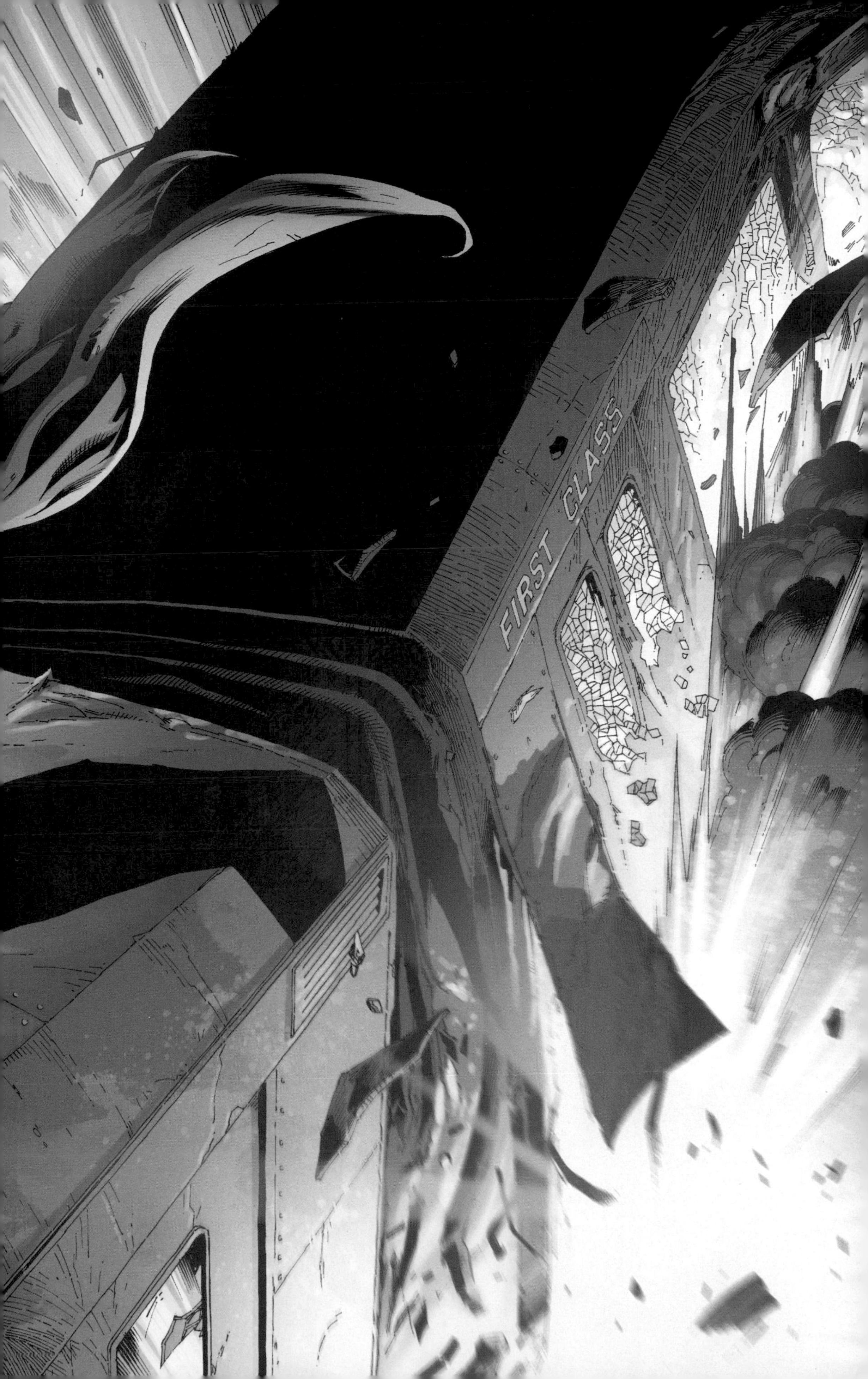
FIRST CLASS

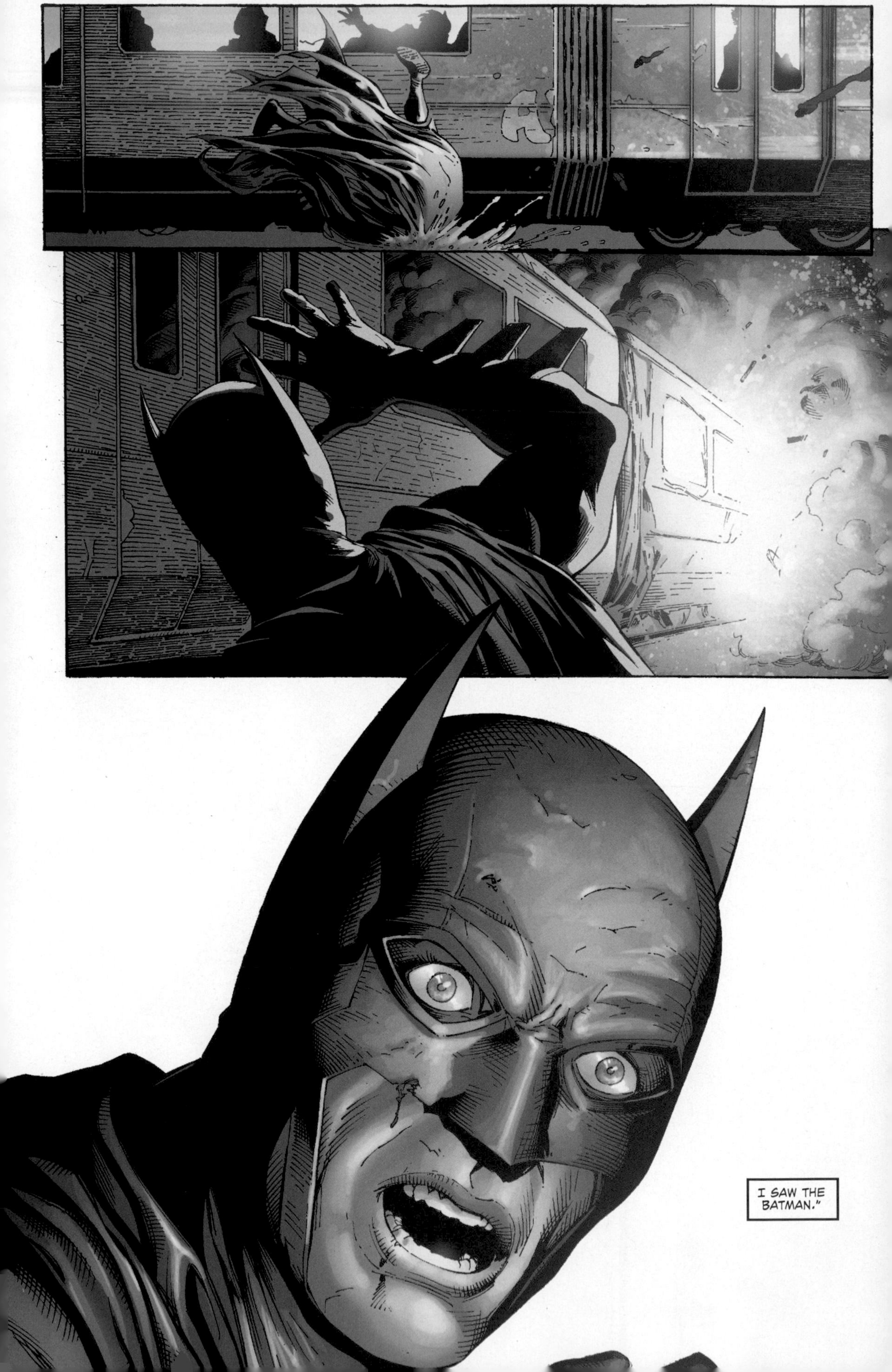
I SAW THE BATMAN."

"HE PULLED ME OUT.

"AND THEN HE STARTED HELPING WHOEVER HE COULD UNTIL YOU GOT HERE."

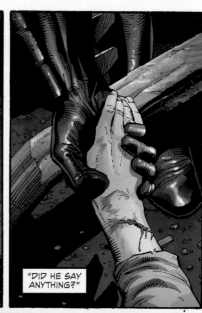

"DID HE SAY ANYTHING?"

"HE SAID HE WAS GOING TO FIND WHO DID THIS."

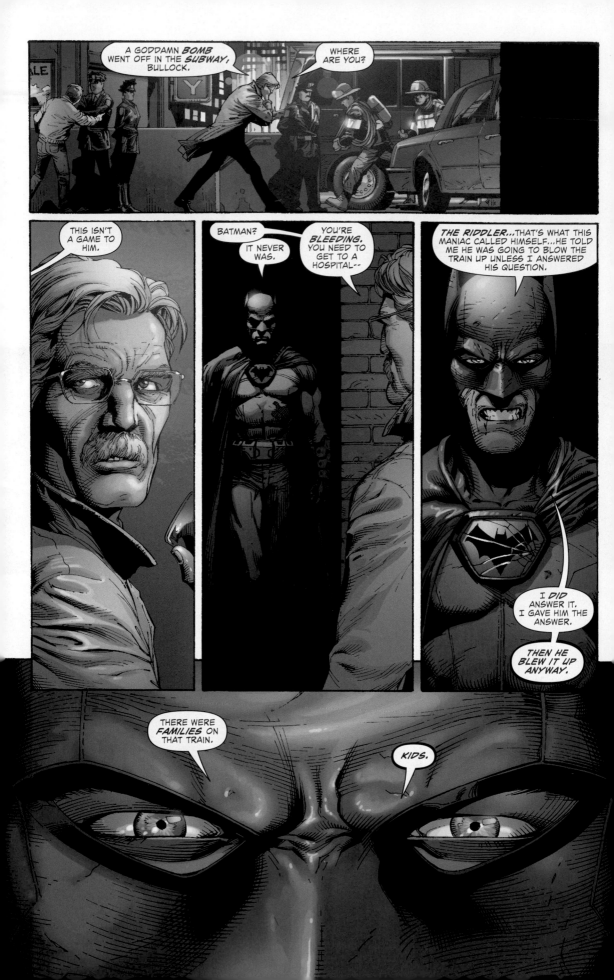

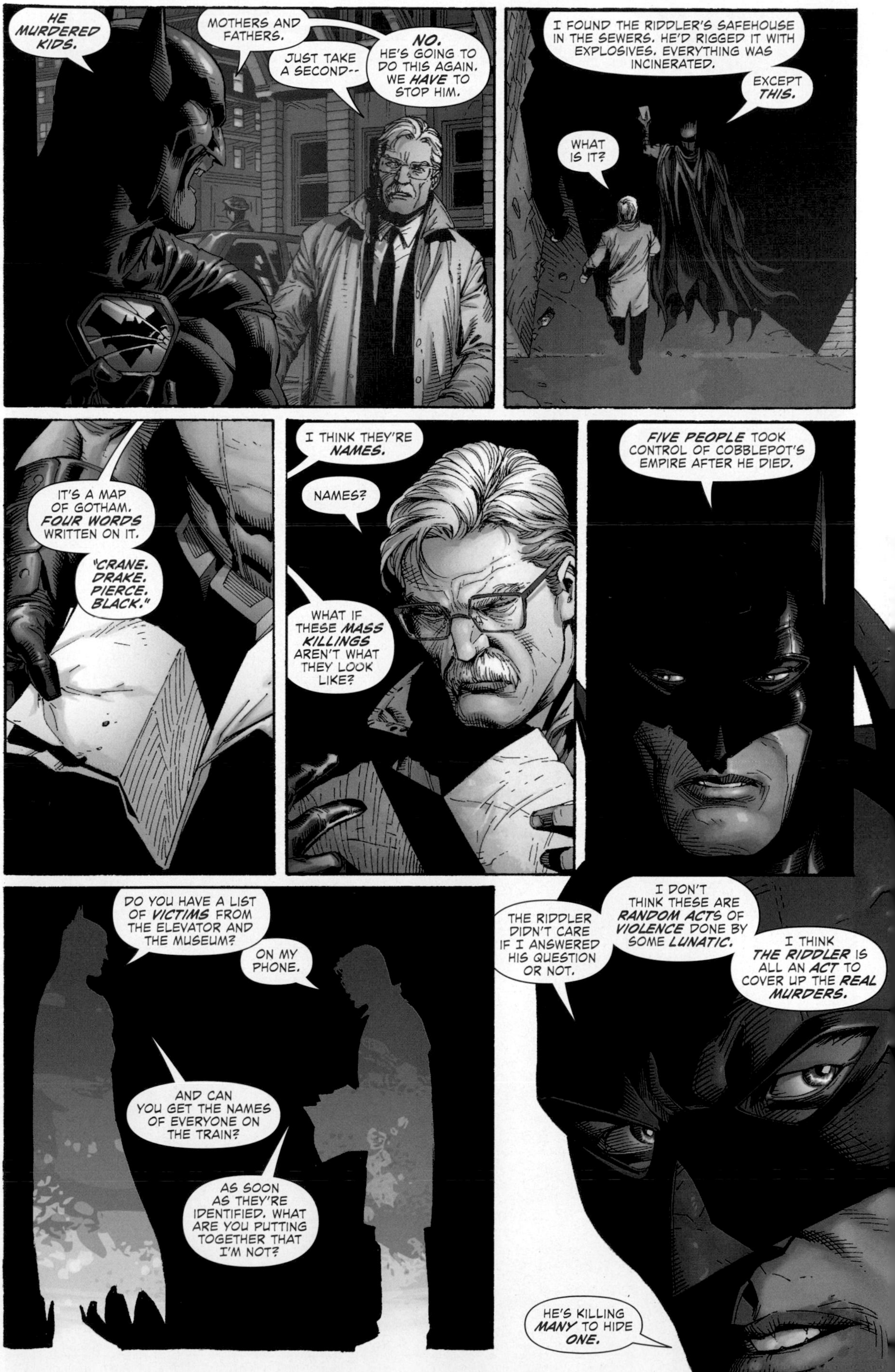
HE MURDERED KIDS.
MOTHERS AND FATHERS.
JUST TAKE A SECOND--
NO. HE'S GOING TO DO THIS AGAIN. WE HAVE TO STOP HIM.
I FOUND THE RIDDLER'S SAFEHOUSE IN THE SEWERS. HE'D RIGGED IT WITH EXPLOSIVES. EVERYTHING WAS INCINERATED.
EXCEPT THIS.
WHAT IS IT?
IT'S A MAP OF GOTHAM. FOUR WORDS WRITTEN ON IT.
"CRANE. DRAKE. PIERCE. BLACK."
I THINK THEY'RE NAMES.
NAMES?
WHAT IF THESE MASS KILLINGS AREN'T WHAT THEY LOOK LIKE?
FIVE PEOPLE TOOK CONTROL OF COBBLEPOT'S EMPIRE AFTER HE DIED.
DO YOU HAVE A LIST OF VICTIMS FROM THE ELEVATOR AND THE MUSEUM?
ON MY PHONE.
AND CAN YOU GET THE NAMES OF EVERYONE ON THE TRAIN?
AS SOON AS THEY'RE IDENTIFIED. WHAT ARE YOU PUTTING TOGETHER THAT I'M NOT?
THE RIDDLER DIDN'T CARE IF I ANSWERED HIS QUESTION OR NOT.
I DON'T THINK THESE ARE RANDOM ACTS OF VIOLENCE DONE BY SOME LUNATIC.
I THINK THE RIDDLER IS ALL AN ACT TO COVER UP THE REAL MURDERS.
HE'S KILLING MANY TO HIDE ONE.

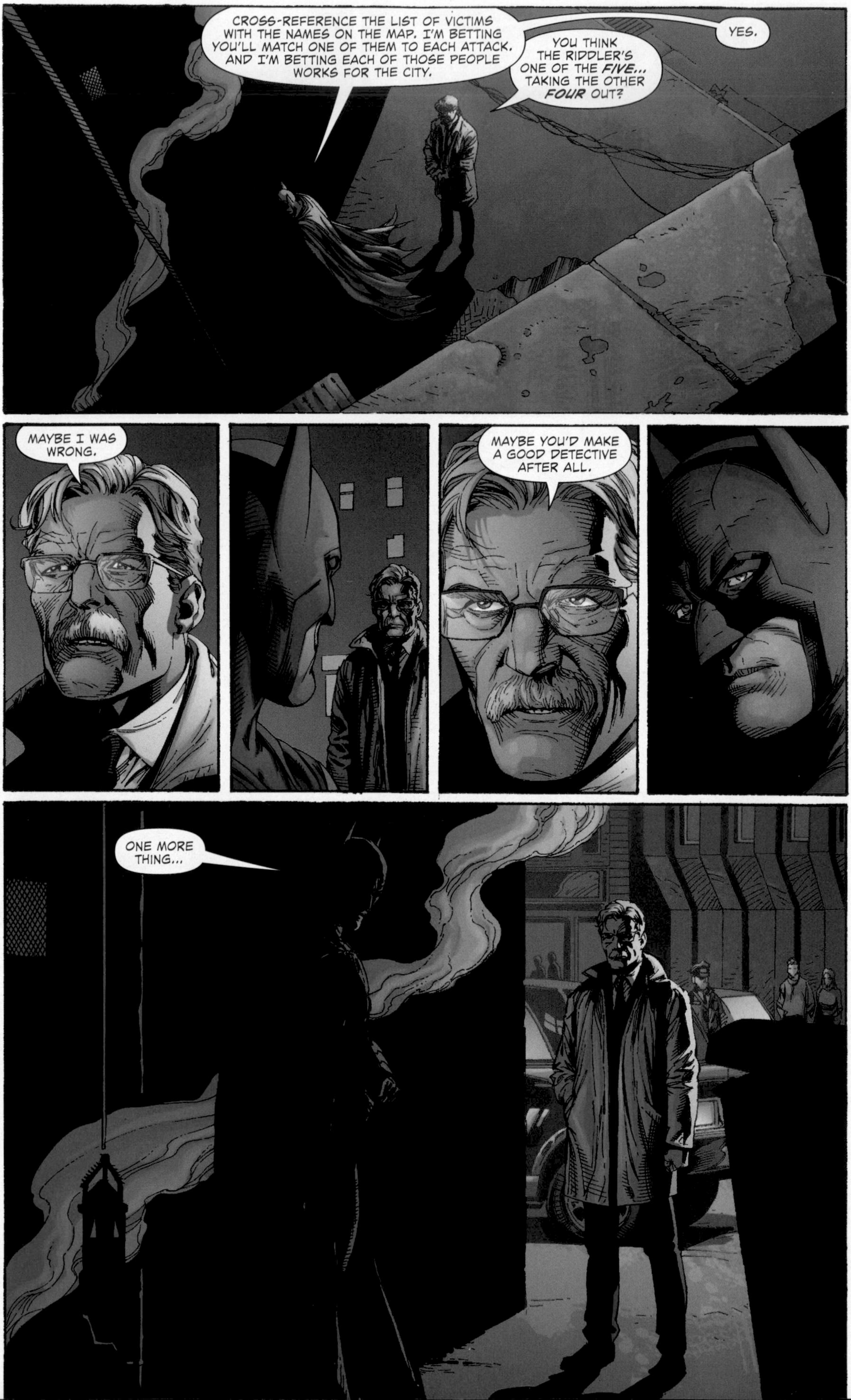
CROSS-REFERENCE THE LIST OF VICTIMS WITH THE NAMES ON THE MAP. I'M BETTING YOU'LL MATCH ONE OF THEM TO EACH ATTACK. AND I'M BETTING EACH OF THOSE PEOPLE WORKS FOR THE CITY.
YOU THINK THE RIDDLER'S ONE OF THE *FIVE...* TAKING THE OTHER *FOUR* OUT?
YES.
MAYBE I WAS WRONG.
MAYBE YOU'D MAKE A GOOD DETECTIVE AFTER ALL.
ONE MORE THING...

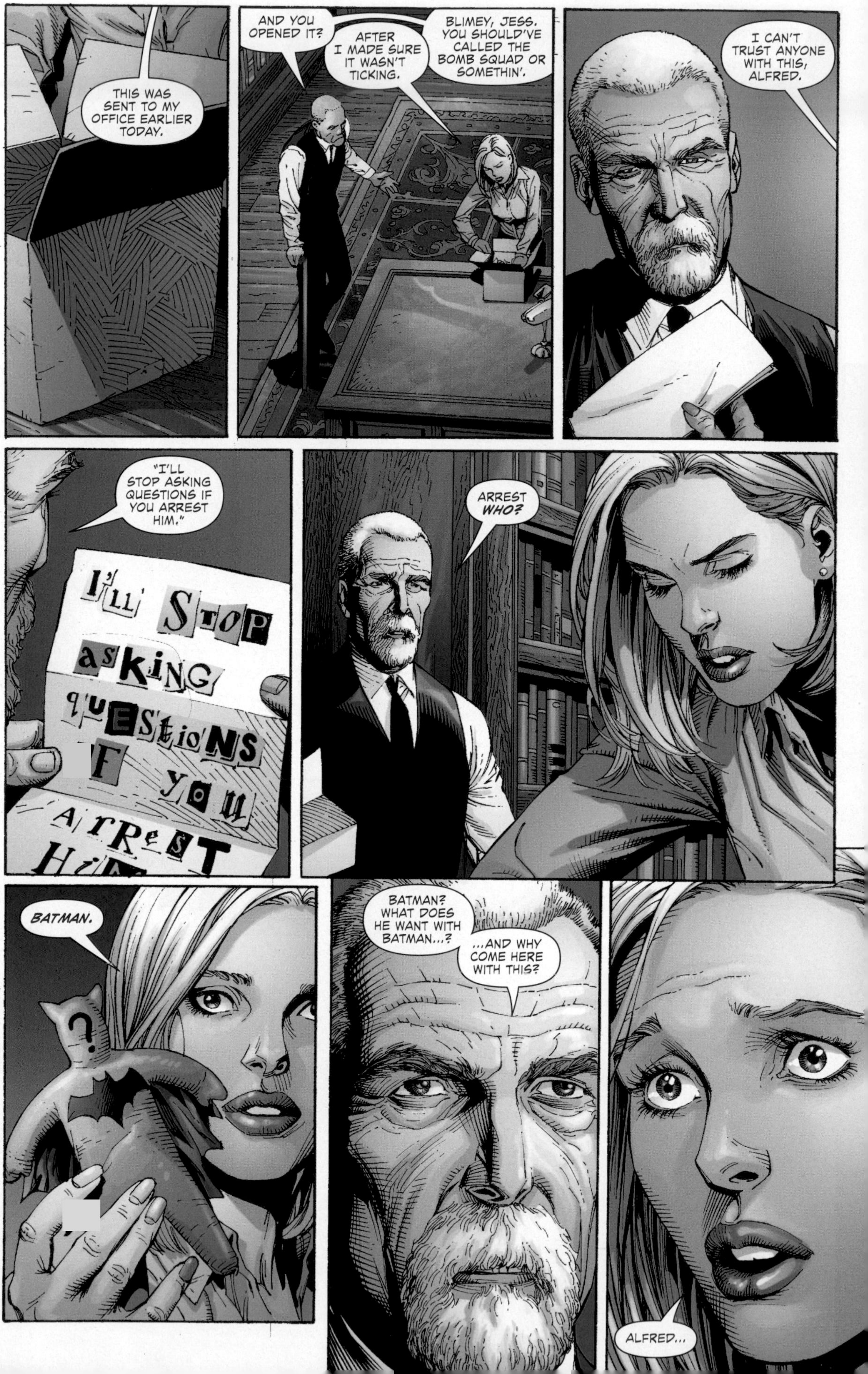

THIS WAS SENT TO MY OFFICE EARLIER TODAY.
AND YOU OPENED IT?
AFTER I MADE SURE IT WASN'T TICKING.
BLIMEY, JESS. YOU SHOULD'VE CALLED THE BOMB SQUAD OR SOMETHIN'.
I CAN'T TRUST ANYONE WITH THIS, ALFRED.
"I'LL STOP ASKING QUESTIONS IF YOU ARREST HIM."
I'LL STOP asKING quEStioNS
you
ARReST
ARREST *WHO?*
BATMAN.
BATMAN? WHAT DOES HE WANT WITH BATMAN...?
...AND WHY COME HERE WITH THIS?
ALFRED...

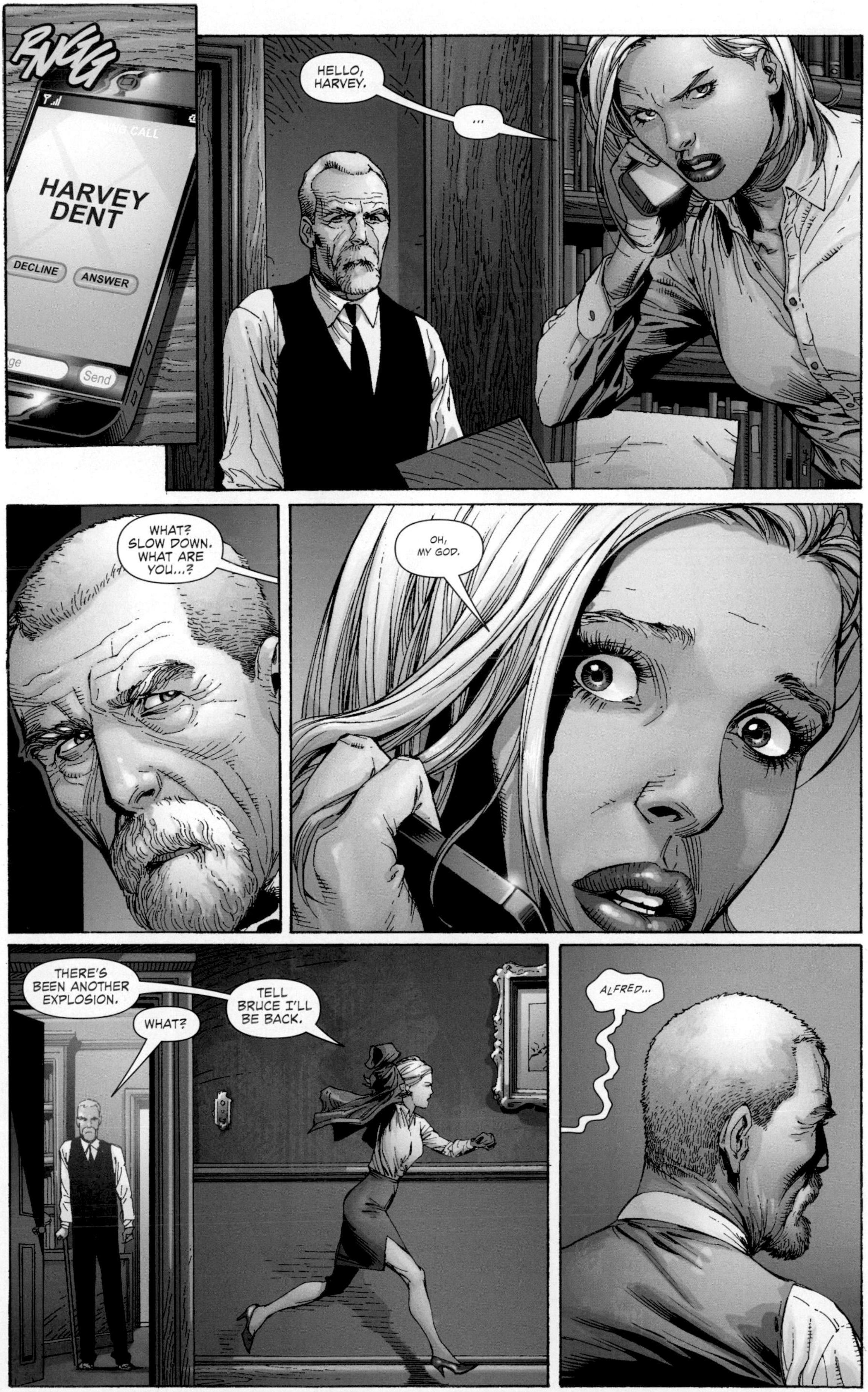
RNGGG
HARVEY DENT
DECLINE
ANSWER
Send
HELLO, HARVEY.
...
WHAT? SLOW DOWN. WHAT ARE YOU...?
OH, MY GOD.
THERE'S BEEN ANOTHER EXPLOSION.
WHAT?
TELL BRUCE I'LL BE BACK.
ALFRED...

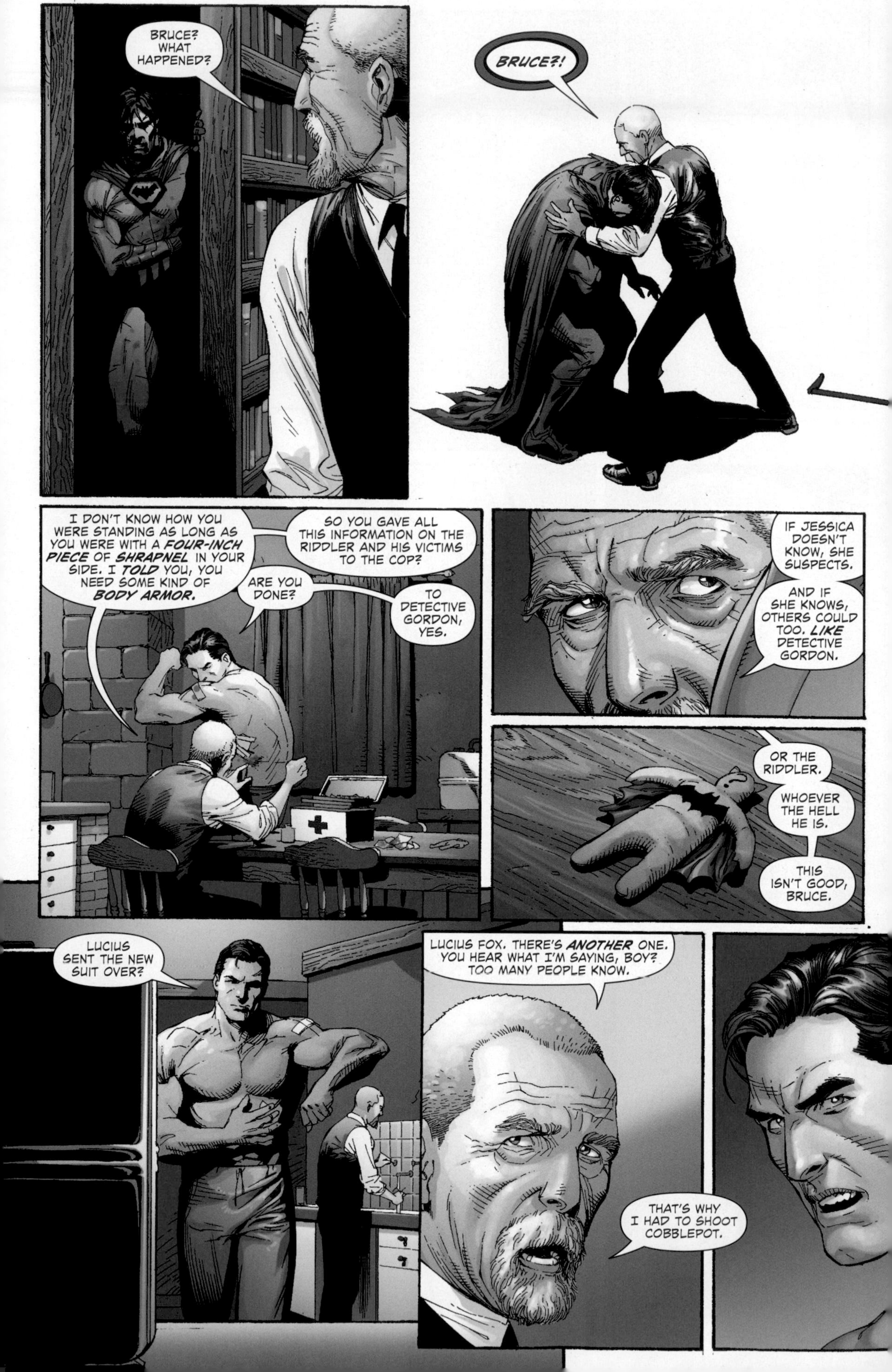
BRUCE? WHAT HAPPENED?
BRUCE?!
I DON'T KNOW HOW YOU WERE STANDING AS LONG AS YOU WERE WITH A FOUR-INCH PIECE OF SHRAPNEL IN YOUR SIDE. I TOLD YOU, YOU NEED SOME KIND OF BODY ARMOR.
SO YOU GAVE ALL THIS INFORMATION ON THE RIDDLER AND HIS VICTIMS TO THE COP?
ARE YOU DONE?
TO DETECTIVE GORDON, YES.
IF JESSICA DOESN'T KNOW, SHE SUSPECTS.
AND IF SHE KNOWS, OTHERS COULD TOO. LIKE DETECTIVE GORDON.
OR THE RIDDLER.
WHOEVER THE HELL HE IS.
THIS ISN'T GOOD, BRUCE.
LUCIUS SENT THE NEW SUIT OVER?
LUCIUS FOX. THERE'S ANOTHER ONE. YOU HEAR WHAT I'M SAYING, BOY? TOO MANY PEOPLE KNOW.
THAT'S WHY I HAD TO SHOOT COBBLEPOT.

YOU TOLD ME YOU SHOT HIM BECAUSE YOU THOUGHT HE WAS GOING TO KILL ME.

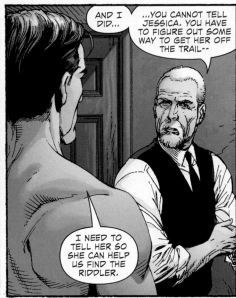

AND I DID...

...YOU CANNOT TELL JESSICA. YOU HAVE TO FIGURE OUT SOME WAY TO GET HER OFF THE TRAIL--

I NEED TO TELL HER SO SHE CAN HELP US FIND THE RIDDLER.

YOU CAN'T HAVE HER AND BATMAN, BRUCE.

YOU MADE THAT CHOICE A LONG TIME AGO, NOT ME.

YOU'RE NOT A MAN ANYMORE.

YOU'RE A WEAPON.

IS THAT WHAT YOU TURNED ME INTO?

THAT'S WHAT YOU ASKED TO BE TURNED INTO.

WEAPONS ARE DESIGNED TO HURT PEOPLE. YOU DON'T WANT TO HURT HER.

VZZD

BATMAN?

I'VE MATCHED THE NAMES.

AND SOMETHING ELSE...

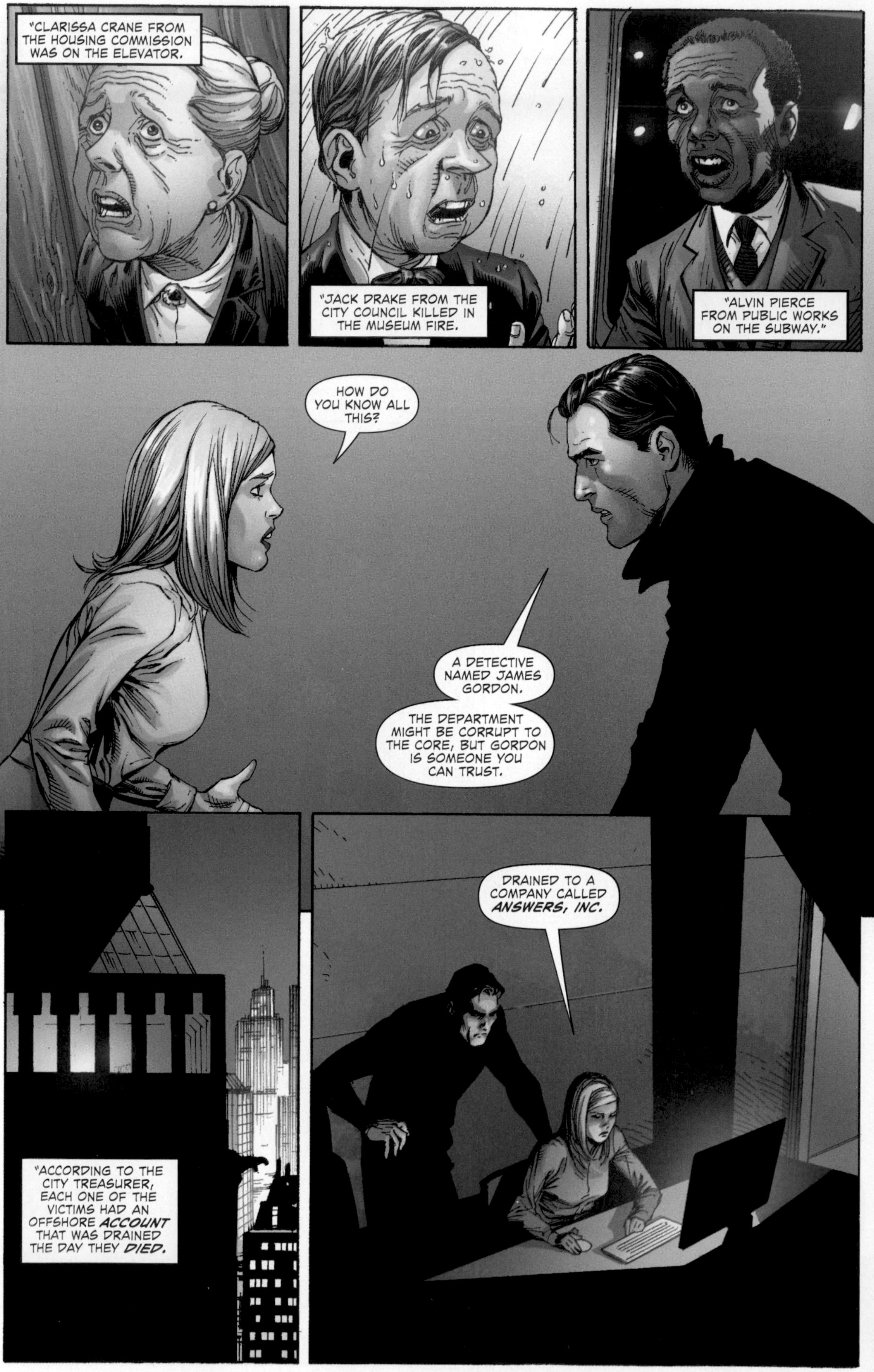
"CLARISSA CRANE FROM THE HOUSING COMMISSION WAS ON THE ELEVATOR.
"JACK DRAKE FROM THE CITY COUNCIL KILLED IN THE MUSEUM FIRE.
"ALVIN PIERCE FROM PUBLIC WORKS ON THE SUBWAY."
HOW DO YOU KNOW ALL THIS?
A DETECTIVE NAMED JAMES GORDON.
THE DEPARTMENT MIGHT BE CORRUPT TO THE CORE, BUT GORDON IS SOMEONE YOU CAN TRUST.
"ACCORDING TO THE CITY TREASURER, EACH ONE OF THE VICTIMS HAD AN OFFSHORE *ACCOUNT* THAT WAS DRAINED THE DAY THEY *DIED*.
DRAINED TO A COMPANY CALLED *ANSWERS, INC.*

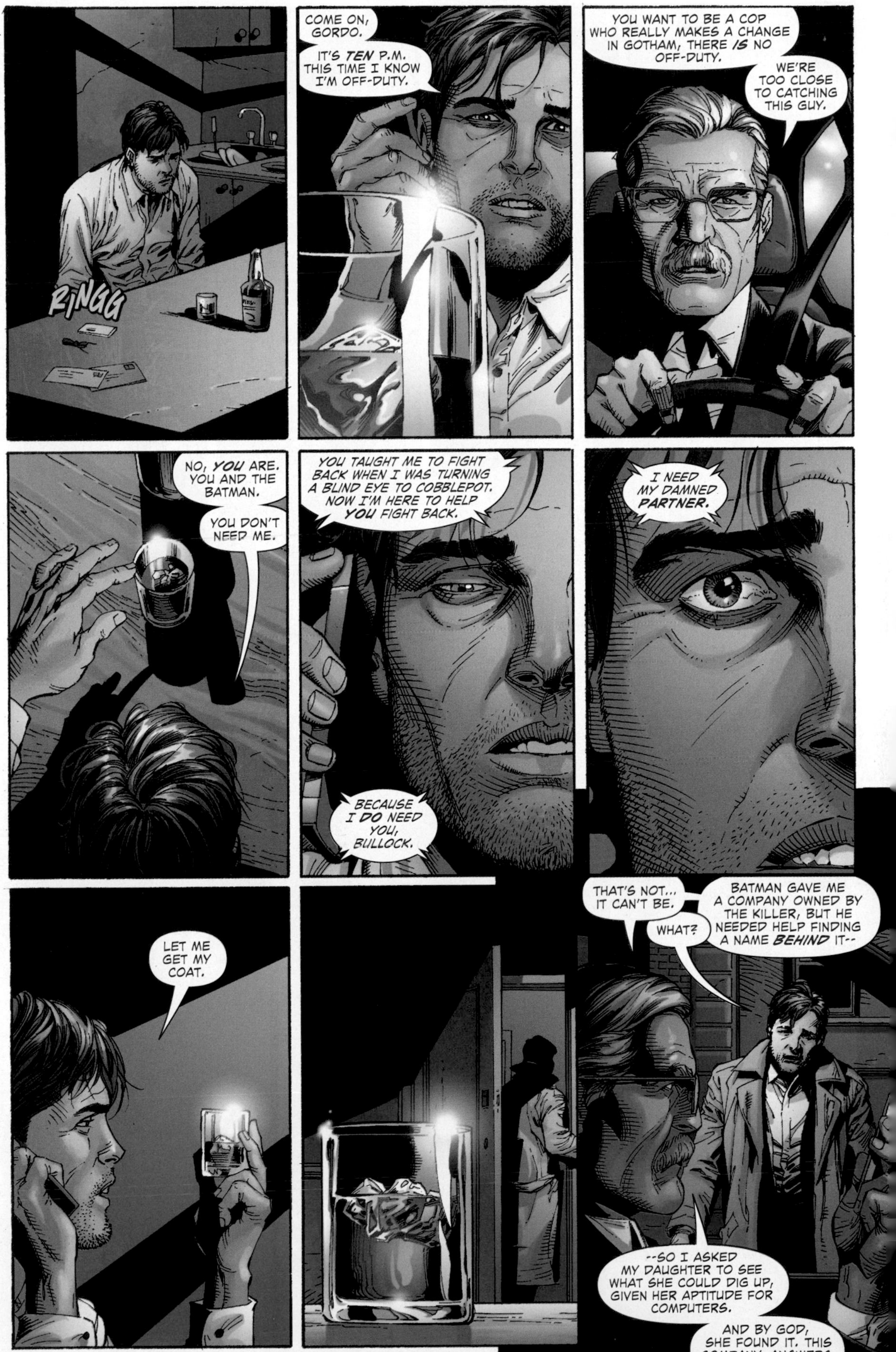
RINGG
COME ON, GORDO.
IT'S TEN P.M. THIS TIME I KNOW I'M OFF-DUTY.
YOU WANT TO BE A COP WHO REALLY MAKES A CHANGE IN GOTHAM, THERE IS NO OFF-DUTY.
WE'RE TOO CLOSE TO CATCHING THIS GUY.
NO, YOU ARE. YOU AND THE BATMAN.
YOU DON'T NEED ME.
YOU TAUGHT ME TO FIGHT BACK WHEN I WAS TURNING A BLIND EYE TO COBBLEPOT. NOW I'M HERE TO HELP YOU FIGHT BACK.
BECAUSE I DO NEED YOU, BULLOCK.
I NEED MY DAMNED PARTNER.
LET ME GET MY COAT.
THAT'S NOT... IT CAN'T BE.
WHAT?
BATMAN GAVE ME A COMPANY OWNED BY THE KILLER, BUT HE NEEDED HELP FINDING A NAME BEHIND IT--
--SO I ASKED MY DAUGHTER TO SEE WHAT SHE COULD DIG UP, GIVEN HER APTITUDE FOR COMPUTERS.
AND BY GOD, SHE FOUND IT. THIS COMPANY. ANSWERS INCORPORATED...

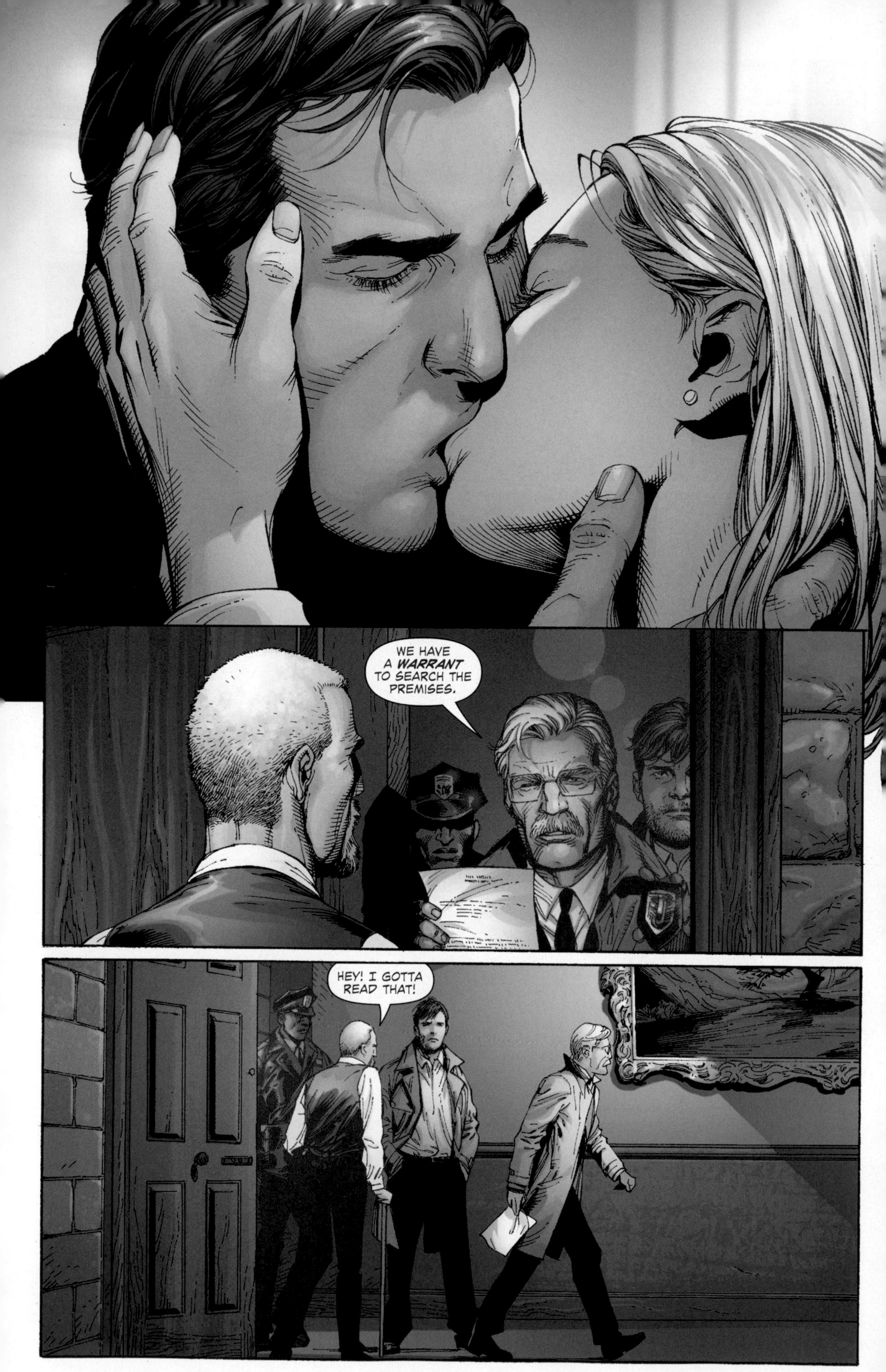
WE HAVE A WARRANT TO SEARCH THE PREMISES.
HEY! I GOTTA READ THAT!

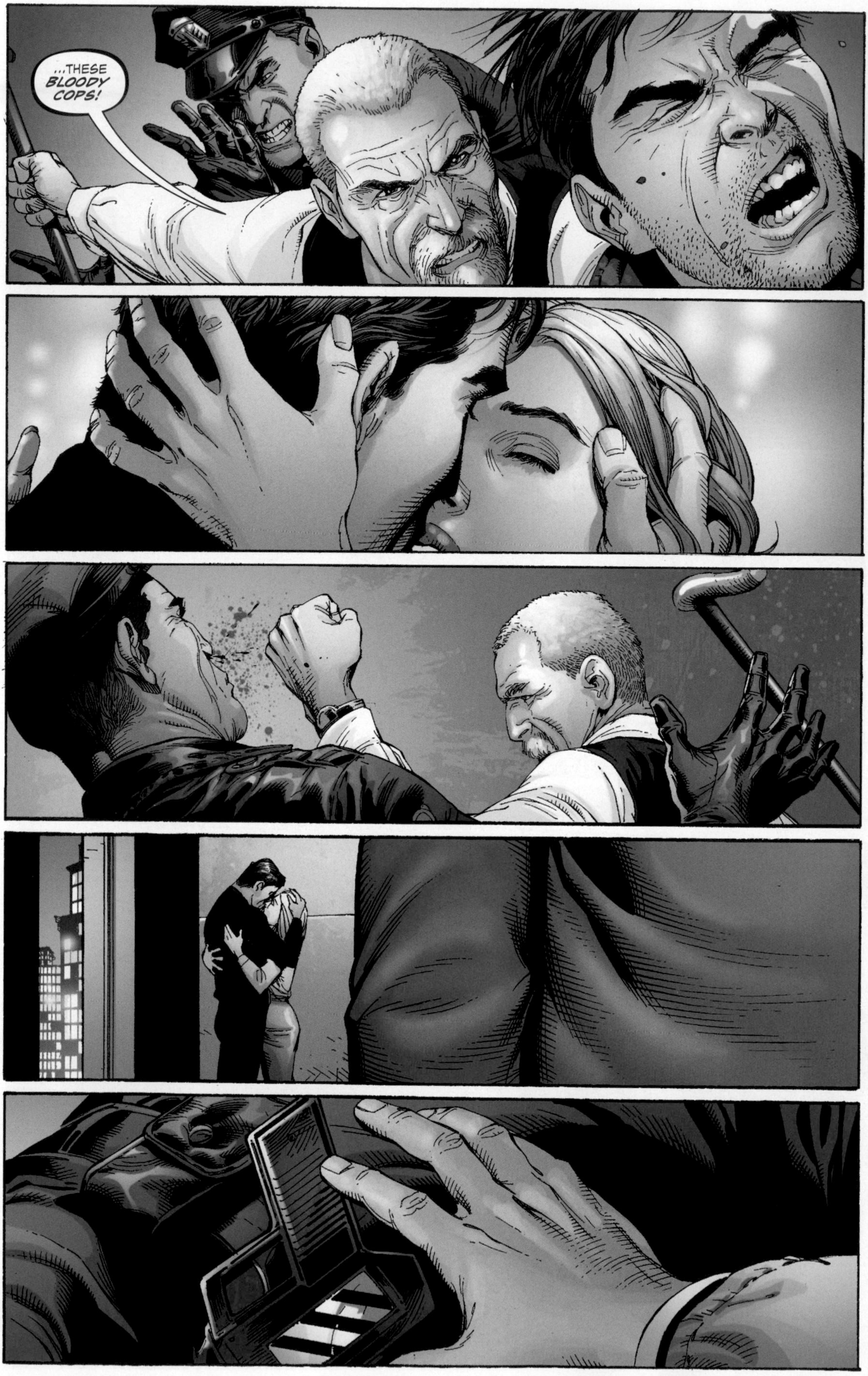
...THESE BLOODY COPS!

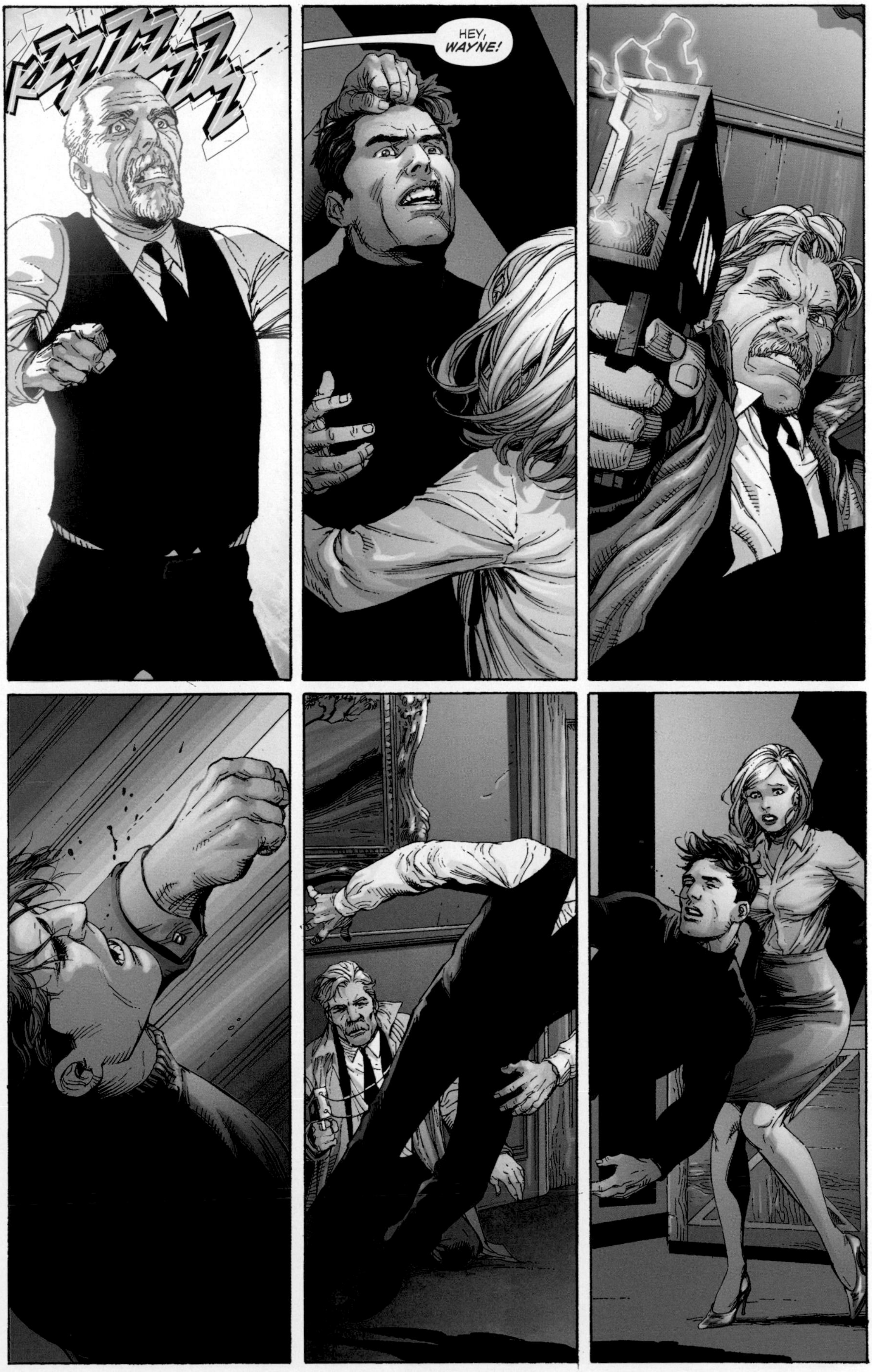
KZZZZZZ
HEY, WAYNE!

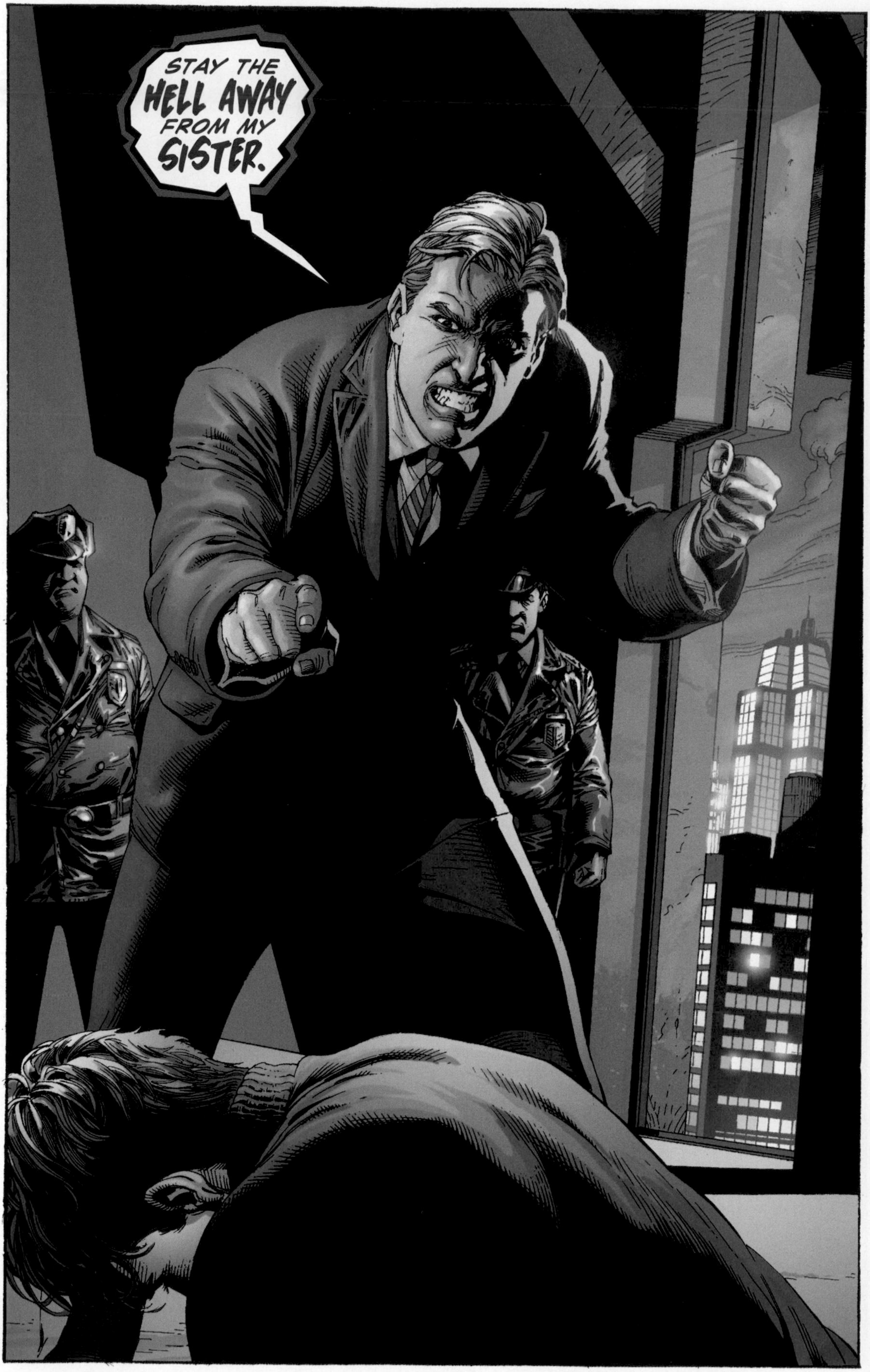
STAY THE HELL AWAY FROM MY SISTER.

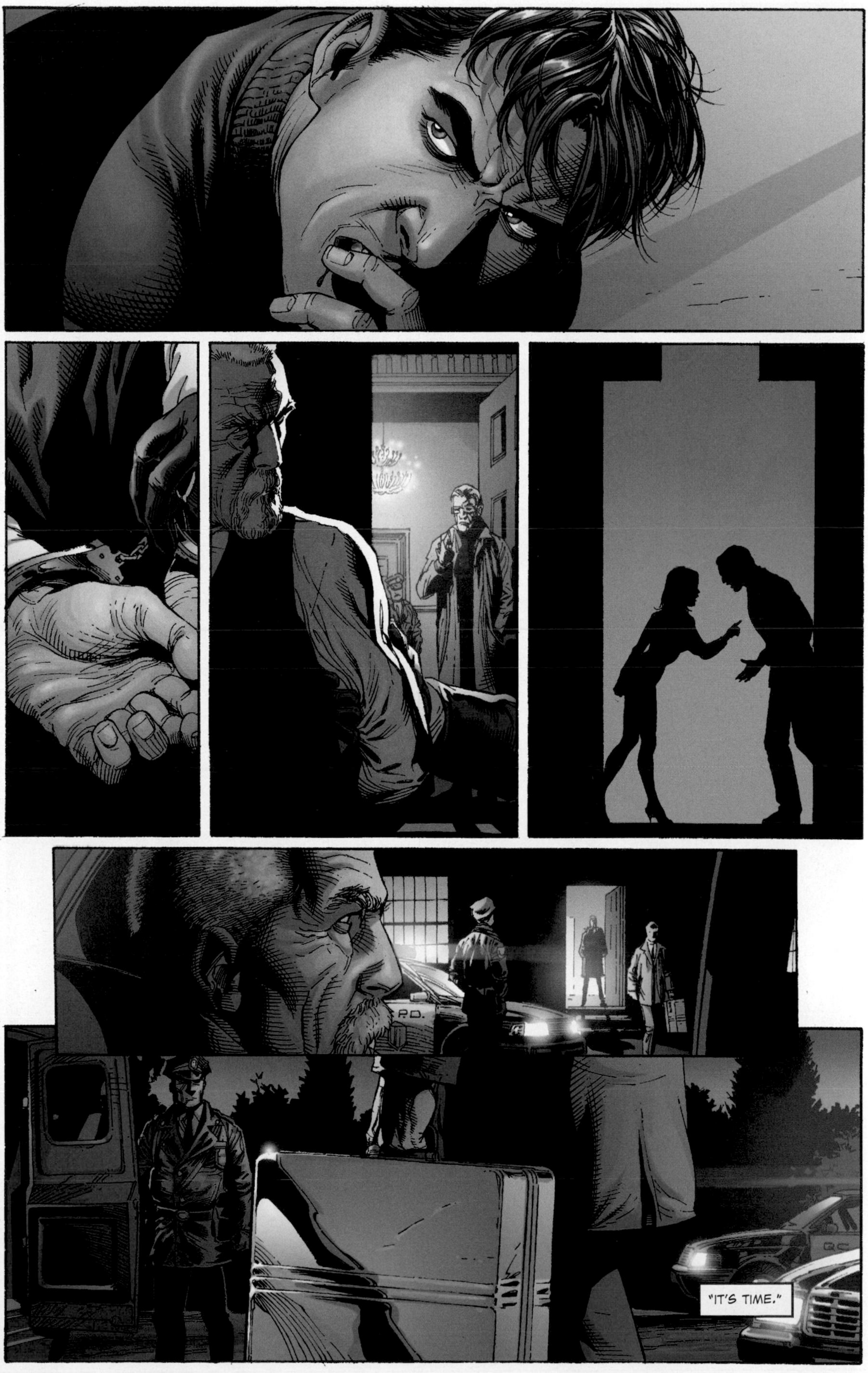
P.D.
"IT'S TIME."

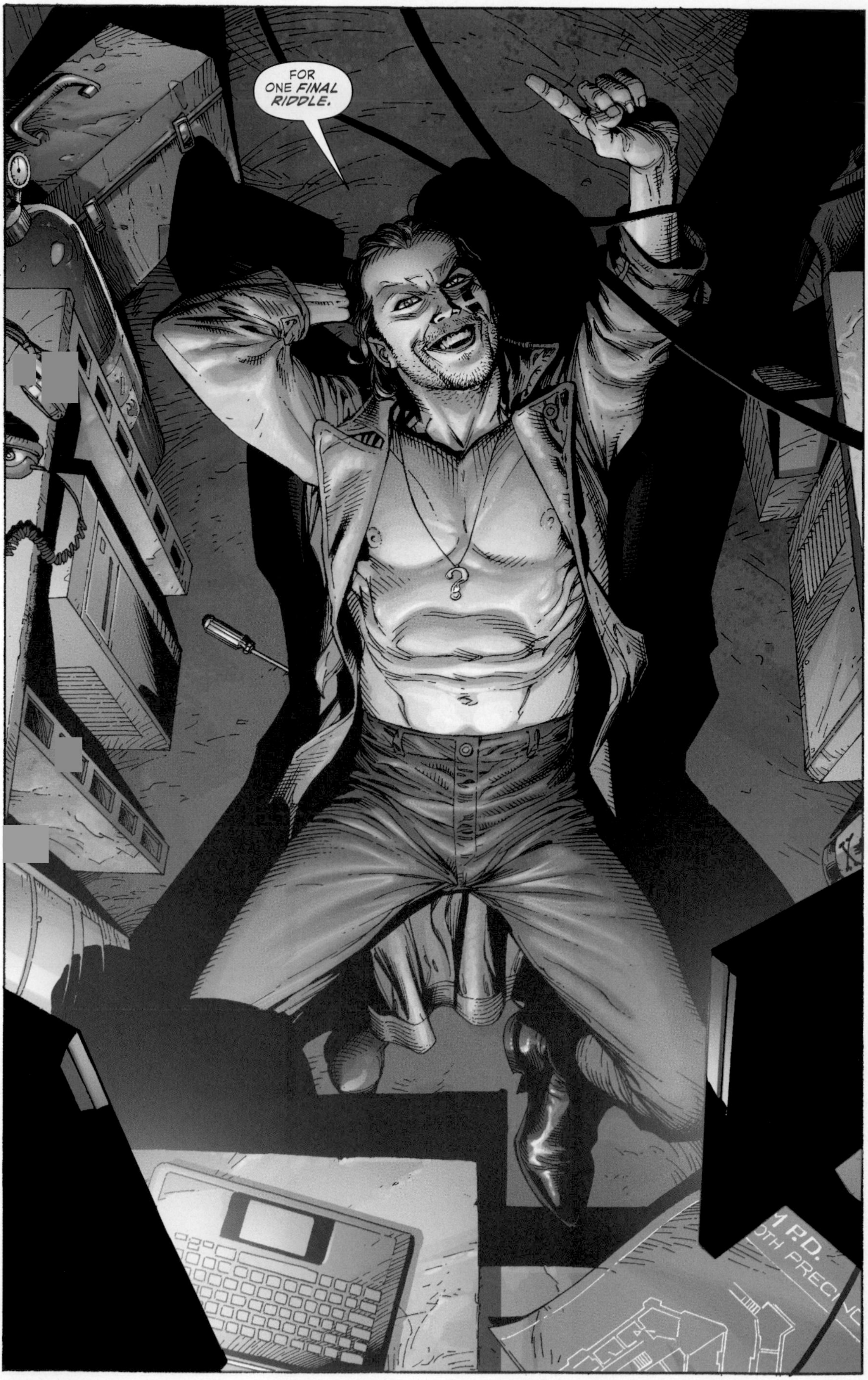
FOR ONE FINAL RIDDLE.

WHAT HAPPENED TO YOU?

ME?

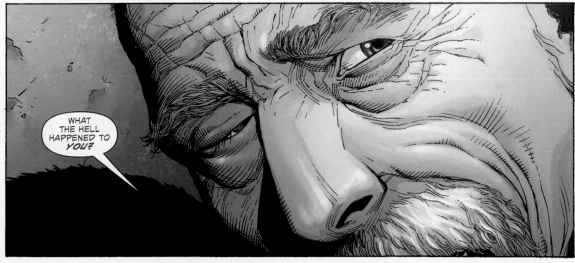

WHAT THE HELL HAPPENED TO YOU?

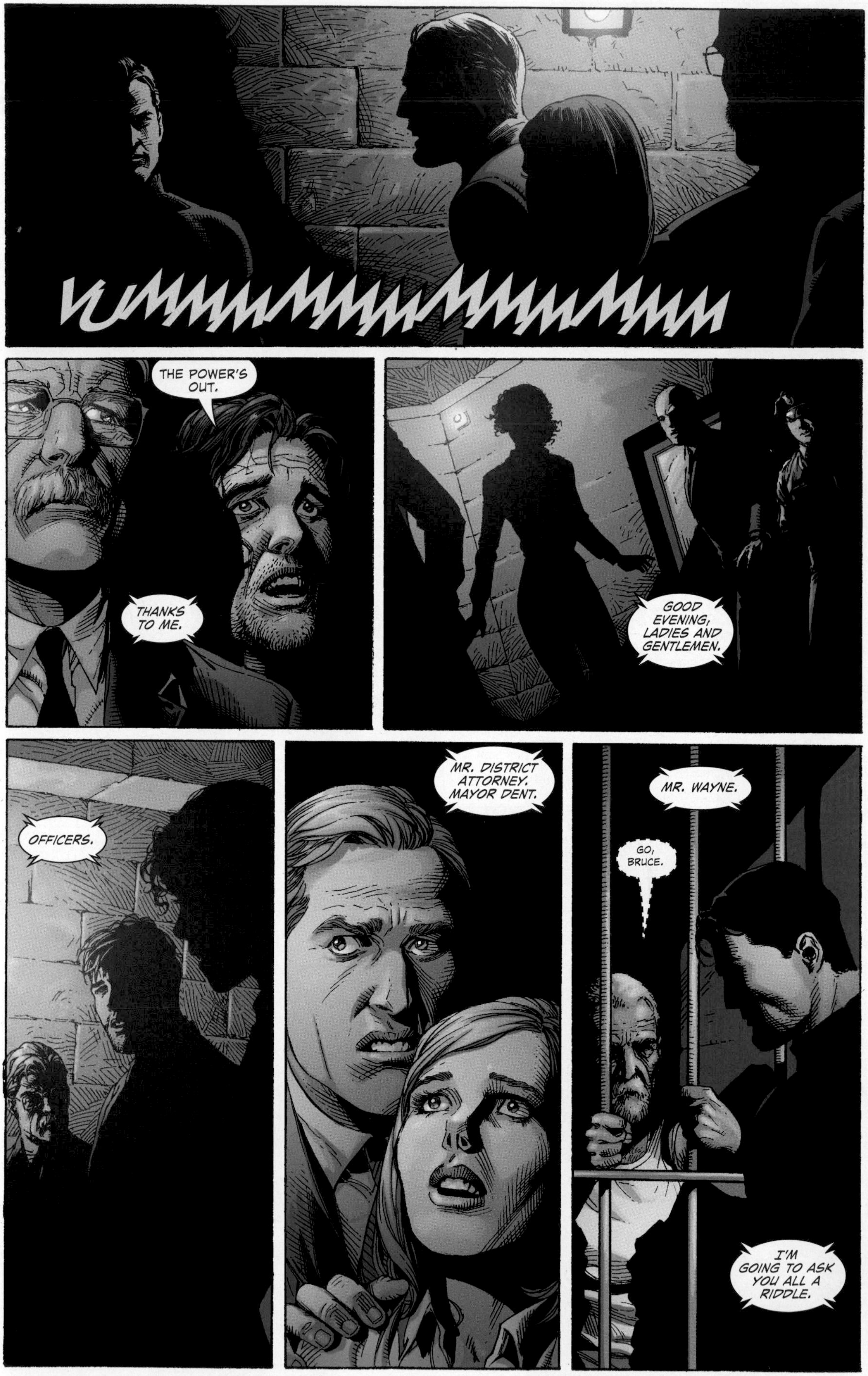
VUMMMMMMMMMMMMMM
THE POWER'S OUT.
THANKS TO ME.
GOOD EVENING, LADIES AND GENTLEMEN.
OFFICERS.
MR. DISTRICT ATTORNEY. MAYOR DENT.
MR. WAYNE.
GO, BRUCE.
I'M GOING TO ASK YOU ALL A RIDDLE.

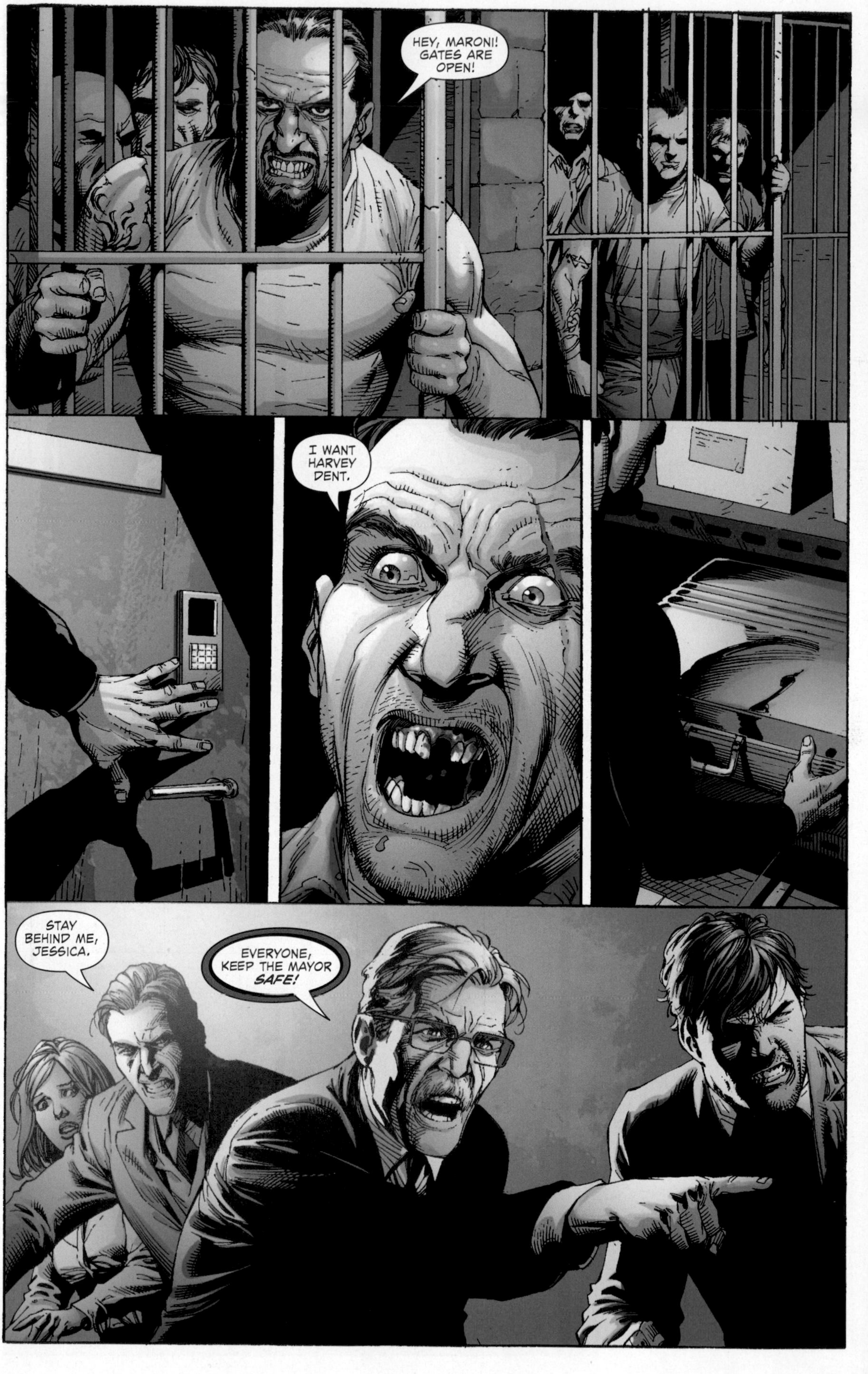
HEY, MARONI! GATES ARE OPEN!
I WANT HARVEY DENT.
STAY BEHIND ME, JESSICA.
EVERYONE, KEEP THE MAYOR SAFE!

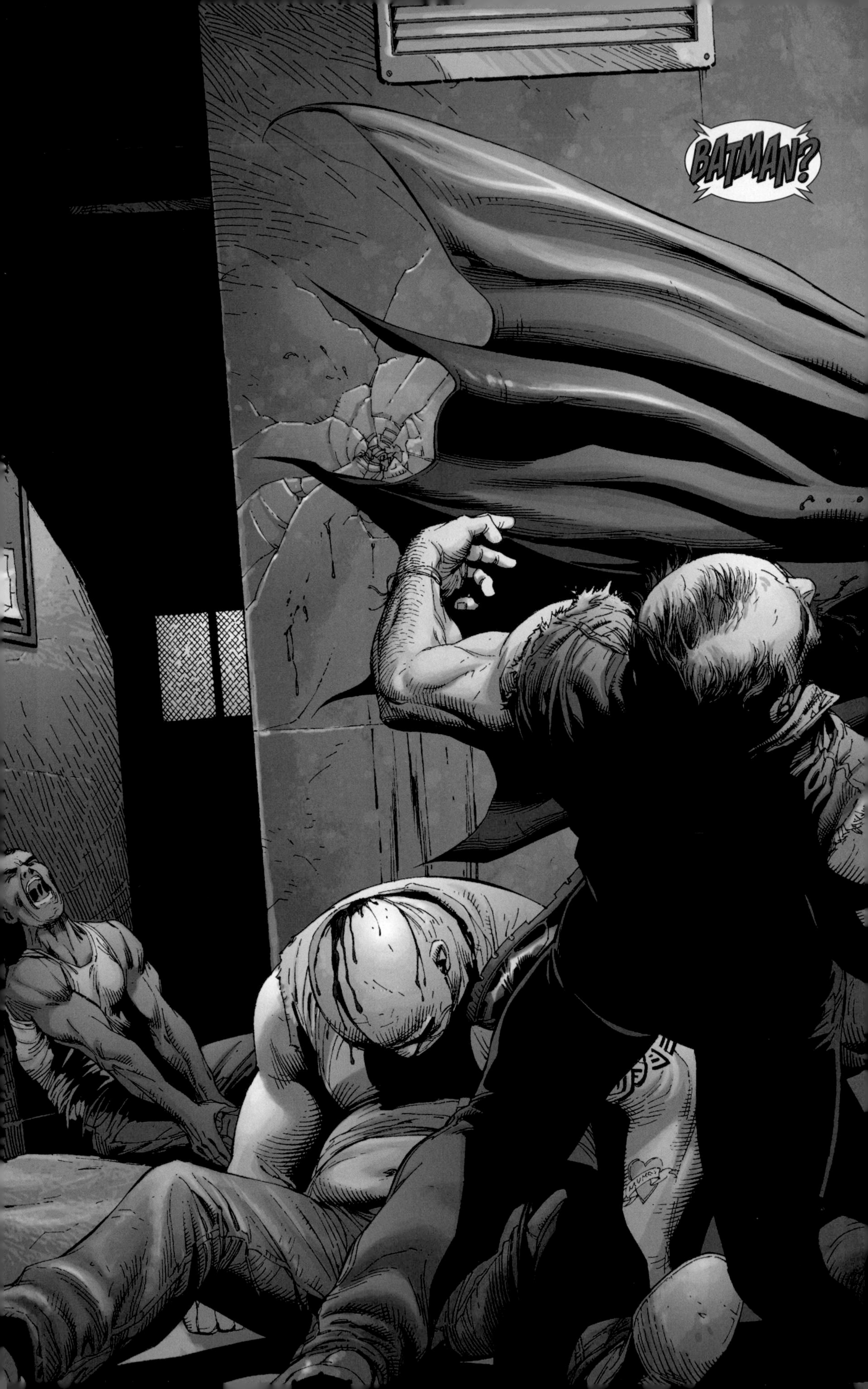
BATMAN?

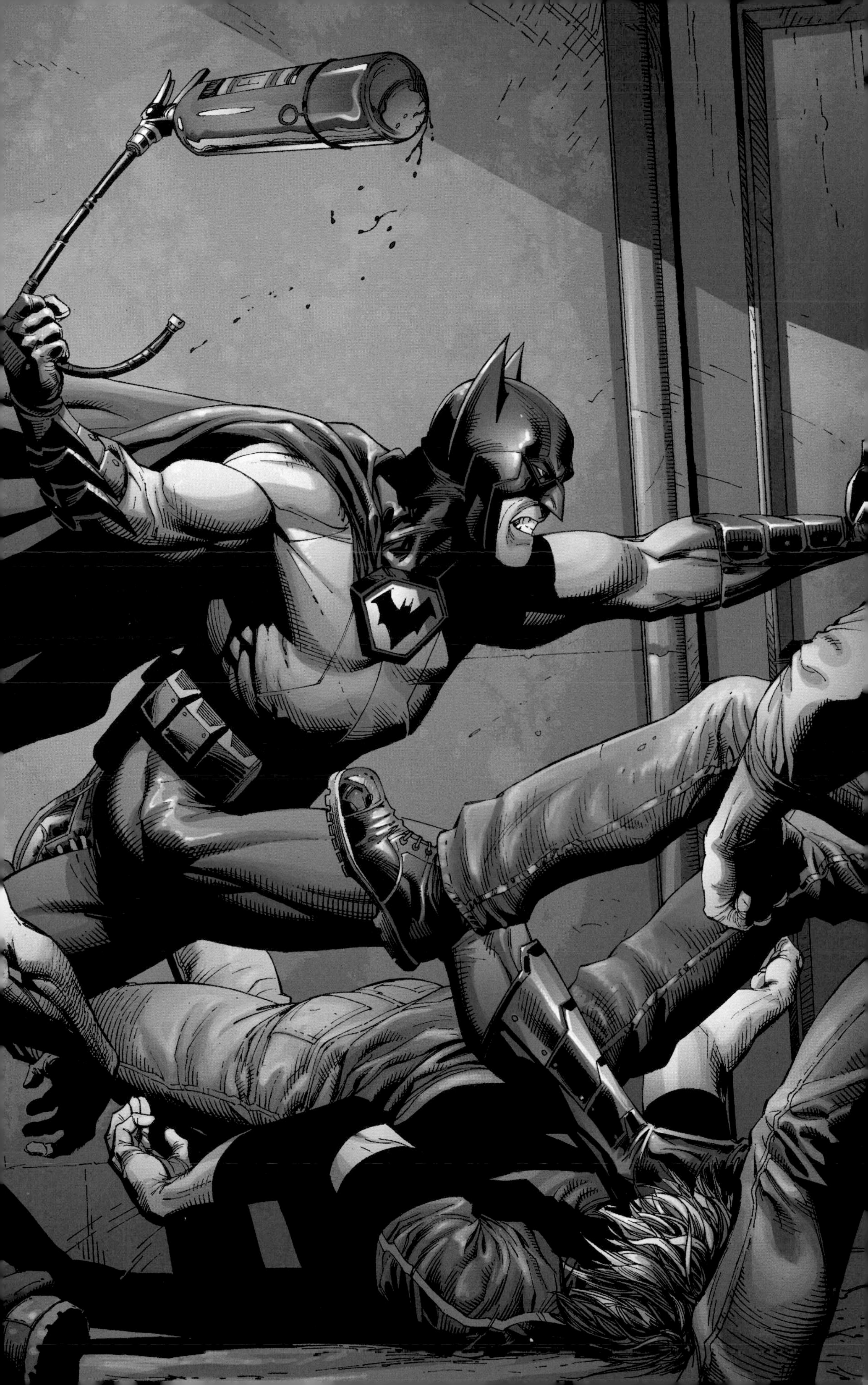

YOU'RE HERE?

KLONK

WELL, *THIS* IS A NICE SURPRISE.

YOU CAN PLAY *TOO.*

THERE'S A CRIMINAL IN A CELL, WANTING TO LEAVE, BUT THERE ARE NO WINDOWS OR CRACKS IN THE WALLS. HE HAS NO TOOLS AND THE DOOR TO HIS CELL IS FIVE INCHES OF SOLID STEEL.

BUT HE STILL ESCAPES.

WE CAN GET TO THE ROOF, JESS. GO DOWN THE FIRE ESCAPE.

YOU HAVE SIXTY SECONDS TO TELL ME *HOW.*

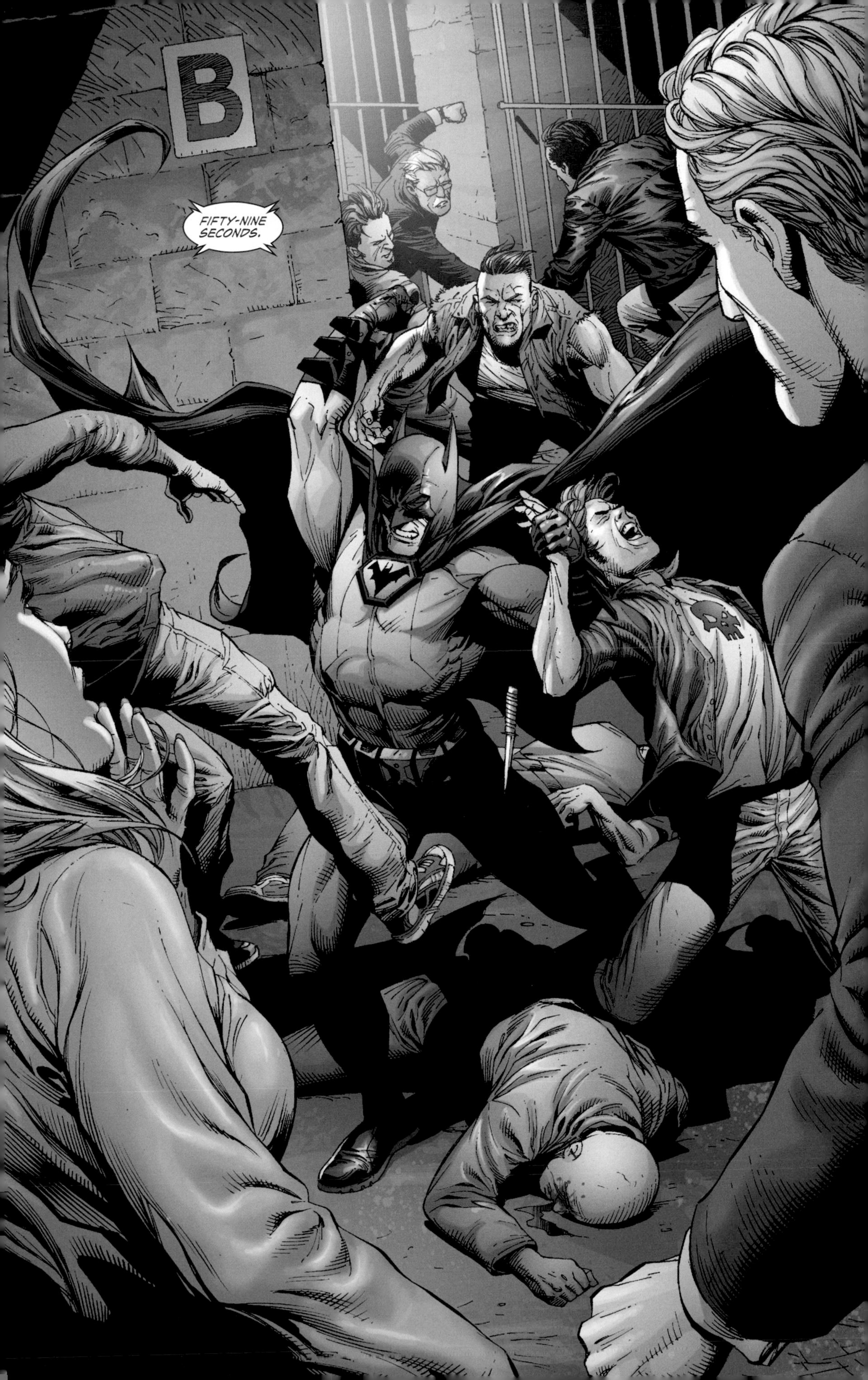
FIFTY-NINE SECONDS.

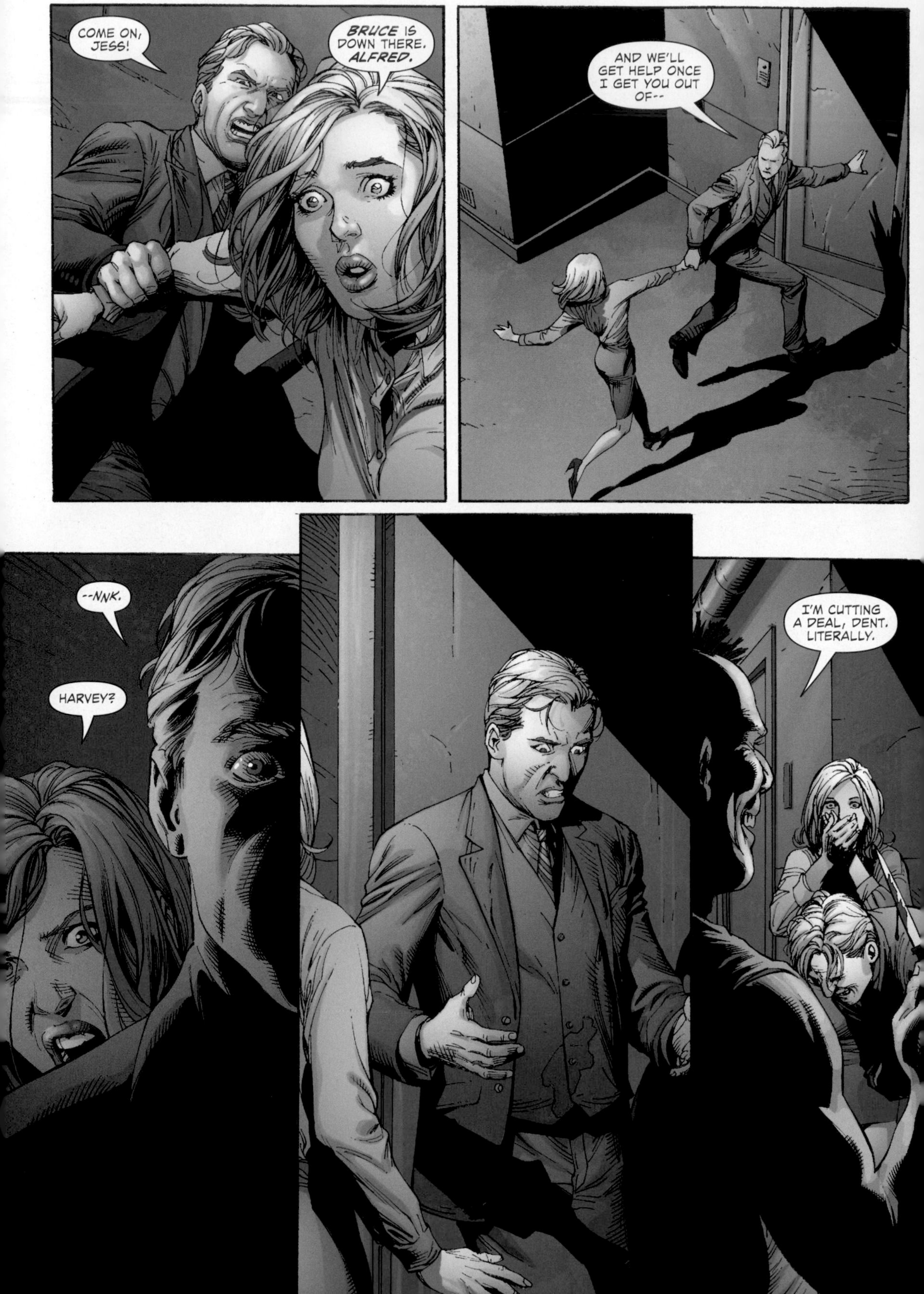
COME ON, JESS!
BRUCE IS DOWN THERE. ALFRED.
AND WE'LL GET HELP ONCE I GET YOU OUT OF--
--NNK.
HARVEY?
I'M CUTTING A DEAL, DENT. LITERALLY.

TWENTY SECONDS.

BATMAN, THE ANSWER--

"THE DOOR WASN'T LOCKED." BUT IT DOESN'T MATTER IF WE ANSWER IT.

HE'S GOING TO BLOW THE PRECINCT UP ANYWAY.

MARONI'S GOT THE D.A.!

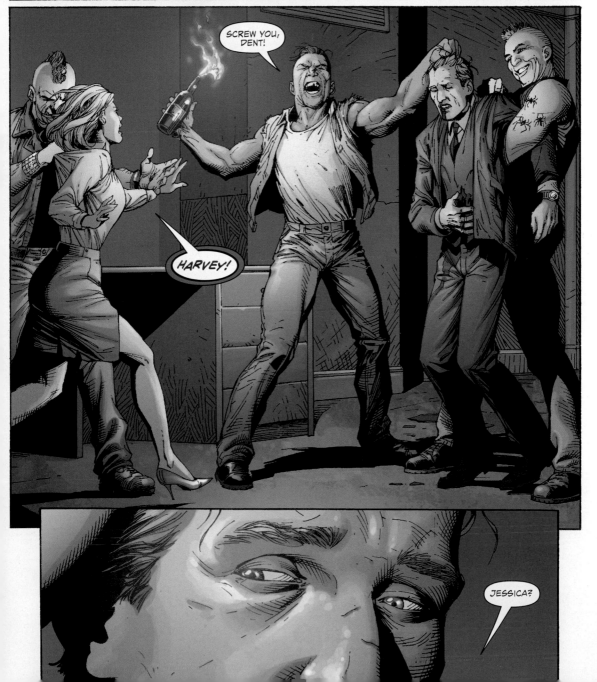

SCREW YOU, DENT!

HARVEY!

JESSICA?

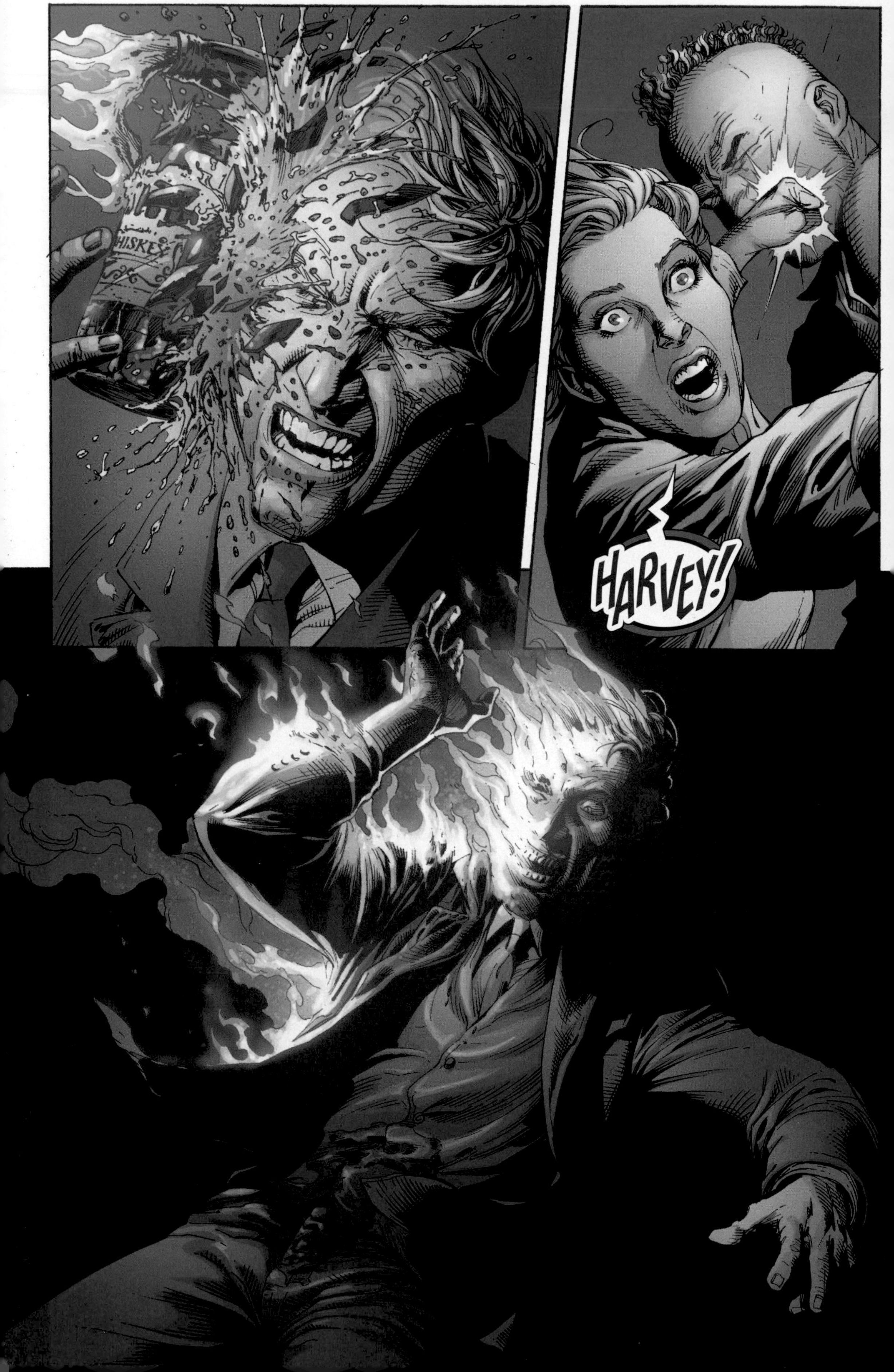
HARVEY!

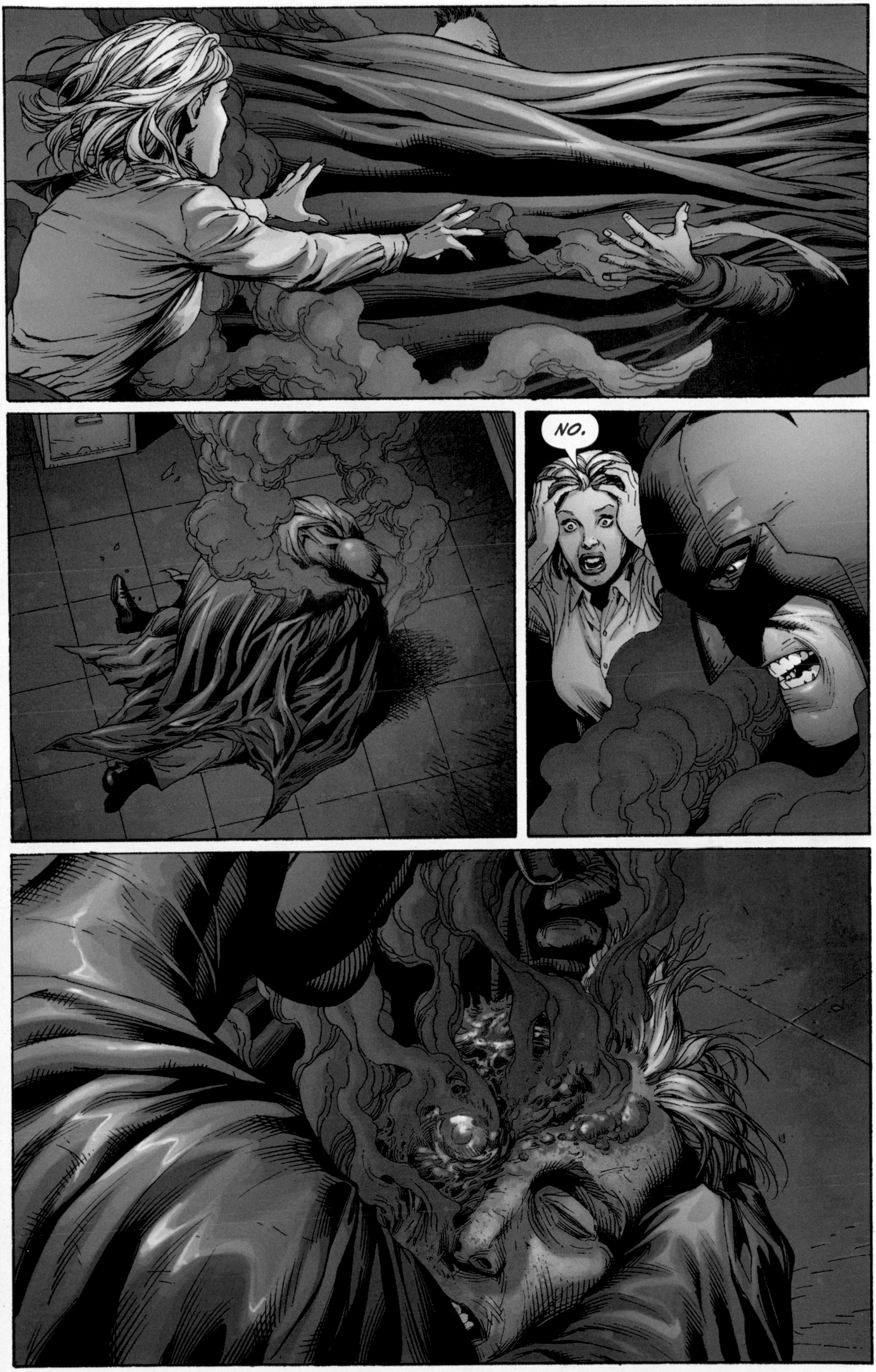
NO.

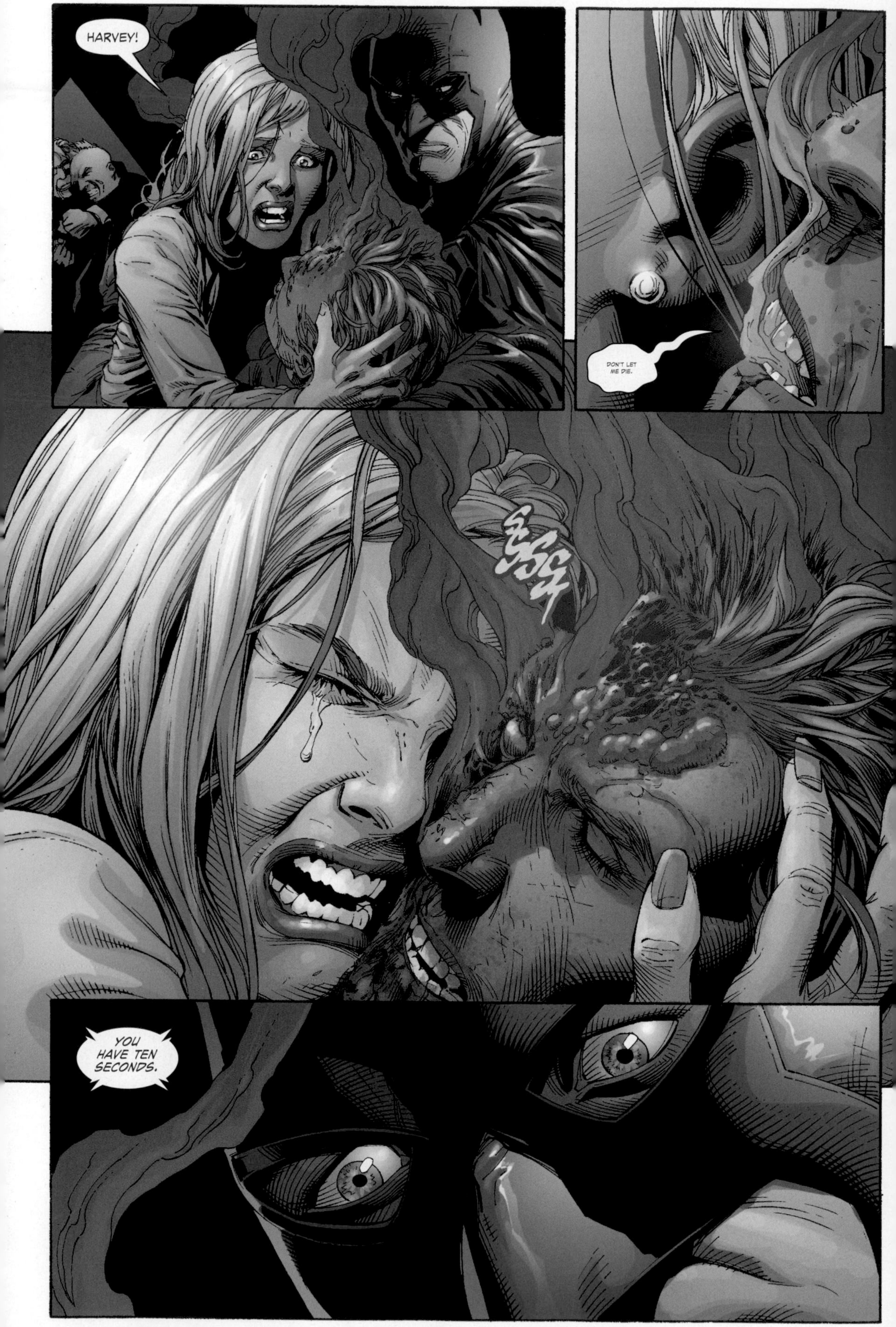
HARVEY!
DON'T LET ME DIE.
YOU HAVE TEN SECONDS.

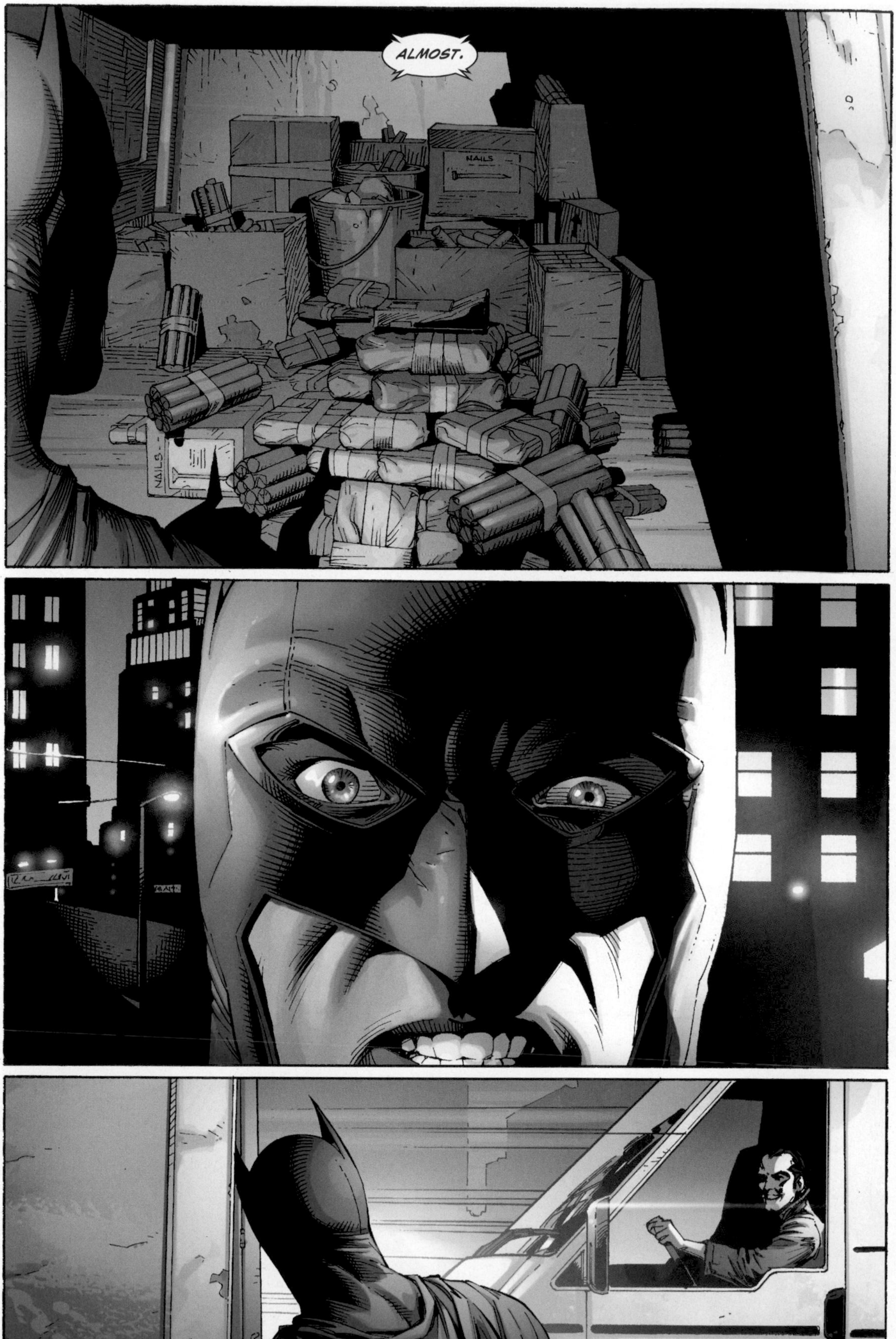
ALMOST.
NAILS
NAILS

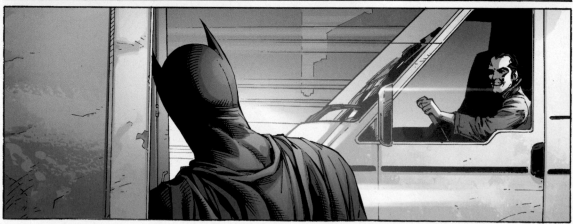

IT'S BEEN FUN, BUT THE GAME'S OVER.

AS SOON AS I DETONATE THAT BOMB, THAT **POLICE STATION**--AND EVERY SINGLE PERSON WHO KNOWS ANYTHING ABOUT ME, YOURSELF INCLUDED-- WILL BE **GONE**--

AND THEN SO WILL **I**.

VR**BOOOMMM**

SKREE

I HAVE A **RIDDLE** FOR **YOU**, RIDDLER.

Hm?

THERE ARE TWO CARS THAT LEAVE THE GOTHAM POLICE DEPARTMENT, ONE **FIVE SECONDS** AFTER THE OTHER, BOTH TRAVELING AT APPROXIMATELY SIXTY MILES AN HOUR. THE ONE IN FRONT HAS A **TRIGGER** TO A **BOMB** CARRIED IN THE SECOND CAR.

THE CARS ARE WITHIN **HALF** A **CITY BLOCK** OF ONE ANOTHER.

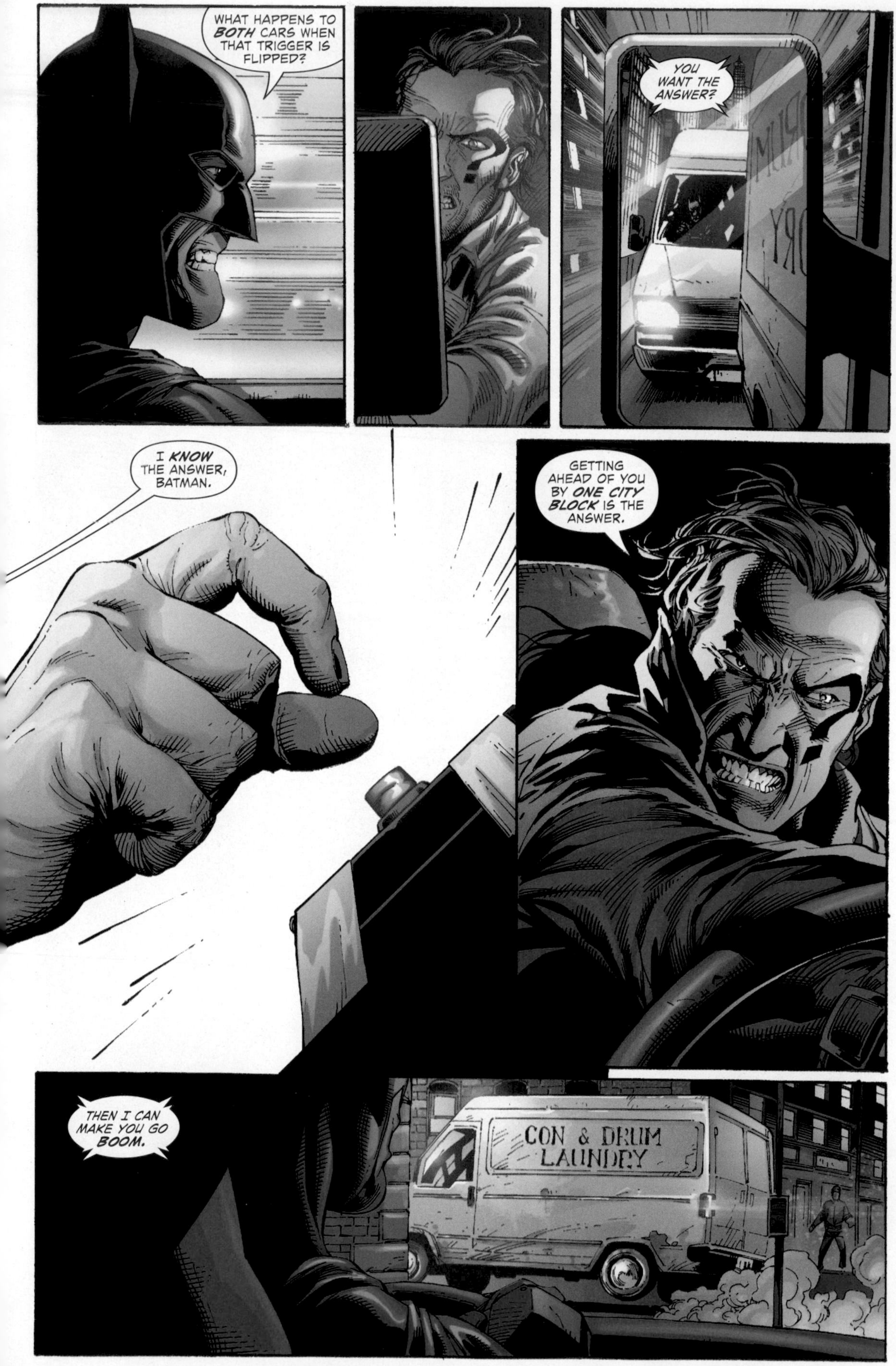
WHAT HAPPENS TO BOTH CARS WHEN THAT TRIGGER IS FLIPPED?
YOU WANT THE ANSWER?
I KNOW THE ANSWER, BATMAN.
GETTING AHEAD OF YOU BY ONE CITY BLOCK IS THE ANSWER.
THEN I CAN MAKE YOU GO BOOM.
CON & DRUM LAUNDRY

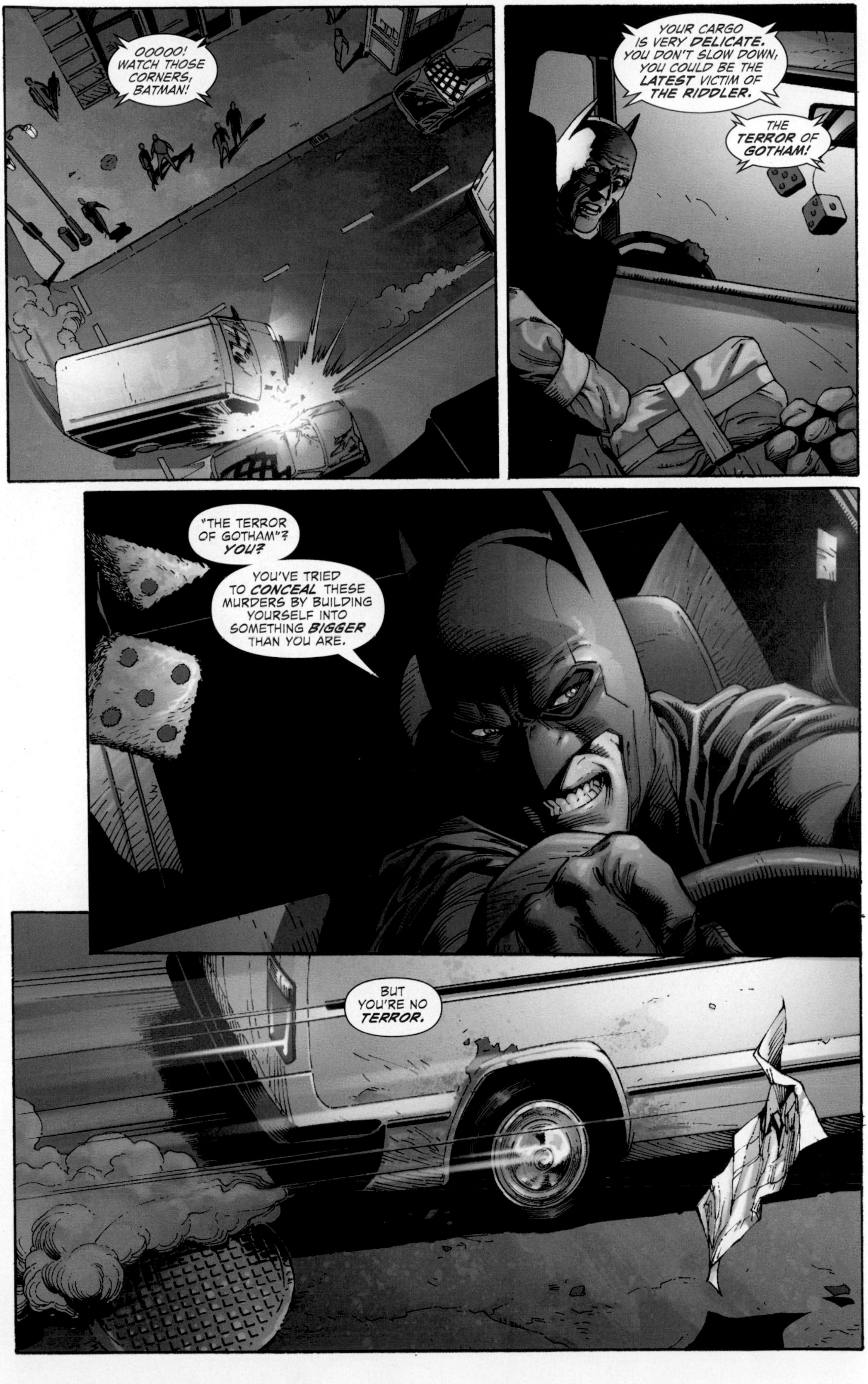

OOOOO! WATCH THOSE CORNERS, BATMAN!
YOUR CARGO IS VERY DELICATE. YOU DON'T SLOW DOWN, YOU COULD BE THE LATEST VICTIM OF THE RIDDLER.
THE TERROR OF GOTHAM!
"THE TERROR OF GOTHAM"? YOU?
YOU'VE TRIED TO CONCEAL THESE MURDERS BY BUILDING YOURSELF INTO SOMETHING BIGGER THAN YOU ARE.
BUT YOU'RE NO TERROR.

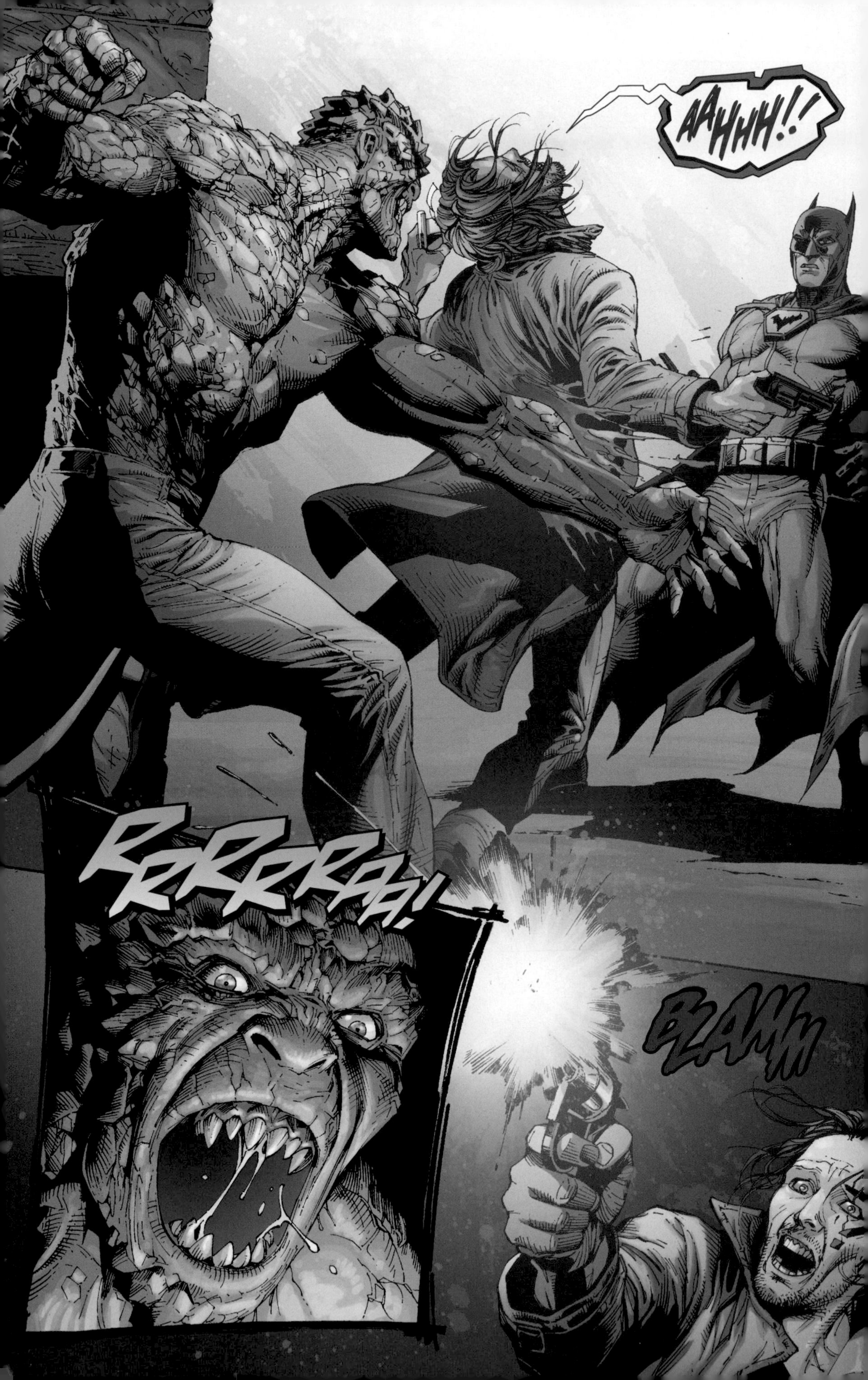
AAHHH!!
RRRRRAA!
BLAMM

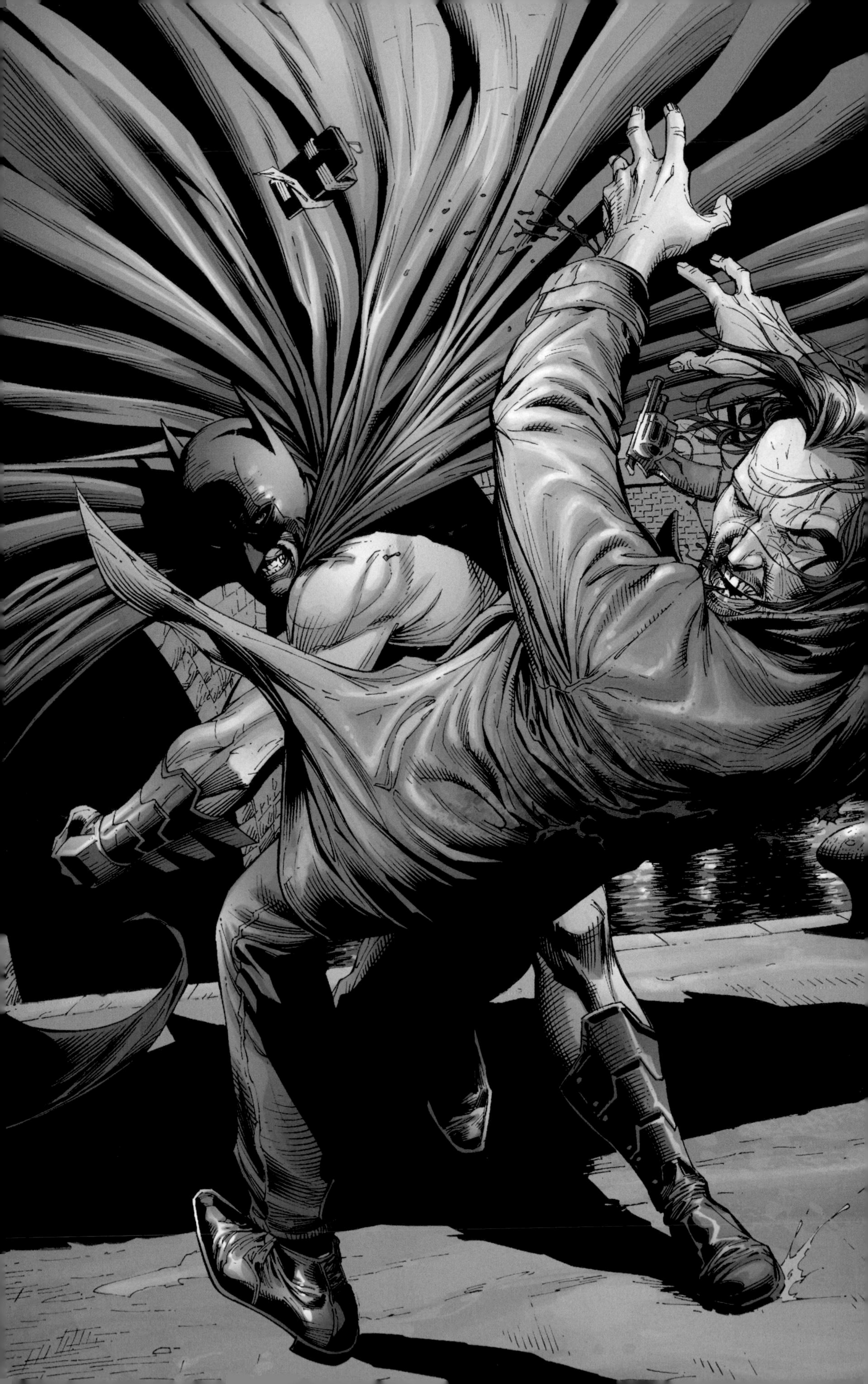

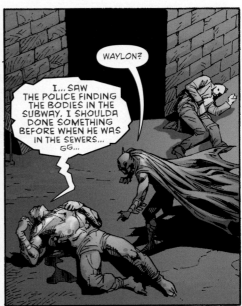

WAYLON?

I... SAW THE POLICE FINDING THE BODIES IN THE SUBWAY. I SHOULDA DONE SOMETHING BEFORE WHEN HE WAS IN THE SEWERS... GG...

...I DIDN'T WANT TO GO BACK DOWN THERE ANYWAY.

KK

"THE RIDDLER, WHOSE TRUE IDENTITY HAS YET TO BE VERIFIED, HAS BEEN CHARGED IN THE DEATHS OF 43 PEOPLE THIS WEEK..."

...WHILE CRIMINAL *SAL MARONI* HAS BEEN CHARGED WITH THE MURDER OF *DISTRICT ATTORNEY HARVEY DENT* WHO WAS KILLED DURING THE *RIOTS* INSIDE THE GOTHAM CITY CENTRAL POLICE DEPARTMENT.

AS THE RIDDLER'S *TRUE MOTIVATIONS* ARE UNCOVERED, ARRESTS ARE EXPECTED TO BE MADE...

"...AMONG THEM *CAPTAIN CHRISTOPHER BLACK*, A HIGHLY DECORATED OFFICER OF THE POLICE DEPARTMENT, WHO IS ACCUSED OF BEING PART OF A NETWORK OF CITY OFFICIALS WHO HAD TAKEN CONTROL OF THE LATE MAYOR COBBLEPOT'S CRIMINAL OPERATIONS.

"OUR CURRENT MAYOR, JESSICA DENT, REMAINS HOSPITALIZED, BUT IS EXPECTED TO MAKE A FULL RECOVERY..."

THEY SAY BRUCE WAYNE IS PAYING FOR ALL THE REPAIRS.

YOU GET THAT, GORDO? WE ARREST THE GUY; ACCUSE HIM OF BEING *THE RIDDLER* AND HE WRITES A BIG, FAT CHECK TO THE *POLICE DEPARTMENT.*

THE CITY MAY HAVE UNDERESTIMATED BRUCE WAYNE. HIS PARENTS WERE GOOD PEOPLE.

YOU'RE GOOD PEOPLE, TOO. WHEN PEOPLE ARE DROWNING IN GOTHAM, THEY DON'T OFTEN GET THROWN A LIFE PRESERVER.

I DON'T THINK I COULD SURVIVE THIS PLACE WITHOUT A PARTNER LIKE YOU.

A *FRIEND,* BULLOCK.

GORDON?

COMMISSIONER WANTS TO SEE YOU.

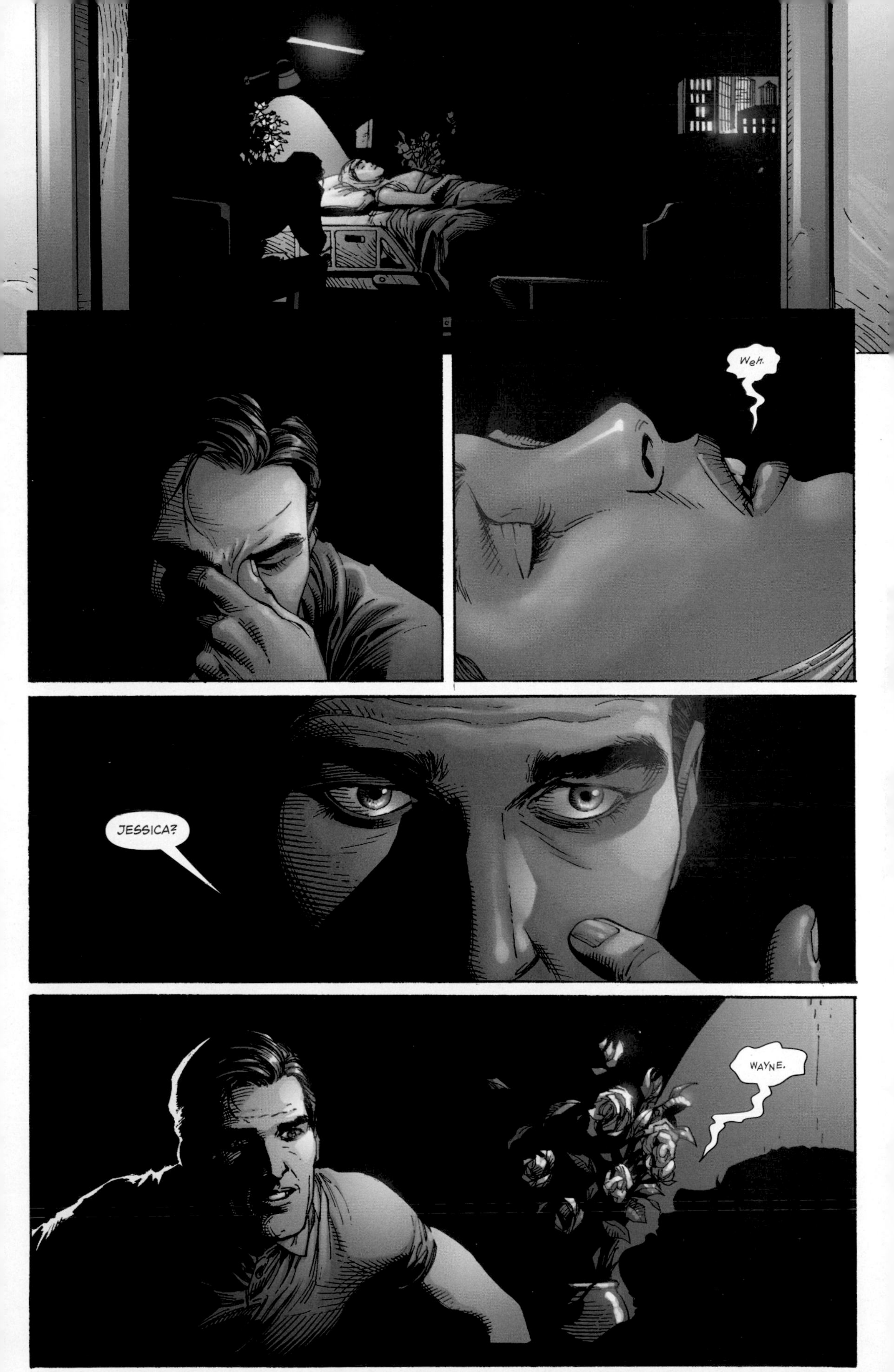
Weh.
JESSICA?
WAYNE.

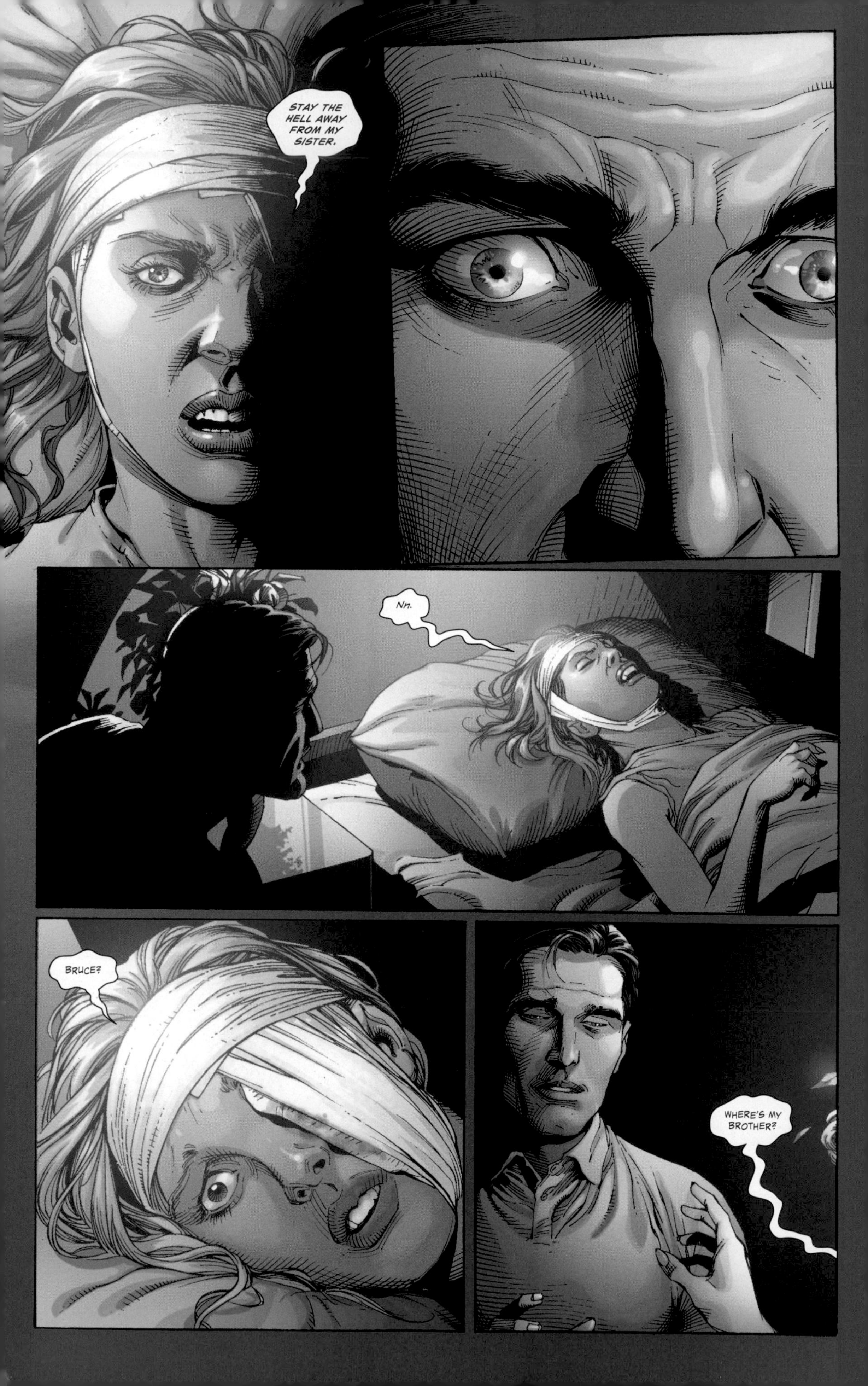
STAY THE HELL AWAY FROM MY SISTER.
Nn.
BRUCE?
WHERE'S MY BROTHER?

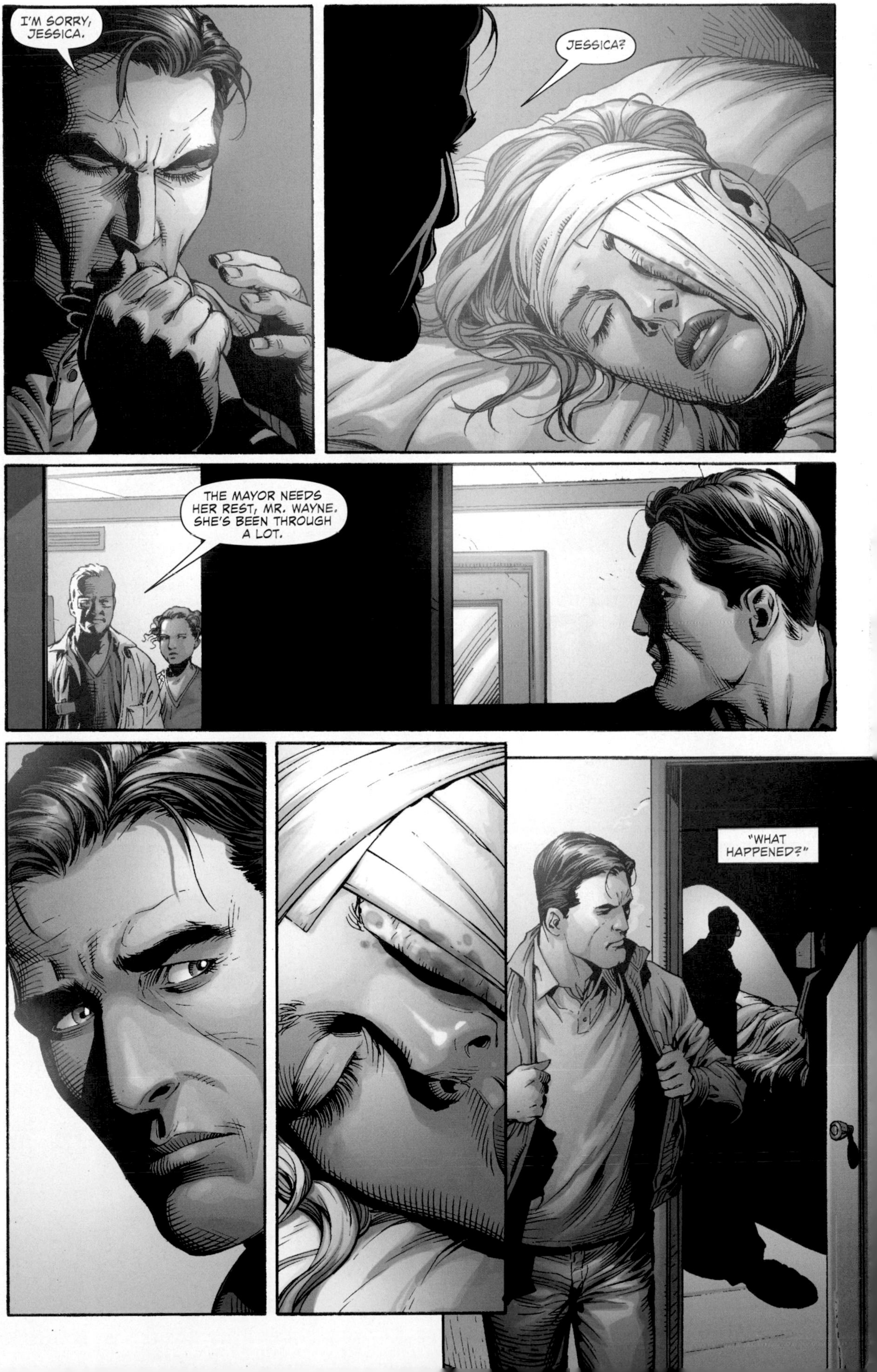
I'M SORRY, JESSICA.
JESSICA?
THE MAYOR NEEDS HER REST, MR. WAYNE. SHE'S BEEN THROUGH A LOT.
"WHAT HAPPENED?"

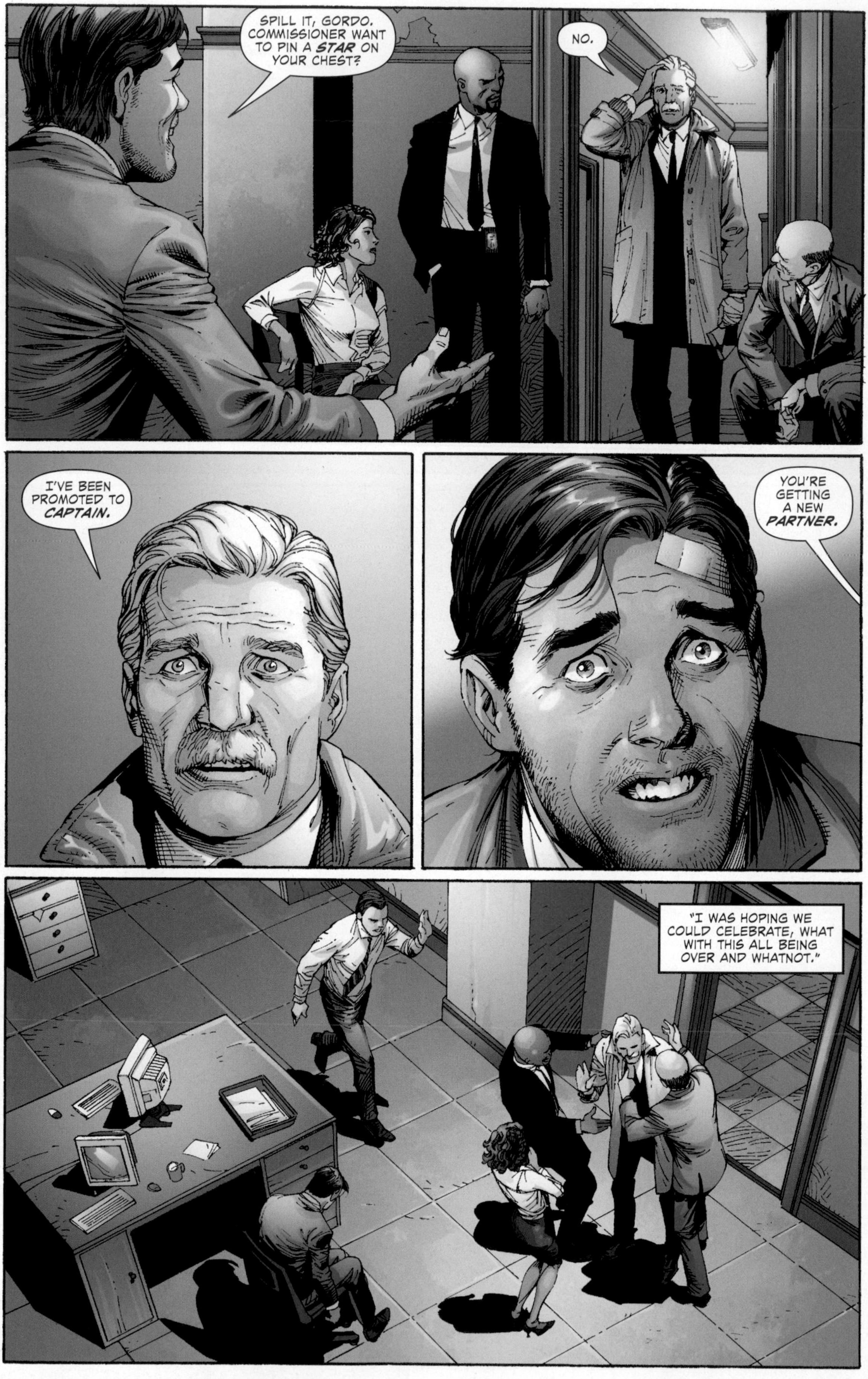
SPILL IT, GORDO. COMMISSIONER WANT TO PIN A STAR ON YOUR CHEST?
NO.
I'VE BEEN PROMOTED TO CAPTAIN.
YOU'RE GETTING A NEW PARTNER.
"I WAS HOPING WE COULD CELEBRATE, WHAT WITH THIS ALL BEING OVER AND WHATNOT."

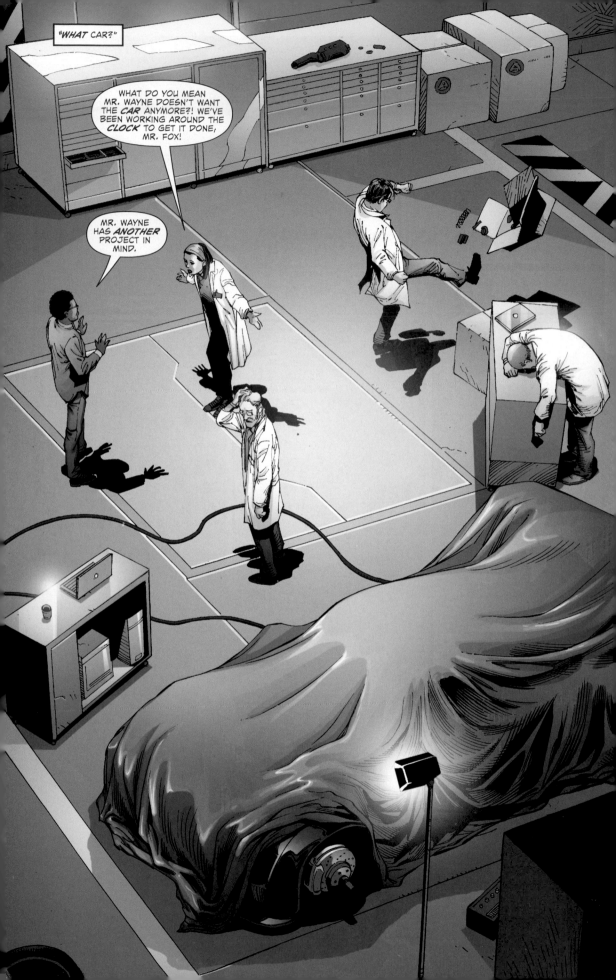

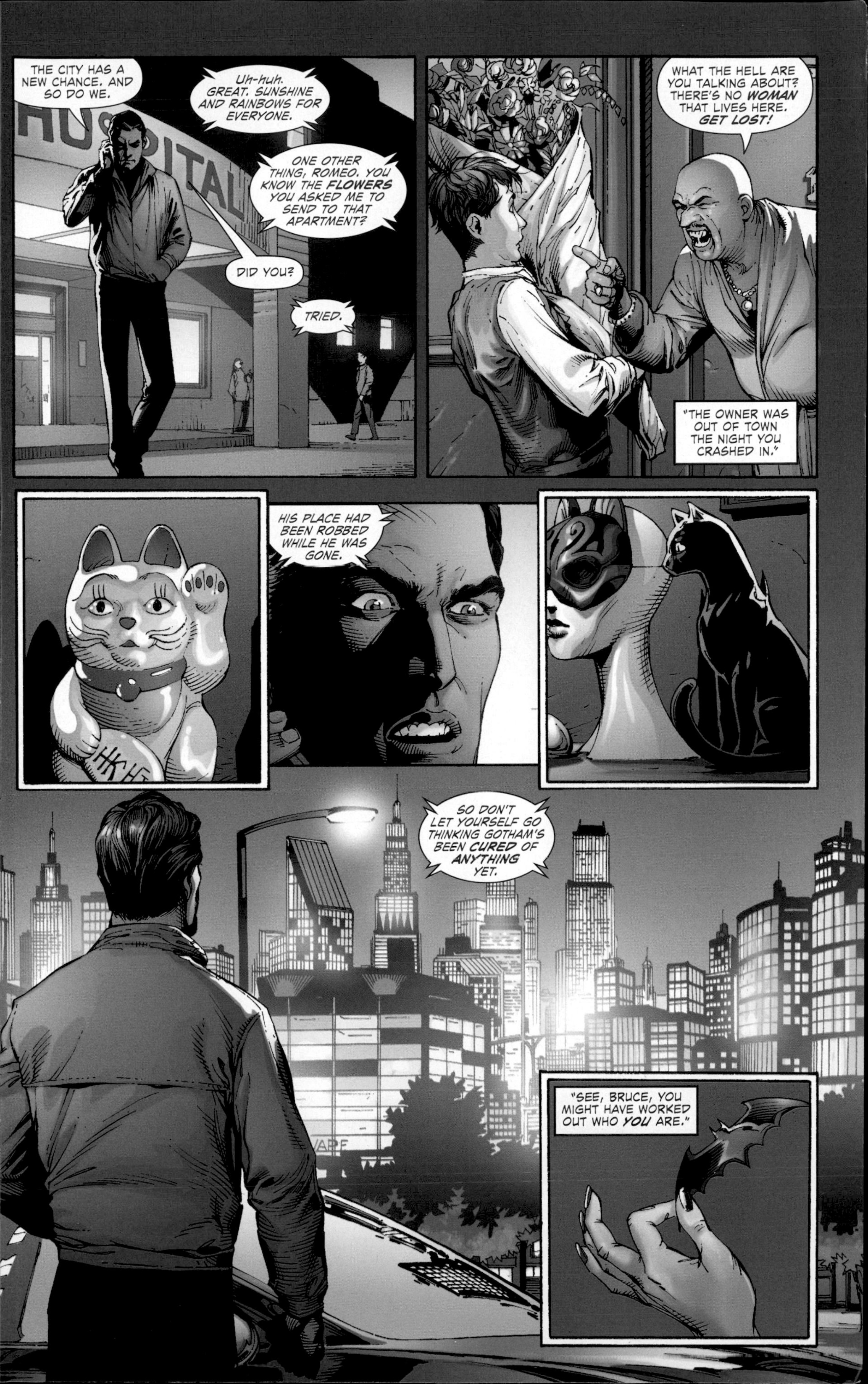
THE CITY HAS A NEW CHANCE. AND SO DO WE.
Uh-huh. GREAT. SUNSHINE AND RAINBOWS FOR EVERYONE.
ONE OTHER THING, ROMEO. YOU KNOW THE FLOWERS YOU ASKED ME TO SEND TO THAT APARTMENT?
DID YOU?
TRIED.
WHAT THE HELL ARE YOU TALKING ABOUT? THERE'S NO WOMAN THAT LIVES HERE. GET LOST!
"THE OWNER WAS OUT OF TOWN THE NIGHT YOU CRASHED IN."
HIS PLACE HAD BEEN ROBBED WHILE HE WAS GONE.
SO DON'T LET YOURSELF GO THINKING GOTHAM'S BEEN CURED OF ANYTHING YET.
"SEE, BRUCE, YOU MIGHT HAVE WORKED OUT WHO YOU ARE."